REZBALLERS AND SKATE ELDERS

REZBALLERS AND SKATE ELDERS

JOYFUL FUTURES IN INDIAN COUNTRY

DAVID KAMPER

University of Nebraska Press
Lincoln

For customers in the EU with safety/GPSR concerns, contact:
gpsr@mare-nostrum.co.uk
Mare Nostrum Group BV
Mauritskade 21D
1091 GC Amsterdam
The Netherlands

Library of Congress Control Number: 2025935052

Designed and set in MeropeBasic
by Lacey Losh.

CONTENTS

ILLUSTRATIONS

ACKNOWLEDGMENTS

In many ways the impetus for this book starts out with my abundantly loving and supportive parents, Mike and Carole Kamper. They instilled a fanaticism for sports in me from an early age, frequently taking me to Lakers basketball games and UCLA football games all throughout my youth. I still have fond memories of falling asleep in the backseat of the car on the way home from a night game in Los Angeles and magically walking up in our garage in Orange County. When I think of sports, despite their many problems, I think of community and family. This book emphasizes how sports are a place to build community and strengthen familial bonds, and I learned this first and foremost from my parents (and all my loving cousins who make discussion of sports a consistent theme at any family gathering). I am grateful for this and for all the love and support you have shown to me throughout my career and my life.

For this project I've had many, many Indigenous and non-Indigenous folks share their time to talk basketball and skateboarding with me. They allowed me to observe them balling or skating, and some even tolerated me "coaching" them. In terms of basketball, from the very beginning, Sam McCracken of Nike's N7 has always been very supportive of this project and wonderful to bounce ideas off of. The leadership at Southern California's incredible youth sports organization, Inter Tribal Sports, has always been such ideal collaborators, generous with their time and always willing to let me hang around their fantastic basketball program. Thank you in particular Brian Van Wanseele, Andrew Masiel Jr., Inez Sanchez Pojas, George Pojas, Ben Foster, Angelina Rentaria, and Isaiah Thompson. Over the years several of you tolerated me as an assistant coach despite my horrible basketball-playing skills and weakness in drawing up plays. Thank you to Joseph Masiel, Dan Sletten, Connor Flores, Andy Silvas, Rob Avila, Jeff Sands, Jose Toscano, Kevin Pretty on

Top, Nate Moore, Josiah Flores, and Julio Marquez. Coaching travel ball and NABI are truly some of the best moments of my life, and I am grateful for the fun that I had with you all and what I learned from you all about basketball. I consider you all great friends to this day. A special thanks to Joey, whom I've been with since the beginning—your willingness to share your community, expertise, and family with me is unmatched, and I'm fortunate for your friendship.

I have been lucky to spend time with many Rezballers as a "coach" and with those who were willing to let me interview them. I'm grateful for your time, patience, and grace. Special thanks to Brandi and Misty Taylor, Rebecca Miles, Jess Becenti, Ruben Rangel, Jacob Andreas, Edward Silgala, Rob, Alec, and Noah Tortes, Gejo Salgado, Raymond Torres (sorry you didn't make the cover), Lexi Lopez, Tehya Marcus, Chase and Chance Thomas, Enrique Fonseca, Alex Arellano, Miles Sands, Thunder Lopez, Zach Balcone, Jacob "Bubba" Duro, Alan Aguayo, Cody Tsosie, Nick Blackburn, Isaac Contreras, Kenny Garcia, John Amago, Aiden Strout, Juan Martinez, Michael Patricio, and Cassius Sands.

So many skaters also tolerated my "hanging out" and letting me ask them some silly and some not-so-silly questions, and for just sharing their stories with me: Joseph Mairena, O'Jay Venegas, Chris Nieto, the Lerma Brothers, Louise Yellowman, Clint Dayzie, Victor Z. Corpuz, Shawn Harrison, JoRey Hernandez, Tony Steele, Trevor Scott, Jeremy Todacheenie, Cecely Todacheenie, Gerald Todacheene, Brandon Hailsey, Jazmine Barney, and Selina Mullen. A special thanks to those who spent extra time with me, on some occasions allowing for more than one interview: Di'Orr Greenwood, Delvan Polelonema, Todd Harder, Douglas Miles Sr., Walt Pourier, Jim Murphy, and Dustinn Craig. Dustinn, I am grateful for your honesty, integrity, and vulnerability and most of all your friendship—it is invaluable. Di'Orr, I consider myself fortunate to be able to help (in some small way) with all the amazing community work you do.

This book took a long time to complete and over the ten plus years that I have been working on it, and I benefited greatly from two different reading groups. First in the late 2010s, Mike Borgstrom, Irene Lara, Kate

Swanson, Mark Wheeler, and Victoria Rivera-Gonzalez were an excellent support group. Although I was by far the last to get full and finish my book, your support during the initial phases was key to helping point me in the right direction for this project. The second writing group was absolutely crucial in getting me over the finishing line: Lydia Heberling, Tony Lucero, Molly Hatay, Joe Whitson, Cassie Comely, Caitlin Tyler-Richards, Cassie Galentine, Richard Pineda, Audrey Beck, Natasha Varner, Jose Cadena, Erika Robb Larkins, Alika Bourgette, and Catherine Ulep. Not all of you showed up every day (me included), but all of you in some ways helped motivate me in the mornings, which would not have been possible without you all. Our "Garage Band" sessions literally changed my life. Erika, thank you for being such a great campus ally. Tony, it is still amazing to me how close I feel to you without ever having met you in person. Cassie G. and Molly, thank you for always making me laugh. Cat and Alika, despite the significant differences in the stages of our careers, your advice, support, and friendship have been rejuvenating—I cannot wait to watch you both get to become "slacker" full professors like me! And Lydia, I love you like a sister. Your partnership and patience with me are invaluable.

A tremendous thank you to my editor at University of Nebraska Press, Matt Bokovoy, who stuck with me through this long process and was always willing to share some fun waves. Thank you also to Heather Stauffer and Taylor Martin for your patience with me. This manuscript was lovingly copyedited by both Molly Hatay and Paige Dawson. Molly, thank you for looking after another "baby" of mine. Paige, your help with this manuscript and keeping me organized and sane during our grant was invaluable. You have a truly remarkable skill set, and I am excited to see how your academic career unfolds. M. Fowler, I am grateful for your photographic help and friendship.

During nearly all this book process I have been the chair of the American Indian Studies Department at San Diego State University. Certainly, this has slowed my work down, but the relationships with fellow chairs and other colleagues have been well worth the twelve years. Special thanks to Bill Nericcio, Maria Ibarra, Adissa Alkebulan, Roberto Hernandez, Doreen Mattingly, Kim Price, Clarissa Clo, Jim Lange, and Luke Wood. My home department has long been a place of refuge that not only made this book possible but also made academic work enjoyable. Thank you to Margaret Field, Linda Parker, Linda Locklear, Cutcha Risling Baldy, Olivia Chilcote, Peter Nelson, Esme Murdock, Brittani Orona, and Oscar Munoz. A particular thanks to Olivia and Esme for your support and your trust and for always laughing at my mediocre jokes. Kate Regan no one (outside of family) has tolerated my scatter-brained energy more than you. There is no way I could have gotten any of it done without you. Kate Spilde, rarely have I found a more fantastic ally; thank you for such a great friendship. So many amazing Indigenous students helped sustain me along the way and made my job worthwhile, but I want to particularly thank students that are now my colleagues: Chris Medellin, Jacob Alvarado, Kellen Hernandez, Kiowa Montoya, Richard Decrane, Ivan Sam, Desmond Hassing, and Raini Tesam-Reading. Your community work, on and off campus, inspires me. And Desmond, our bimonthly breakfasts have been so grounding in getting me to debate something other than my research.

Thank you to the recently created Surf/Skate Studies Collaborative at SDSU; your work and partnership in this area continue to sustain me. BCB for life! And to my newest colleague and "BFF," Neftalie Williams, it has not been that long, but it feels like a lifetime and that it was meant to be. I cannot wait for all the amazing things we will do together. And Rogers, it took us years to figure out how to collaborate academically, and I am so grateful that we finally have. Lastly, I must thank Rod Labrador. When we began this academic journey together nearly thirty years ago, we dreamed that we could somehow study what we loved most, sports and hip-hop—thank God we made it.

Above I thanked my parents, but I also must thank Michele and Jim Brooks. I know a lot of what I did for "work" did not quite compute with you, but nonetheless you have always supported me and our family. Ella America, you are the best fieldwork companion that anyone could ask for. Rosa Lucille, you are the best take-a-work-break and chill companion that anyone could ask for. And to you both, I am so proud to have finished this book, but nothing could ever make me half as proud as I am to be your father. You are both remarkable people with great journeys ahead that I am grateful to get to celebrate with you. Finally, Joanna Brooks, my ride or die—and what a ride this has been. During the time I have been writing this book, we have both learned so much about who we each are and who we are together. I can overcome anything with your love and support, and I thank you for continuing to challenge me to be better.

REZBALLERS AND SKATE ELDERS

INTRODUCTION

It was a gorgeous early August day in 2019, warm, bright, and colorful. Three hundred and sixty degrees around me was festive activity, smiles, cheers, and happiness. I was standing on the edge of the concrete bowl of the WK 4-Directions Skatepark in the town of Pine Ridge on the Pine Ridge Indian Reservation—which is sandwiched between what the U.S. settler state labels as the Badlands National Park and the state of Nebraska. The skatepark was built with the help of the Native-owned Wounded Knee Skateboards company and two nonprofits, the Stronghold Society and Montana Pool Service.[1] The WK 4-Directions Skatepark is part of a larger outdoor recreational complex in the heart of the reservation. As I stood at the park on this beautiful day in August: to the east of me was a softball game being played with the leisurely intensity that can only be found in softball; to the south kids were throwing a football around on an open field, no organized game, just running routes for fun; to the west was a pickup basketball game at which one teenager just arrived, riding bareback on his horse, to join the game despite wearing jeans; and to the north was the tail end of a community parade consisting of elders and tribal council representatives smiling, waving, and throwing candy from "floats" being pulled on trailers behind large pickup trucks or from the backseat of convertibles. Behind these floats were several powwow dancers marching or dancing in the parade wearing full regalia. This particular day was the annual Lakota Wicipi, a thoroughly community-based multiday event that combines powwow, rodeo, sports, and the promotion of Lakota culture in all forms and varieties. There was much joy in the air.

The Lakota Reservation at Pine Ridge is a singularity in the public imagination of Indian Country. It often stands in for all the Indigenous communities in North America, as a synecdoche or prototype for American

Indian reservations—at least from the perspective of non-Natives. With good reason though, given the number of historically significant events that took place on this land. Events that are keenly representative of different eras of Indigenous resistance to and suffering from North American settler colonialism. Yet at the same time this overrepresentation of Pine Ridge speaks to particular settler narratives of Indians being either barbaric savages that needed subduing or noble warriors who fought hard to maintain traditional lifeways. Either way, these tropes of "primitivism" have always marginalized Indigenous communities, making them seem to be out of time or irrelevant to the modern, civilized world. The overrepresentation and oversimplification of Lakota society, and Indian Country as a whole, as merely synonymous does harm to all of Indian Country by distilling the diversity of American Indian history, culture, and communities to a few simple tropes of barbarism. More recently, an overemphasis on Pine Ridge and the challenge it is to live on this reservation is frequently employed as a metaphor to highlight the tragedy and suffering of American Indians. Since the mid-twentieth century Pine Ridge has frequently been used as either a cautionary tale of poverty, addiction, and trauma or a halfhearted critique of (or semi-admission of blame for) the history of U.S. white supremacy and federal Indian policy (see the *Bury My Heart at Wounded Knee* book and film, *Thunderheart*, and countless documentaries, books, and academic articles). This overemphasis on Pine Ridge is deployed to code Indigenous spaces as devastated, depraved, and depressed. Certainly, these terms have some utility in describing part of Indian Country, but all too often damage-centered narratives obscure and override the true joy, happiness, and vibrancy that pulses through Indigenous communities (Tuck and Yang 2014).

This book attempts to highlight that joy, happiness, and vibrancy (without ignoring the pain and intergenerational trauma) of Native American communities by focusing on just two of the many things Native people do for fun: play basketball and skateboard. As an integral part of nearly all localized communities, sports sustain communal and individual life by building solidarity, promoting physical and mental health, and socializing youth (in both collaboratively beneficial and hegemonically problematic ways). On a regional and global scale, professional and Olympic sports play a major role in contemporary consumer capitalism, producing massive revenues from event-based competition and entertainment and providing far-reaching venues for the marketing of ancillary products and services (Carrington and McDonald 2009; Zirin 2009, 2016; Boykoff 2023). Despite the increasing global-facing articulation of professional sports, local community-based sports are still a significant part of communities all over the world, though this tends to be more in the realm of leisure, not professionalization.[2]

American Indian communities are no exception when it comes to communal expression of sport. Sport has been a key part of Indigenous life well before and long after contact with European settlers. American Indian communities have always combined the physical with the spiritual to maintain a balance between mental, emotional, and corporeal health. Kinesthetic ability and endurance are key parts of the ceremonial-, leisure-, and sustenance-based activities of Indigenous peoples. Arguably, this holistic approach to health is the reason why what is now called "sport" has been so prevalent in American Indian communities. Yet I also take caution not to romanticize Native American participation in sports and physical activity. Historically discourses of Indians as "natural athletes" have been used to sustain settler colonial agendas pitting primitive versus civilized, ancient (and vanished) versus modern (see Deloria 2004). This book illustrates that there is much to suggest that contemporary Native folks participate in and conceptualize sports in ways that are hardly distinguishable for the rest of mainstream America. However, I seek to highlight the many and really important ways that certain sports, which may have originated outside of Indian Country, have become indigenized by Native athletes—that is, interpreted through Indigenous values and become an intricate part of Indigenous communal life.

This process of indigenization is what most interests me, and it is for this reason that this book deals with two sports that started outside of Indian Country. Basketball was introduced to tribal communities mainly through the effort of the boarding school system, whose main prerogative was to assimilate Indians into Americans. This "civilizing mission" began almost simultaneously with the advent of basketball itself, meaning that Indians were there basically from the beginning of basketball. James Naismith is conventionally credited with the invention of basketball, but Native people have made it their own, from its inception. Skateboarding, on the other hand, was embraced in Indian Country in far less intentional ways than basketball. It was not brought in as part of an assimilating project per se, but rather picked up and adapted by Indigenous kids in ways that were similar to how skateboarding has spread globally. Rather than a collective or systematically promoted sport, for much of its history skateboarding has been an outsider activity that attracted creative and adventurous personalities who were either looking for something different or, already feeling alienated, were drawn toward something that would confirm their outcast or oppositional identity. In many ways, there are no more outsider communities in the United States than reservation ones, and so early on Native skaters were sort of the outcasts of the outcasts. But, as more and more Native kids began skating, youth advocates and tribal governments began to promote skateboarding in unique ways that channeled Indigenous creative expression and intentional values through the artistry, inventiveness, and persistence inherent to skateboarding.

When describing my research on basketball and skateboarding to people in ordinary conversation, there is often considerable surprise about the popularity of these activities in Indian Country. Indeed, to borrow the language of renown Native scholar Philip J. Deloria (2004), to most people it is truly unexpected to find Indians in the places of basketball and skateboarding. This probably says more about misperceptions of Indians, per se, than it does about basketball and skateboarding, although each of these activities conventionally is associated with specific racial communities in the United States: urban African American communities for the former and white middle-class suburban communities for the latter.[3] That is, as Deloria has illustrated, Indians are often thought by white folks as being out of place in contemporary American society. An Indian engaging in modernity is often read as a novelty that can be both amusing and a sort of exception that proves the long-held settler colonial rule: Indians exclusively are people of the past, while the present and future belong to white folks. However, Deloria also explains that, like any other community, of course Indians absolutely engage in cultural change and do, in fact, inhabit the present and the future. Moreover, there are some very clear transformative moments and articulations where American Indians combine tradition and contemporary expression of culture in ways that allow Indigenous people to simultaneously occupy the past, present, and future. What I hope this book chronicles is not merely the greater exposure of something many might not know about (the broad popularity of basketball and skateboarding in Indian Country), but more importantly how basketball and skateboarding provide a venue for these transformative moments.

Basketball and skateboarding are certainly not the only venues for this kind transformative joy in Indian Country. What's more, the characteristics unique to basketball and skateboarding do not necessarily and inherently induce more happiness than other venues in Indian Country such as powwows, tribally based ceremonies, all forms of music, language, arts and crafts, rodeos, or any other sport. Basketball and skateboarding just happen to be popular and relatively ubiquitous. For sure, some of this has to do with historic circumstances or the relatively small amount of resources needed to participate in each of these pastimes, but this book is far less of a *why* of basketball and skateboarding than a *how* of basketball and skateboarding in Indian Country. To that end, much of this book is descriptive of what I've seen, what I've been told, and what I participated in. Additionally, there are moments where I will make arguments about the way in which these sports coincide with specific Indigenous values and meet specific needs of contemporary Indigenous communities. However, I resist arguments of exceptionalism that would seek to answer why basketball and skateboarding over running, lacrosse, or football. Certainly, these sports too have a long history and long traditions in Indian Country.

Moreover, I think it folly or at least untenable to argue what is a "traditional" sport versus what is not. In this same vein, I am not interested in defining discrete borders around what are mainstream American skateboarding and basketball and what are Indigenous expressions of these activities or, rather, in distinguishing the difference between Indians who just happen to play basketball or skateboard and what is often called "Rezball" or a "Native" skate company. In many cases, there are very clear expressions of indigeneity suffused through these activities, such as skateboard companies explicitly referencing tribal names or culture as part of their brand and art or basketball tournaments that begin with powwow drummers rhythmically parading the teams on to the court Grand Entry–style. But other articulations might not be so explicit. For example, Indigenous people just participating in these sports, that are clearly a part of modern life, is a statement of Indigenous presence, even if these athletes do not outwardly assert their indigeneity. An assertion of Native presence in contemporary life has always been a struggle for Indigenous people fighting the overwhelming settler discourses of vanishing. Moreover, participation in these activities that originated outside of Indian Country is not a rejection of tradition or an assimilation to mainstream American culture. Deloria explains this paradox of racial boundaries that always haunted Indianness this way:

> White Americans valued Indians for an authenticity located outside of modernity while demanding that they evolve socially and culturally such that they could be assimilated into it. Indian authenticity rested on the ground of unchangeable racial difference. . . . Indian people were faced with the contradictory demand to both eliminate and preserve their difference (Deloria 2019, 236)

This passage comes from Deloria's fantastic recent monograph, *Becoming Mary Sully: Towards an American Indian Abstract*, in which he is referring to a time, one hundred years ago, when his Dakota great aunt was an emerging modernist artist. Nonetheless, this challenge still exists for American Indians today, including those who have avidly immersed themselves in the culture of basketball or skateboarding (see also Povinelli's [2002] and Spilde's [1999] characterization of this paradox). In contemplating the life and art of Mary Sully, Deloria conceives of thinking around this temporal double bind of Indianness. He modifies the logic of "indigenizing" through an inverted turn of phrase. He suggests that rather than declaring that Mary Sully indigenized modernist art—taking something from outside her Native tradition and making it her own by incorporating it into her Indigenous cultural values—we ought to think of Marry Sully as *native to modernism* (Deloria 2019, 21). This tweak suggests that she was a cocreator of the artistic category that white culture conventionally labels as "modernism" and associates with early twentieth-century artists (of all genres) in Europe and the United States. That is, as Deloria (2019) puts it, Sully "staked a native claim to modernism" (5). Following Deloria, I believe it is worthwhile to think of the Indigenous folks I chronicle in this book as *native* to basketball or *native* to skateboarding. The Native athletes and cultural practitioners who engage in basketball and skateboarding are not just taking it and making it work in their own communities, but in a sense these activities are integral to contemporary Indigenous ways of being, and we should think of Rezballers and Native skaters as key to the constant process of (re)producing the activities we call basketball and skateboarding.

There is another reason why I argue it is germane to state that these athletes are *native to* skateboarding and basketball, and it is a concern for Indigenous futurity. Deloria's (2019) formulation draws upon Mark Rifkin's (2017) contention about Indigenous temporality, and his warning that as we work against the discourses that have confined American Indians to the past, we must be cautious to not naturalize or authorize settler colonial notions of time by asserting that a settler present and future is the same as Indigenous present and future. Decoupling Indigenous present and future from settler present and future can provide more potential for hope and joy that is of Indigenous making, not settler authorized or generated. In exploring basketball and skateboarding in Indian Country, I have encountered a great deal of joy and hope in Native people around these activities (and to be sure some frustration and disappointment as well). Joy and hope are the temperaments of a healthy present and healthy future, respectively. Therefore, I contend that continued engagement in basketball and skateboarding, on their own terms, leads to joyful futures in Indian Country.

A SKATE POSER AND A BAD BASKETBALL PLAYER

These two things describe me to a tee. I have owned skateboards my entire life, but I have never been any good at skateboarding. For sure I can balance, push, kick, and cruise comfortably on a skateboard, but probably have only pulled off three or four clean ollies in my entire life. My basketball playing career pretty much ended in grade school when playing on Boy's Club teams where I only saw playing time during the mandatory two of four quarters that the coach had to play me—and somehow, I still managed to foul out of several games. But because I was born and raised in sunny Southern California, these two sports were always a part of my life, though mostly just as a fan and avid follower of the cultures of basketball and skateboarding. So as my academic career developed and I was lucky enough to spend more and more time in Indian Country and around Native people, I discovered that many shared my enthusiasm for basketball and skateboarding. To be sure basketball is more ubiquitous than skating in Indian Country, but it can be found all over if you just know where to look. I was continually thrilled at this discovery and could not wait to get to a point in my career where I could make this one of my main research focuses. For the last twelve years, since I finished my first book, I have been exploring basketball and skateboarding in Indian Country. This has comprised countless hours hanging out at skateparks, all over the western United States both on and off reservations, watching Indigenous skaters or hanging out and interviewing them in between skate sessions. Similarly, I have logged hundreds and hundreds of hours among Rezballers, attending Native tournaments, at practices and games helping coach all-Native teams, and interviewing them. This book comes out of twelve years' worth of this hanging out, trying to skate and hoisting too many bricks. I am grateful for all the Native people who laughed at my feeble attempt to participate and then were patient enough to let me hang out and ask them some questions. The material in this book comes from consent-based recordings of interviews and individual reviews of text from those consultants I reference. All I worked with were willing to use their actual names.[4] Skateboarding and basketball are so vast in Indian Country that there was much I had to leave out of this book, so apologies in advance to important contributors to these sports whom I have left out.

This book is divided into two parts based on each pastime. In the first chapter, I survey the general terrain of Rezball, chronicling some of its older and more recent history, looking at the various venues in which it is played and the overall importance of basketball in Indian Country. Clearly the title of chapter 1, "Ball Is Life," alludes to the critical role basketball plays in many Indigenous peoples' lives. Moreover, this chapter most explicitly describes the way Rezballers are native to basketball, as I describe the way Native people locate themselves in relationship to the invention of basketball. Chapter 2, "Some Days It's a Good Day to Play Basketball," documents the various instances that Rezball has found its way into the artistic life of Indian Country. Particularly, I interpret the various references to basketball in Native literature. Basketball is so ubiquitous to American Indian life that it is not just that so many Native people play it, but also there is Indigenous commentary and secondary literature on Rezball. Chapter 3 explores how Rezball provides hope and joy for Native folks. It addresses the very real intergeneration trauma in Indian Country and how basketball is not just an alternative to some of the struggles of reservation life but provides moments of joy right alongside the pain. Chapter 3 is also where I begin to delve deeper into the lives of Rezballers whom I have come to know (often as a coach) in order to give voice to their personal connections to Rezball. This ethnographic mode is carried into chapter 4, where I focus more specifically on female Rezballers and explore the way basketball is gendered in Indian Country and how Rezball has the potential for more gender equity than found in the mainstream expressions of basketball.

Chapter 5 begins the skateboarding half of the book. It provides a background on skating in American Indian communities by attending to some key moments and events that popularized skateboarding across

Indian Country. These developments helped many previously isolated Native skaters see that they were not the only ones skateboarding but were in fact part of a larger culture movement throughout Indian Country. I also discuss some of the attributes of skateboarding that make it native to Indian Country. That is, there are many spatial and kinesthetic aspects of skateboarding that provide fruitful models for the development and expression of Indigenous notions of place, space, and the processes of skill development and maturity. Chapter 6 returns to biographic and ethnographic modes of chapters 3 and 4, as I detail the lives of key figures in the Native skate scene. Here I explore how the outsiderness of skateboarding has been a draw for many Native youth who experience a sense of alienation provoked by the acute way settler colonialism affects reservation life. I compare the counterculture narratives of skateboarding's original rebels, the Dogtown crew, to Indigenous people's more potent rebellion against normative American values. I do this by looking at the way Native skaters have used the palate of the skate deck art and their own skate brands to express Indigenous culture and a history of resistance. Chapter 7 explicitly explores the concept that I have coined "skate elders." These are Native skaters who use skateboarding to mentor Indian youth in ways that conform to Indigenous conventions of cultural transmission, of knowledge and skill production, and of the development of balanced lives. Although these skate elders may not be quite as old as the elders that we generally find in Indian Country, they similarly look out for the generation of skaters behind them, seeking to guide them toward healthy lives. Lastly, as in the basketball section, in chapter 8 I conclude the skateboard section with a discussion of gender in Native skateboarding. I seek to understand how Native skateboarding is gendered differently and similarly to skateboarding outside of Indian Country. Skateboarding has long been an ambivalent space for women and nonbinary folks. Some aspects of skate culture lend to tolerance of all identities and subjectivities in skateboarding's effort to not conform to authority and mainstream conservative values. Yet, at the same time the movement toward extreme risk taking has only reified the hypermasculinity found in many mainstream normative American sports.

Through conversations with female and nonbinary identified Native skaters I discuss skateboarding as a venue of gender equality and equity in Indian Country.

Perhaps the most important goal of this book is to emphasize the fun people have in Indian Country and the fact that this fun is not frivolous but is crucial to American Indian vibrancy. Much of the project of America has been directly or indirectly based on suppressing Indigenous identity, culture, and history. This has caused a lot of pain and trauma in Native spaces, but nevertheless Indigenous communities continue to thrive in large part because of the persistent desire to have fun, experience joy, and maintain hope. Basketball and skateboarding play a small but important part of this persistence.

Since the spring of 2014 I have been volunteering as an assistant coach for the Inter Tribal Sports (ITS) All-Star travel basketball team. The first season I joined the team I offered to help in any way they needed me. I told the cohead coaches, Joey Masiel and Dan Sletten, that I would even be happy to be a ballboy—retrieving balls during jump shooting practice or refilling water bottles, whatever was needed. It did not matter to me; I just wanted to be a part of the experience and help in any small way I could. However, within two practices everyone began calling me "Coach Kamper" or just "Coach." At first this seemed like just a measure of respect that the coaches were demanding of the fourteen- to eighteen-year-old boys because of my age. Joey, a tribal member of the Pechanga Band of Luiseño Indians, at the time in his early thirties, has been playing Rezball his whole life. He was there from the beginning as his father and uncle helped found what would become ITS as they organized basketball games against other neighboring Southern California tribes, ultimately creating a local, Native basketball league (Joey Masiel, interview, July 31, 2015). Joey is an excellent basketball player (having starred in high school and played for a while at a local community college) with a keen sense of the game and the needs of the youth in his community. Dan, who had been working at the Pechanga tribal rec center with Joey for two years, also played a great deal of basketball in his high school years and since then had gone to school for athletic training. Despite not being Native he was generally well accepted in the community as a friendly face always around to help and to run community-based programming. He had a great deal of experience coaching youth sports and excelled at designing practices and workouts. The two had great chemistry and teamwork in coaching together (Dan Sletten, interview, July 31, 2015).

Within a few weeks I had earned enough of Coach Joey's and Coach Dan's trust that they had me participating in and helping run the practice drills. My own basketball skills are minimal, having only played organized ball through the eighth grade; however, all of my life I have been an avid fan and follower of the sport at all levels. Moreover, I have done a great deal of coaching of youth sports on my own (mainly soccer), so many of my skills were easily transferable to this context. All the same, I made certain to stay out of Dan's and Joey's way and ventured to quietly gain the players' respect with my consistency of showing up and willingness to do the tiring (and sometimes mundane) drills and the discipline-based wind sprints along with the boys, even though Dan and Joey were not doing them.[1] Although this level of participation often set me apart from Joey and Dan, who assigned the drills and sprints, I hoped it would be an opportunity for me to show the kids my commitment to the task at hand—even if on more than one occasion I could not finish all the sprints or had to step outside the gym and catch some air so that I would not vomit in front of them!

Soon Joey and Dan were inviting me to make brief remarks to the boys' when the team would huddle to reflect on a key part of practice. After the two of them would make their suggestions, encouragements, or admonitions to the boys, Joey or Dan started asking me if I had anything to add. I only occasionally took this opportunity to address them and tried to keep it brief whenever I did. Every now and then they would even let me interrupt a drill to make a brief observation or correction to what I saw the players doing. As time with them went on, some of the boys even began to listen to my one-on-one suggestions to them despite the fact that they could see that I was actually awful at playing basketball myself. It was not long before I became a regular fixture of the team. I mark this acceptance both by willingness of the boys to attend to my comments and, more importantly, to them being comfortable enough to tease me about my own play and skills. Often this kind of joking rapport is the best part of being on a team and certainly what I enjoy most. Moving from observing the games in the stands to more actively participating with the team at biweekly practices and sitting on the bench at games provided me with a much greater understanding of Rezball. It was through this kind of participation that I began to more deeply comprehend several things: how much Rezball meant to the players and the Indigenous communities for which they played, how hope can live right alongside desolation and frustration, and how activities such as Rezball can create joy and desire in a community in spite of other social, economic, and political challenges.

Take, for example, Jacob and Edward, two teenagers from the La Jolla Band of Luiseño Indians. Jacob and Edward have been playing basketball in this community most of their lives. La Jolla is a proud community up the Palomar Mountain foothills geographically separated from the rest of the other San Diego County Luiseño tribes who reside further down the valley. Life is a bit of a paradox for the youth of this tribe in that while many of their Native classmates, friends, and even cousins are members of some of the most successful governmental gaming tribes in the country, the La Jolla tribe's economic enterprises are more modest, consisting of a campground, river tubing, and zipline operation.[2] La Jolla folks live just five to ten miles from some of the largest tribal casinos in Southern California, yet their tribe has far fewer resources and job opportunities than their closest tribal neighbors.[3] Rounding out this paradox is the fact that due to the popularity of basketball in this small community, the tribe secured grants from the LA '84 Foundation and Nike N7 in the early 2000s to build a state-of-the-art, gorgeous outdoor basketball facility including a weather-resistant rubberized court made from recycled sneaker soles, Plexiglas backboards, breakaway rims, and adjustable height stanchions.[4] This is by far the nicest outdoor facility in San Diego Indian Country and would rival most other courts through-out San Diego County. The court is a testament to how much people from La Jolla value basketball and how Rezball is a symbol of hope in a community that has many challenges. This is the community in which Jacob and Edward grew up, inheriting a love for basketball from uncles, aunts, older siblings, and cousins and playing as much as possible with their peers (Edward Sigala, interview January 19, 2016; Jacob Andreas, interview March 15, 2016).

One Saturday morning in 2014 when I was helping coach the ITS Boys All-Star team, Jacob and Edward showed up bleary-eyed and mussy-haired for the 8 a.m. van that was to take the team to play in a local Southern California travel ball tournament. Our team had to play two games that day and one, potentially two, the next day. When asked why they looked so exhausted and if they had had much rest the night before, they demurred and mumbled something to the effect of "not really." These were two of the best players on the team (our top on-ball defender and our leading scorer), and they both were key to any game plan we might employ in the tournament. Upon being pushed a bit further for an explanation, they regaled us in an epic tale about how they had no ride from their home at La Jolla Reservation to the Pechanga Reservation, where they had to meet the team that morning. Wanting to make sure that they were on time and did not miss the van to the tournament, at around 9 p.m. the previous night, Edward and Jacob just decided to start walking toward Pechanga. Along the way they got ahold of one of their cousins, who was able to drive them about half of the twenty-five-mile distance. That still left them with a ten- to fifteen-mile trek that included a low mountain pass separating the Pala and Pechanga Reservations. At nearly 5 a.m. they finally made it to a community park near where they were to meet the van. Realizing they had time to kill until they had to meet the rest of the team at 8 a.m., they decided to try to catch a few hours of sleep by lying down on concrete park benches. Hence, their semi-frazzled look when the coaches and the rest of the team met up with them.

To me, this is a very powerful story of desire—desire to play basketball, desire to be with friends, and desire not to let down teammates, coaches, and themselves. Jacob and Edward could have very easily just bailed on the tournament or the game for that day, but basketball meant too much to them. The fact that they had to walk the last ten to fifteen miles to get to the meeting point illustrates their lack of resources but more importantly their dedication. This is how badly they wanted to play: it meant more to them than sleep, than physical safety (the road they had to walk is quite narrow and does not have sidewalks), or than breakfast (waking up in the park instead of home meant no food). In

the handful of times Edward and Jacob repeated this story the morning
after their walk, and have each retold it to me since, they tell the story
as if it was noteworthy but not terribly remarkable. To them, they were
just doing what they had to do in order to play ball.

REZBALL

In this basketball section of the book, the chapters that follow exam-
ine what basketball means to Native communities and the Indigenous
individuals who comprise them. What is the process of indigenizing
basketball—or what has come to be known as "Rezball"? Objectively, in
terms of the style of play or tactics employed, Rezball likely appears to
the average observer as indistinguishable from basketball played anywhere else. In fact, when asked what is unique about Rezball, most Native
people speak in generalities or assign it vague and ambivalent qualities.
However, what is most significant is that Native people distinguish the
basketball they play as something Indigenous to Indian Country. Style
of play seems less important than the community created by playing
Rezball. Rezball connotes a tight-knit, cultural ethos of playing *in the
community*—as opposed to other more mainstream places where basketball is played—and playing *for the community*—as opposed to using
one's individual basketball skill as an opportunity to exit the community.
Furthermore, while Rezball can be just as competitive as games found at
the highest levels of the sport, the games are also always about collective
fun and enjoyment.

A common idiom found on T-shirts, on social media posts, and even
on tattoos in Indian Country is "Ball Is Life." This phrase is a turn on
Indigenous traditional teachings about ecological balance such as "Water
Is Life"; "Sheep Is Life"; or "Salmon Is Life." The idea being, not only is
basketball a super important part of the life of the people promoting
this idiom, but also, just like water, sheep, or salmon, basketball gives
life to a community. This is what this section (and arguably this whole
book) is about, how basketball (and sport in general) provides vibrancy
for Native communities.

Basketball can obviously be played solo, as lone individuals shooting hoops for practice, or a handful of players challenging each other out on the court. Rezball in these formats certainly provides an outlet for physical expression and all the positive attributes that accrue from exercise. However, basketball has its most positive effect when it engages the community writ large. Basketball has been played in Indian Country for just over a hundred years. In the span of fifty years, it has become something more than just a fun way to get physical exercise, but rather a way to celebrate survivance, local heroes, and a collective spirit and values. All year round tribes or community groups host games and tournaments. Some are affiliated with seasonal ceremonial celebrations and others with fundraisers; some are the games between reservation high school teams; and others are to crown regional or national bragging rights for the best Indigenous community-based team of the year. Regardless of the reason for the games, they almost always turn out large Native crowds to cheer on their kin, to enjoy displays of skill and athleticism, and to catch up with old friends and family members. Rezball provides an important venue for Indigenous people to enact their common connections and values — the things that help shape their Indianness.

BASKETBALL (AB)ORIGINALS

In Milos Forman's award winning 1975 cinematic adaptation of *One Flew over Cuckoo's Nest*, one of the early pivotal scenes is Jack Nicholson's Randle McMurphy attempting to teach Will Sampson's "Chief" Bromden basketball in a fenced-in yard of their mental asylum. At first "Chief" seems unable to get the hang of this modern American sport, as he stoically stares at McMurphy and the wild gesticulations he is using to explain to the Indian how the game is played. An African American orderly looking on with the skepticism of a basketball aficionado sneers, "McMurphy! What the hell are you talking to him for? He can't hear a fuckin' thing." The lesson ends in failure. All "Chief" can do is hold the ball and stare at McMurphy despite his many attempts to engage the (putative) deaf-mute Indian. The next time they are out on the court, several scenes later, "Chief" begins to pick up the game rather quickly. It is also the first time we see cracks in his deaf and dumb Noble Savage persona. Here Bromden shows the first signs of having the capacity to enjoy himself, smiling and skipping up and down the court. We soon find out that Bromden has been merely performing white expectations of primitive Indianness—even down to the appellation "Chief." (*Spoiler Alert!*) He is only pretending to be a deaf-mute, and, of course, he knows how to play basketball.

In the first scene McMurphy sardonically introduces basketball to Bromden as an "old Indian game . . . called, uh, put the ball in the hole." McMurphy and the other bystanders presume the game is too modern and too "American" for him to have any knowledge of it. However, Bromden comes to demonstrate Indians are very well versed in and proficient at the sport. In the latter basketball scene, he dominates the patients' pick-up game against the African American orderlies.[5] McMurphy's ignorance of the ubiquity of basketball as a twentieth-century expression of Indianness is what leads him to expect "Chief" to be too simple for this modern sport—at the time this film is set, Indigenous people had long enjoyed and excelled at basketball in their communities for at least three-quarters of a century. This settler colonial ignorance, in large part, is what allows Bromden to perpetrate his deaf and dumb "Chief" ruse with all others in the asylum. It is only deep-seated racist stereotypes of Indigenous people, as Noble Savages from the past, that prevent mainstream society from equating basketball with Indianness. Ironically, McMurphy does not know how correct he is when he calls basketball an "old Indian game."

Consider, on the contrary, the ESPN documentary by Maura Mandt and Josh Swade (2012) entitled *There's No Place Like Home*. This film details the Sotheby's auction of James Naismith's original list of rules to the game of basketball and the battle between wealthy Duke University and Kansas University alumni to purchase this artifact for their respective basketball-blueblood universities' collections. Naismith is considered to be the creator of basketball as, in late 1891, he was looking for an indoor, winter sport to channel the abundant energy found in the youth under his charge at the Springfield, Massachusetts, Young Men's Christian Association. Seven years after inventing the game, Naismith went on to work at the University of Kansas, where he helped grow his game to national attention and participation. Mandt and Swade's documentary chronicles the contemporary fate of his "rules" as one of Naismith's descendants attempted to sell this document in order to solve his own financial insolubility. In the movie Swade relates a key part of the story: a private bid to acquire the document in advance of it ever being auctioned at Sotheby's. *There's No Place Like Home* discloses that an unnamed American Indian tribe from Oklahoma, "rich with casino profits," attempted to purchase the rules for over ten million dollars with the intent of using the rules as a centerpiece for a basketball museum they had planned to build. Irrespective of the potential apocrypha in this tale, it signifies the value that many American Indians put on not just the sport of basketball but its origins as well. We can read this attempt to purchase the rules as an effort by at least one Oklahoma Native community to claim the beginning of basketball, and thereby the sport itself, to be Indigenous. It reveals a deep-seated connection to the sport and a desire to extend that into antiquity, to make basketball a part of American Indian history, not merely U.S. history. Purchasing the historic document of James Naismith's original rules of basketball would have indigenized the rules by making them the figurative and literal possession of Native people. Ironically, this is the reversal of the way that U.S. settler colonialism assimilates Native antiquities into general American history in order to increase the claim of U.S. national longevity and naturalize the dispossession of Native land and culture.

TOURNEY TIME

While basketball ostensibly originated outside of the Indian Country, Rezball allows American Indians to engage the modern world in ways that both reinforce a historic Indigenous virtue of social interconnection and underscore Native peoples' perpetual vitality to reinterpret these historic values through contemporary practices. This adapting of the past to meet the needs of the present is the epitome of American Indian vibrancy. Take, for example, the annual Lakota Nation Invitational (LNI) basketball tournament, held just off the Pine Ridge Reservation, and how this Rezball tourney embodies the use of a contemporary form to revitalize historic culture and language.

The LNI was founded in 1977 and has grown into one of the largest Rezball tournaments in the country. It started as an innovative, Indigenous solution to the perennial problem of reservation border town racism in the Dakotas. The turmoil experienced by Indians in this region of the country was disturbingly similar to that of African Americans in the Jim Crow South. Residents of the all-white towns just off reservations in this area of the country consistently discriminated against Indians. For much of the twentieth century it was commonplace to see handmade signs in restaurant and store windows reading, "No Dogs or Indians Allowed." Moreover, the regular occurrence of vigilante groups of white men beating Indians to death outside of bars and saloons was not at all dissimilar to lynchings in the American South.

In early 1973, fueled by the growing revolutionary ideology of Native civil rights activism and the tension surrounding internal political strife on the Pine Ridge Reservation, local Indians had had enough and responded radically to the bloody assault and death of a local Lakota man by a white man. When the white assailant only received a one-day sentence of involuntary manslaughter for killing the Lakota man, Native activists responded by forcefully seizing the hamlet of Wounded Knee. The location was specifically chosen to symbolically connect the current treatment of Indians in the Dakotas to those Indians massacred by the U.S. Calvary on the same spot in 1890. One indirect result of this seventy-one-day armed standoff between Lakota activists and federal authorities was increased distrust and prejudice from white folks surrounding the reservation. This white distrust of Lakotas and the fear of violence in Native communities had some very practical and quotidian effects in these communities. One such byproduct connected directly to local Rezball.

There are several high schools, predominantly Native, on the various Lakota reservations throughout North and South Dakota and Nebraska.

One such school, Pine Ridge High School, had Bryan Brewer (a future Oglala Sioux tribal chairman) as their basketball coach. In 1977, four years after the Wounded Knee incident, Coach Brewer could not convince non-Indian basketball teams to come to the reservation to play the Pine Ridge High School team (Klein 2020). In the four years since the Wounded Knee occupation, there had been ongoing intra-tribal tension and violent repression of activism at the hands of the FBI (Churchill and Vander Wall 2002); consequently, "athletic directors from school districts across South Dakota refused to let their athletes play ball" at Pine Ridge—so much so that for a few years Coach Brewer's team could not even complete a full season's schedule (Klein 2020). Brewer knew his kids were desperate for the normalcy that comes from playing basketball. His solution: call around to Native and reservation high schools up to hundreds of miles away from Pine Ridge, entreating them to come to a basketball tournament that he would host in mid-December. This tournament became the Lakota Nation Invitational. The event caught on quickly and became so large and successful that they had to move it to the border town of Rapid City, South Dakota—the very kind of place that was home to the anti-Indian racism that generated the necessity of the LNI in the first place. Within five years the tournament became so popular and showcased such high-level basketball games that non-Indian teams began petitioning to play these Native teams and get into this Rezball tournament. Ultimately, LNI created a bidding system where only two of the sixteen teams could hail from non-Indian communities.[6] Now, it is the LNI tournament directors who decide which teams play and where, not the white high schools' athletic directors. This turnabout is a quintessential illustration of how success in basketball can translate into Native pride, legitimacy, and authority—all qualities that generate vibrancy in a community.

Brewer's innovative spirit in creating this tournament as a solution to anti-Indian racism has only flourished as the years have passed. Under his leadership today the tournament is a massive cultural and community-wide event that includes a powwow, a cheerleading contest, traditional hand-game competitions, a wrestling tournament, an art show, a "business plan" competition, an academic quiz competition, and a Lakota language bowl (challenging contestants' knowledge of the Indigenous language). All of this in only four days! And it is projected that the LNI brings in five to six million dollars every year to the local community that hosts the tournament (Rickert 2019). Basketball is the foundation of this event, but through it Native youth, and the local community, celebrate tradition as well.

Equally popular, if not more so, than the LNI is the Native American Basketball Invitational (NABI) held annually in the Phoenix Valley. NABI was started in 2003, and although NABI has not been around as long as the Lakota tournament, it has become much larger and broader reaching than the regional LNI event. NABI averages 120 to 160 teams every year that come from as far away as the Florida Seminole Nation, Native Alaska villages, and Maori communities in New Zealand. The tournament is so large that each year there are four full brackets of tournament play—two for high school boys and two for high school girls. During the last week of June and the first of July it is not uncommon to see several white, federal grant-funded passenger vans in the parking lots of junior high schools, high schools, community colleges, or tribal rec centers all throughout the Phoenix Valley. These white "commodity" vans can be seen lined up in the parking lots bespattered with dust, bugs, and blotches of chipped paint that have been collected during their treks from rural reservations to Phoenix for the biggest Rezball tourney of the year. Native youth, ages fifteen to eighteen, pile out of these vans into gyms of all sizes and amenities, some with unspoiled parquet floors well-maintained for likes of DI college or professional ballers, others with faux wood vinyl flooring efficiently constructed for junior high schools and community centers. These Native kids come to compete in a guaranteed minimum of four games, sometimes often playing two or three games a day, all in hopes of being crowned the best youth Rezballers in the country.

The basketball is almost always played at a breakneck pace. Defenses play full- or half-court pressure, trapping the ball all over the court in an effort to force turnovers that quickly switch the direction of the game with sprints up the court or lob outlet passes for fast breaks, earning acrobatic twisting lay-ups, wide open transition threes, or even the occasional slam dunk.[7] And when forced into half-court offenses, more often than not players are looking to chuck up as many three-point shots as possible. This is Rezball at its pinnacle expression. Undoubtedly, a spectator might find similar elements of play in any high school, college, or even professional game around the world (especially with the increasing awareness of the statistical value of the three-point shot over a long two-point shot or a contested post-up shot),[8] and, indeed, there are a lot of similarities, but on the whole Rezball is a more consistently fast-paced game where teams usually frantically run all over the court when playing both offense and defense. But in many ways Rezball is less about a style of play than it is an ethos.

At an average NABI game parents, relatives, and friends fill the bleachers cheering on their favorite team, shouting out para-coaching instructions, and frequently bellowing disapproval at the referees. Despite the competitive spirit in the gym, fans are always supportive of both teams. Sometimes scores can get quite lopsided—30- to 40-point deficits, occasionally even worse—but both teams always play to the final buzzer, and fans cheer on players all the way through the game. I have seen fans cheer enthusiastically when a Rezballer works hard to hit an open three even though her or his team is down 35 points, and there are only one and half minutes left in the game. Moreover, although there is no shot clock used for these games, teams with only narrow leads of 3 and 4 points hardly ever try to stall out the game.[9] They always show respect for the opposing team by playing hard themselves, working for a shot all the way until the end of the game.

Winning is certainly very important, but by no means is it the only thing that matters. Make no mistake, the players want to win, but they also recognize and enjoy the benefits of just participating in NABI. Being a part of the event and the Native community at the tournament and having fun seem just as important to these Native youth. Rarely do most of them get to interact with so many Indigenous people of their age all in the same place, or even get an opportunity to travel more than fifty to a hundred miles away from their reservation. Among the highlights of the tournament are the pool and dance parties at the host hotel, which can feature 500–750 Indigenous kids from all over the country enjoying each other just by acting like normal teenagers. These dance or pool parties are known to occasionally even generate romantic relationships that can last long after the tournament is over. Additionally, each team is required to attend a college fair and three "Educational Seminars" on topics such as college admittance, financial planning, and mental and physical well-being. Although players often begrudgingly attend these seminars, they do so as a team with many other teams in stuffy hotel ballrooms and bond over the "necessary evil" of the seminars. Of course, these seminars speak to the effort of NABI's organizers to use basketball to broaden the horizons of these Native youth and provide them with additional life skills. Moreover, every year NABI gives out thousands of dollars in college scholarships to the most academically inclined NABI Rezballers. Hence, as in many other instances across Indian Country, Rezball is a contemporary opportunity for Native youth to reenact the process of community building and maintenance, something crucial to all communities, but particularly Indigenous ones surviving the ongoing ravages of settler colonialism.

INTER TRIBAL SPORTS

A third iteration of Rezball tournaments can be found in Southern California in the form of an intertribal youth sports league that features basketball as one of its premiere sports. Inter Tribal Sports (ITS) officially began in 2002 as organized flag football, basketball, and softball leagues for five Native community teams (three tribally based). Over the proceeding fifteen years, ITS has grown exponentially to include twenty-two tribal communities from San Diego, Riverside, San Bernardino, and Imperial Counties and has served up to three thousand Indigenous youth per year. ITS has provided these youth with opportunities to play a multitude of sports that now includes soccer, lacrosse, cheerleading, golf, and cross country, in addition to the original three. But basketball has always been a mainstay for the program—the one that gets some of the highest participation from athletes and fans. I discuss ITS Rezball in much greater detail in chapter 2, "Some Days It's a Good Day to Play Basketball," as I chronicle the experiences of some of the many Rez-ballers who play with ITS. However, considering ITS on a macro level, its efforts to strengthen Indigenous community and culture make it a leading program in Indian Country and one that many consider setting an example of best practices. Indeed, as an organization with some of the most seniority of any Nike N7 grantees, ITS is always held up by Nike as a model for other programs seeking to earn an N7 grant.

One thing that sets ITS apart nationally and locally is the tremendous amount of community support it enjoys. Although not every Southern California tribe participates or is able to participate on a permanent basis, ITS still garners a near unprecedented level of support compared to other Southern California intertribal organizations. Likely, this has to do with the fact that sport is not as easily politicized as governmental, economic, linguistic, or cultural networks in Southern California Indi-an Country.[10] But the fact remains that almost all uniformly agree that ITS is an excellent organization because of the way in which it brings the larger community together and is a positive outlet for Native youth to channel their energy and enact a commitment to something larger than their individual lives. Support for ITS is made most manifest at the weekly game day events during basketball season when Indians from several different communities meet at one tribe's rec center for up to nine hours of Rezball. These game day events (described in more detail below) are significant for Southern California Indian Country because they bring family and friends together in ways few other things do, and they rival community Rezball tourneys anywhere in Indian Country.

PARQUET POWWOWS

Given the intra- and intertribal ways that Rezball can bring Indian peo-ples together, it is worth considering organized basketball events, such as ITS, NABI, and LNI, in comparison to a contemporaneous, popular In-digenous event that also functions as a lynchpin of tribal and intertribal community wellness: the powwow. On a surface level, there are some very fundamental similarities between Rezball events or tournaments and powwows. They are both ritualized, periodic events that draw large audiences of community support and participation. Another similarity is the way Native participants look forward to powwows and Rezball games with great anticipation. Rarely are people mere occasional participants in Rezball or powwow; rather, these two expressions of indigeneity become significant life commitments. It is often declared that *powwow is a way of life* (see Ellis 2003; Ellis, Lassiter, and Dunham 2005). The sentiment behind this assertion mirrors the notion "Ball Is Life." This lifestyle commitment can be seen quite clearly in both activities. Participants dedicate themselves to honing and practicing their craft during their individual free time. They plan their weekly, monthly, and annual schedules around powwows and Rezball tourneys. Both demand not just a resource of time, but also money. Regulars save up their money in order to travel to national and regional iterations of Rezball and powwow. Moreover, just as powwow dancers (and their families) invest a great deal of care and money in their regalia, buying supplies for or commissioning the fabrication of parts of their outfits and then storing the regalia in protective and respectful ways, so do Rezballers make an investment in their gear. Intense attention is paid to on- and off-court attire and how these clothes function and look, and the need to save money to buy the best gear. The most obvious example can be found in "sneaker culture" and its expression in Rezball—who has the freshest shoes, who sports the classic ones (and when), and whose are kept in the best condition (requiring constant cleaning and strict avoidance of scuff marks) are frequent topics of attention and discussion. Additionally, Rezballers will collectively invest in smart-looking jerseys in order to match and appear collectively sharp as a team. Just as powwow dancers attend to every detail of their regalia, so too do Rezballers, often debating the merits of what, from the outside, might seem insignificant: the functionality and style of gym shorts, headbands, and even socks! While Rezballer gear might not have the same (conventionally) "Indian" cultural symbolism or value that most powwow regalia maintain, it is no less important to Rezballers, and most wear their gear as an expression of who they are, proud Indigenous people who play basketball mostly in Indigenous contexts.

There are other spatial and kinesthetic connections between powwows and Rezball. For example, in powwows that cannot be held outside, due to weather, usually the dancing takes place indoors on the same court or floor that is normally used for basketball. Additionally, it is not uncommon to see Native folks either practicing their dances or conducting community powwow classes in tribal gyms on the same basketball court where (and often simultaneously with) Rezballers practice their shots or running drills.[11] On some level this is a matter of convenience; however, there are strong similarities to the way the physical space and floor are utilized by participants of these two highly popular Indian Country activities. Holding a powwow is often seen as sanctifying a space even if the space is an echoing gymnasium with basketball stanchions hanging from the ceiling. Dancers make the courts in these gyms their own sacrosanct arena by enacting modern interpretations of tribal traditions and Indigenous communal life. The embodied kinesthetic activity, collective participation (in terms of dancing, signing, and spectating), shared sense of respect (the value on doing things "in a good way") for the activity happening within the physical space, and the arrangement of the Native bodies and movements all temporarily transform basketball gyms into socially and culturally relevant areas during the duration of a powwow.

These same worn slabs of hardwood also frequently provide refuge for Rezballers. There is a similar visceral and kinesthetic connection to space and place that Rezballers maintain in tribal gyms. The bodies and limbs of Rezballers equally reenact ritual movements in real time in ways that garner praise (or silent disapproval) from the audience. Moreover, a shared sense of collective engagement with a contemporary expression of Indianness exists in Rezball games and tournaments just as in powwows. Participants expect the basketball in this setting to be enacted with a certain sense of dedication, effort, and pace, all leading to the ritualization of behavior and activity that indigenizes basketball.

The connections between these two kinds of Indian Country events are not lost on a group of Rezball fanatics who, in 2010, created the Native American All Indian Shoot-Out. This tournament is now held annually in an auxiliary gym on the campus of University of New Mexico (UNM). This tournament is always scheduled for the same weekend as "Gathering of Nations"—the largest powwow in the world. Tens of thousands of people travel globally to attend "Gathering" and dance (or watch the dance) in UNM's renown basketball arena, affectionately known as "the Pit."[12] Simultaneous to powwow dancers and singers performing on UNM's premier basketball court, hundreds of Rezballers are intensely competing on UNM's smaller, older, secondary gym that holds the intramural basketball courts. These two events are far from mutually exclusive; many Rezballers, dancers, and spectators go back and forth between these two events during Gathering weekend as a dynamic way to celebrate two of the most vibrant articulations of contemporary Indianness.

At the LNI, powwow culture plays an even more central role than at the Native American All Indian Shoot-Out. On Saturday night, the most important night of the four-day tournament, there is a set of public events on the main court before the girls' and boys' championship games that mirror the form and structure of powwows. A local powwow drum group is hired to play for the festivities. Just as in a powwow, they start by playing a flag song as Native veterans march on the court in military uniforms, powwow regalia, or street clothes. Accompanying these forty-some some veterans is a color guard, eagle staff holder, and a handful of men's Traditional or Grass dancers and a few younger girl Jingle or Traditional dancers. Everyone in the arena welcomes this assemblage with the utmost respect for the veterans, and the MC announces each veteran's name, tribal community, and in which war they served. Then the drum group is asked to play an honor song as the tournament officials recognize the community service and achievements of longtime coaches, teachers, or officials connected to LNI. The events conclude with what LNI organizers have appropriately labeled a "grand entry." This term is borrowed directly from powwow culture and follows the same format. The MC introduces each high school team as they enter the arena, parade around the court, and fall into formation until the entire court is filled with all thirty-two teams. During this whole approximately twenty-minute process the drum group is playing, and an MC is entertaining the crowd in much the same way a powwow MC would call out the groups of dancers in a powwow grand entry, organized by dance style. The color guard and small contingent of powwow dancers return to the court to lead the teams in along with the tournament organizers. As in a powwow, LNI organizers mark out a time and space for the entire community to appreciate the spectacle of the event and to show gratitude to the tournament organizers for creating this opportunity for communal celebration and to honor the participants for their commitment and hard work on the court.

Since the second half of the twentieth century, powwows have been a mainstay of tribal and intertribal life. In his seminal monograph *A Dancing People*, Clyde Ellis (2003) tries to sort out the complex and varied significance of contemporary powwows by interviewing several active participants. One such Dakota tribal dancer tells him, "'While I don't have an overly romantic view of powwows . . . I do know they are places where senses of family and community are enriched. In the twenty-first century they offer one of the few places we can take our kids and let them run around knowing they will be safe. This is not to suggest that anything mystical occurs there . . . indeed, political disagreements are prevalent as are gossip and jealously'" (Ellis 2003, 6). Ellis's consultants relate how powwows have generative power to reinforce and reconstruct a sense of community. Ellis argues that powwows "are intensely meaningful, perhaps because . . . participants and spectators are more or less tightly knit by kinship and a sense of community that is expressed daily in numerous ways outside of the powwow" (5). Another dancer tells him, "'Here [at a powwow] . . . I remember what it means to be a member of this family, this tribe of people, I wouldn't miss it for the world'" (4). Nearly all of the Native folks Ellis worked with comment on the sense of belonging that is produced by powwows. Even if powwows occasionally invoke tensions in Indian County, Ellis's research illustrates how they can also be a venue for people to peacefully work out conflicts in tribal communities and contested notions of Indianness (see also Ellis, Lassiter, and Dunham 2005). Indeed, he clearly illustrates how powwows constitute much of the sociocultural fabric of contemporary Indian life.

While not explicitly built from the same traditional cultural material as powwows, Rezball games and tournaments can conjure this same sense of intergenerational, communal identity and connectivity by providing a space for people to collectively express indigeneity. Through interviews with and anecdotes from Rezballers, the chapters that follow reveal how the games and events surrounding them reinforce implicit tribal values such as diligence, strong family relations, and working collectively to achieve goals. At Rezball games players compete in ways that allow them to demonstrate to each other, and the fans they represent, that their tribal community is so important to them that they willingly exert massive amounts of time and energy to gain approval and respect. Equally, the games allow the fans to reaffirm kin relationships by cheering on the players, representing their community, and reconnecting with friends and family in the stands during the game. In trying to understand the draw of powwows, Ellis cites Gloria Alese Young's dissertation explaining that one of the main functions of powwows is to "raise the quality of life of its participants through improved mental health and social contacts" (quoted in Ellis, Lassiter, and Dunham 2005, 11). Rezball serves this exact same purpose, bringing a sense of wellness to the players and fans who participate and providing a healthy and productive activity to which they can dedicate their time and energy. In essence, Rezball has become a new version of powwow; not a replacement per se, but rather an additional form of commitment to tribal life and Indianness in the contemporary era.

MONEY(REZ)BALL

It is equally relevant to note the economic similarities between powwows and Rezball. The events and transactions surrounding these performances of physical skill and coordination can be a very important manifestation of local Indigenous economics. I comment above on a comparable effect on personal finance, noting how Native people dedicate their own (and their family's) money and time in order to fully participate in pow-wows and Rezball. Additionally, both of these activities have become a hub for the circulation and redistribution of community-wide resources. This economic impact can be illustrated in several ways. Among the most obvious for powwows are the giveaways and "blanket dances" that are a key component of nearly every powwow. In the former, families seek to honor a member of their family (or kin network) by gifting various types of items to selected powwow organizers, participants, and spectators in order to commemorate an accomplishment or life cycle milestone of this family member. In the blanket dance a specific song and dance is set apart from others as a blanket is placed in the center of the arena, and participants and spectators are encouraged to place small monetary donations on the blanket while a drum group plays a song. This collection of loose bills is used variously: to pay for a drum group's performance or to defray their travel costs; to assist with other logistic expenses associated with the powwow; or to help local families undergoing extreme hardships. These customary practices of powwow help circulate resources and wealth throughout a community so that successes and burdens are shared evenly, not disproportionately. Another standard-bearer of powwow culture are vendor booths that are always set up on the periphery of the arena, selling all kinds of food, arts and crafts, and clothing. These provide a vital means for enterprising Native peoples to supplement their income, and in some cases it might be their sole source of revenue. Similarly, many powwows offer financial prizes to dancers or drum groups for winning competitions at powwows. This can be a valuable source of income for many dancers who traverse what is known as the powwow "circuit" or "trail," traveling across the country entering competitions. Finally, powwows commonly have raffle-based fundraisers where vendors are asked to donate an item or two that they would normally sell, and participants buy raffle tickets for a chance to win these items. Money from these raffles frequently goes to the same causes as funds raised in a blanket dance. The popularity of powwows helps successfully circulate money throughout the community in a way that is culturally grounded.

Rezball games and tournaments provide analogous examples of these localized economic transactions. For example, while something akin to giveaways or a blanket dance is rarely featured at Rezball events, it is very common for Rezball tournaments to raise money through entrance fees from the teams playing. These fees sometimes go toward a local cause — often to cover the cost of a Native youth basketball team's travel or entrance fee to another regional or national tournament or the costs of uniforms or shoes for a youth team. Similar to the competition prize money common at certain powwows, many Rezball tournaments have cash prizes for the winning team. It should be no surprise that as this prize money increases the number of teams in a tournament, it also increases the competitive level of play, not unlike powwows with large prize money. Additionally, many of the same food and clothing vendors who sell at powwows also find that they can make money at Rezball tournaments. Although Rezball events rarely have as large of a congregation of vendors as exists at powwows, it is normal to see three to four booths outside of or in the foyer of the tournament gyms. The LNI tournament has a large number of vending booths (twenty to thirty), which is on par with most significant-sized powwows. Additionally, a handful of small companies have been created to sell basketball clothing and apparel marketed specifically to Rezball players and fans. Not only do these companies show up to tournaments, but they are increasing their online vending as well.

Considered from another angle, we can read the construction of large elaborate basketball gyms or high-tech outdoor courts as a crucial financial commitment on behalf of a tribal government (and the people it represents). Putting profit from tribal enterprises toward projects that the whole community can enjoy and at which a great deal of time is spent illustrates a very powerful investment in community. The Pechanga Band of Luiseño Indians in Temecula, California, for example, has used profits from their highly successful casino to build a gym with basketball courts as nice as any in California — including as nice as the training facilities of a few of California's NBA teams. About 650 miles east of the Pechanga reservation sit the twin towns of Ft. Defiance and Window Rock at the Navajo Nation. These slightly more modest desert towns together have a little over 7,000 residents. Yet, given that fans start lining up at 10 a.m. to vie for tickets to a 7 p.m. high school basketball game, it's no wonder the tribal government felt that building a 6,500-seat, state-of-the-art basketball arena for the local team was a necessity. And there are two other high school basketball arenas at the Navajo Nation that are nearly as big, in Shiprock, New Mexico, and Chinlee, Arizona.

Finally, it is worth considering the WNBA team, the Connecticut Sun. In 2002 the Orlando Miracles franchise was in jeopardy of folding. At this time in the history of the WNBA, the NBA began to end the practice of underwriting the women's franchises, and the Miracles' "brother" team, the NBA's Orlando Magic, declined its option to take over the operation and expenses of the Miracles. In stepped the Mohegan Tribe of Connecticut. Relying on the popularity of women's basketball in the Connecticut area and Native connection to the sport in general, the tribe became the first Native nation to own a major professional sports team.[13] The team was immediately moved from Orlando to the Mohegan reservation and renamed the Connecticut Sun after the tribe's casino and cultural symbol. While the Sun does not necessarily fit the conventional notion of Rezball—none of the players are Native, and they do not necessarily play the fast-paced style characterized by the ball played in tribal communities—it is hard to argue against them being an indigenized team given the ownership. Indeed, the Sun is the only professional sports team to play at or be owned by a Native nation[14] Their arena is situated in the middle of the tribe's casino, and the team's professional staff (coaches, trainers, and advisers) are considered tribal enterprise employees. The Mohegans' investment in the WNBA represents as significant a commitment to basketball as any in Indian Country. Its existence allows the tribe to redistribute to tribal community members the revenue that comes from a mostly non-Indian fan base through ticket sales, TV broadcasts, and marketing deals. Each one of these tribal governmental investments in the construction of extravagant spaces for

Rezball amounts to an institutionalized recognition of the importance and value of basketball in Indian Country.

CONCLUSION

When chatting about my research to colleagues or nonacademic friends, who are generally unfamiliar with American Indian communities, I am often struck by how frequently people are either surprised or puzzled by Indians' participation in basketball.[15] My response is almost always to take out my phone and show them a picture of the Ft. Defiance, Arizona, high school arena and to relate how small the town is and how early people line up for games. Generally, it is not until I tell them that there are also two other basketball arenas this big on the Navajo reservation that the significance of the sport in Indian Country really begins to sink in for them. This response of surprise toward Rezball likely comes from what Philip J. Deloria (2004) describes as normative cultural "expectations" for who Indians are and what they commonly do. Most non-Indians are still conditioned to think of Indians as people of the past (as some combination of uncivilized, violent "savages" and simplistic, romanticized "noble" exotic others). Delimiting Indigenous people to the past comes from the presumption that they engage in "traditional" behaviors, rather than practices characteristic of the modern world. To some extent this bias comes from a general Western blindness to seeing "tradition" as anything other than static (see Hobsbawm and Ranger 2012). When it comes to Native peoples, this invariable notion of tradition racializes Indigenous peoples, solely defining them by culture and ideology thought to be unchanged for millennia. Indigenous peoples are caught in a double bind whereby outsiders use static notions of "tradition" to determine Indigenous authenticity, thereby delimiting the only real Indians to the past. Hence contemporary expressions of indigeneity that might engage modernity are deemed to be anomalous and inauthentic (Deloria 2004; see also Vizenor 1994; Povinelli 2002; Raibmon 2005). This is a particularly potent tactic of settler colonialism because it provides the logic to disavow Native peoples contemporary political, legal, and resource rights commensurate with indigeneity.

One fundamental way Indigenous people fight such settler logic is to embrace this contradiction and insist that tradition and modernity can be engaged simultaneously—that they are not in opposition to each other. The most obvious example of this is when Native communities continue (or revive) ceremonies and practices that they have done for thousands of years. An alternative is when Native communities adapt things from their contemporaries and indigenize them, make them their own, and claim these behaviors as just as integral to the community as those being practiced for millennia. While often overlooked as the defining features of an Indigenous community, the latter practices of adoption and incorporation have just as much potency for community as the former practices thought to live in the community since time immemorial. Moreover, the latter sort of practices can implicitly combat settler colonialism in a way the former practices often fail to do, because an engagement with modernity forces non-Indians to thoroughly consider what contemporary Indigenous life looks like—not a romanticized notion of people only doing the same things they have been doing for thousands of years. I see this transformative potential every time I show the picture of the Ft. Defiance gym to someone, and their eyes get big, and a light bulb seems to go off inside their head realizing, "Wait, Indians are still here and their communities are vibrant?" I believe the ubiquity of Rezball is one of the clearest expressions of this vibrancy.

The follow-up question to these casual conversations about my research is almost inevitably, "But why basketball? Why not lacrosse or running?" The implication behind this question is "why not something *more traditional?*" (often these exact words are used!). This question is intended both for me as a scholar (in terms of the research I choose to undertake) and for Indians as athletes (in terms of the sports in which they choose to participate). Setting aside the way that this question just betrays and reifies people's expectations that Indians should be playing something else that is "more traditional," there are a multitude of answers to this question of why basketball: people play multiple sports;

basketball is not a resource-intense sport and can be played with just one or two people; some boarding schools introduced it early on to Native communities, to name a few. Invariably when I ask Rezballers when and why they start playing basketball, they will say it is because their older siblings, cousins, or aunts and uncles played so they just started to play also. In my estimation this even further illustrates the integral and ubiquitous nature of Rezball. It is habitual participation that gets passed down generationally without question as to why it happens or why that kind of practice. Because of this habitual participation, this book is less interested in the question of *why* basketball (particularly the one of why basketball as opposed to another sport). The answer is because this is what people do: playing or watching Rezball is part of what it means to an Indian in the twenty-first century in the United States. A more interesting question to me is, what does playing Rezball do for individuals and the community as a whole? I explore this question in the next several chapters.

SOME DAYS IT'S A GOOD DAY
TO PLAY BASKETBALL

The title of this chapter comes from what many still consider to be the definitive cinematic depiction of contemporary reservation life despite the fact that the film itself is over twenty years old. Chris Eyre's (1998) film *Smoke Signals* (with a screenplay by Sherman Alexie) sought to capture everyday life on the reservation, so of course it includes Rezball. One of the earliest scenes in the movie is a pickup game in a reservation gym. This scene is used to establish both a sense of place and the tension between the two main characters, Victor and Thomas. The former is playing pickup with two other friends inside the tribal gym, while the latter watches on and tries to interject in the conversation from the sideline. Soon they take a break from playing, and one of Victor's friends rhythmically bounces the ball on the hardwood court to replicate a powwow drum and sings a "49" about playing basketball against General Custer.[1] They then begin to have a discussion about who is the best basketball player of all time. Nearly every basketball player or fan has had this debate with their friends at least fifty times, yet in Indian Country the flavor of the debate is often different. Victor claims that Geronimo was the best ever, which leads to some back and forth banter about whether Geronimo was tall enough to be a great basketball player. Significantly the question is not whether or not Geronimo actually played basketball. To most outside of Indian Country, this is where the debate would begin and end; however, the Rezballers in Smoke Signals accept the fact that he was a hooper to be a given. By choosing Geronimo and then not having their characters question if he even played basketball, but rather how good he was at it, Alexie and Eyre stake a claim that basketball is an Indigenous sport. This is just another iteration of the way Alexie (and others) use fiction to indigenize basketball and absorb it into Native history and culture (indeed, there are other crucial scenes in the movie that take place on basketball courts).

The debate about Geronimo's skills is summed up by one of Victor's Rezball buddies as he says, "Some days it's a good day to die, and some days it's a good day to play basketball." This is a witty riff on an Oglala Lakota adage, "Today is a good day to die," that warriors would purportedly say before going into battle to proclaim their willingness to defend their community even if it meant dying. Recognizing that the only real source of this quote is from white accounts of Lakota warriors, Alexie's screenplay drolly reclaims this phrase from white, racist, "noble savage" stereotypes by the suggestion that only *some days* is it a good day to die and others it is a good day to do other more joyful things like playing basketball. Suggesting instead that there are all kinds of other, very quotidian, things that Indian people do (other than dying) undercuts the dehumanizing nature of "noble savage" representations that make all Indians valorous, stoic warriors defined mainly by their willingness to do battle that will result in valiant martyrdom. Recognizing that it is a good day for all kinds of things that Indians generally do is what makes them human. For example, later in the film Eyre and Alexie have Thomas Builds the Fire assert, as he sits down for a big meal of pancakes, "Sometimes it's a good day to die, and sometimes it's a good day to eat breakfast." What makes this turn of phrase so insightful is that it not only mocks "noble savage" imagery, but it also captures the balance between the harsh realities of colonization when Native people died defending their communities and the fact that everyday life—like eating breakfast—still went on and continues to carry on in reservation communities in spite of settler colonialism.

The realization that "some days it's a good day to play basketball" illustrates the balance between the momentous and the mundane, between the tragic and the hopeful. Much of Alexie's literary work also draws out this relationship and tension between despair and joy in contemporary Indian communities. Settler colonialism, intergenerational trauma, and poverty have wrought an abundance of challenges and despair to Indigenous communities; yet at the same time the continuation of cultural practices, language revitalization, and the various ways people have enjoyed themselves and have fun empowers hope on reservations. Rezball is one of these embodiments of hope and joy in contemporary Indigenous life. Edward and Jacob's story (from the last chapter) of their trek to make it to the meeting spot for the van to the basketball tournament is an expression of this hope and desire for joy. They did not have the resources to get to the meeting spot, a product of desolation and poverty; nonetheless, their desire to play was strong enough that they figured out a way to get there. This chapter explores how Rezball, because of its ubiquity in Indigenous life, has become a venue for hope and joy. Promoting such practices is critically important to the wellness of Indigenous communities and is an inherent recognition that these communities are not merely spaces of deficit.

THE JOY AND HOPE OF REZBALL

In the previous chapter I compare Rezball to powwows, but I am not suggesting that the former is replacing the latter. Rather, looking at the growth, popularity, and function of powwows is instructive for understanding how collective gatherings centered around what are essentially kinesthetic expressions can be vital for the mental health and well-being of an Indigenous community. It is important not to underestimate the impact of Rezball on youth and adults and how this ostensibly "fun" activity keeps Native peoples connected to and engaged in their community. As Clyde Ellis (2003) observes of powwows:

> Today, some critics are disdainful of powwow people who, in their estimation, spend an awful lot of time building elaborate dance outfits and chasing contest dollars instead of devoting their time and energy to more serious things like political activism. (7)

The same superficial critique might be leveled at Rezball. Yet this underestimates the importance of everyday activities and the joy that can be found in the quotidian. An activity does not need to be the most explicitly political or "traditional" to help build a strong, healthy Native community. As Ellis puts it, "expressions of kinship and community define the powwow as an event that draws Indian people together in a profoundly meaningful way" (14). This praise could also be ascribed to Rezball. In a highly positive manner, Rezball connects people not only within specific tribal communities, but also across all Indian Country. And given the contemporary challenges in Indian Country that are the lasting consequences of settler colonialism, healthy community interactions are invaluable. Activities such as Rezball can provide a counterweight of fun and happiness to the settler colonial burdens of substance abuse, domestic violence, suicide, unemployment, culturicide, ecocide, and so on.

This balance of joy and despair in quotidian life is particularly acute in Indian Country. Perhaps no Native author or thinker captures this better than the Coeur D'Alene–Spokane fiction writer and essayist Sherman Alexie. His lyrical depictions of reservation life deftly humanize the way Indigenous people find happiness and peace in the face of despair caused by significant life challenges. Rezball and Rezballers make many appearances in Alexie's narratives, due in part to his own self-proclaimed love of basketball and in part to his recognition of the ubiquity of basketball in Indian Country. Alexie has also made the connection between Rezball and powwows; in one short story he describes his protagonist as a connoisseur of "many of the general American Indian ceremonies like powwows and basketball tournaments" (Alexie 2000, 183). Making Rezball and Rezballers the narrative foci helps his stories connect with Native people across the country, not solely the Spokane Reservation where he grew up. Alexie employs his own intimate familiarity with the sport—having played it most of his life—to make several metaphorical observations about contemporary Native life (see Grassian 2005; Goldstein 2009; Jaskulski 2014). Perhaps most powerful is the way Alexie uses basketball as a symbol of hope in the face of desperation.

Take, for example, Alexie's short story "What Ever Happened to Frank Snake Church?" from his National Book Award–winning collection, *Ten*

Little Indians (2003). Although it is set in urban Seattle, not a reservation, Alexie skillfully captures the multilevel displacements common to Native peoples' lives and the depressing effect of these displacements. The story's main character, Frank Snake Church, was considered the best high school basketball prospect in Seattle, where he "averaged forty-one points a game during his senior year . . . and had received 114 scholarship offers from colleges all over the country" (202). But then his mother dies the summer before he was to begin playing for the University of Washington men's basketball team.

> To honor her and keep her memory sacred, Frank knew he had to give up something valuable. He had to bury her with one of his most important treasures. So he buried his basketball dreams. On the morning of her funeral, Frank walked to the local park and shot one hundred jump shots and made eighty-five of them. He left the ball at the park, helped bury his mother that afternoon, and had not played the game since. (202)

Alexie puts an Indigenous twist on the all-too-familiar story of a star basketball player's career cut short by injury, substance abuse, tragic death, or inability to keep academic eligibility. In this case it is his commitment to Indigenous tradition and culture that ends Frank's career.

While Frank sacrifices his playing days, basketball still remained a complex part of his life. This is a significant narrative choice by Alexie. In doing this he makes certain to not counterpose basketball in opposition to Frank's Spokane Native culture. This would create a false dichotomy of primitive Native (traditional culture) and contemporary American life (basketball). Here and in several of his other works, Alexie challenges conventional historiography of basketball in Indian Country and counters the assimilationist narratives that white reformers tried to tell with basketball when they first brought it to Indian boarding schools in the early twentieth century. Like many other purported "white" sports taught in boarding schools, white reformers thought basketball could be a key way to assimilate Indians' primitive instinctual physicality with the modern mode of civilized athletic order (see Bloom 2000; Deloria 2004; Jenkins 2007; Peavy and Smith 2008). Alexie's literary use of basketball refutes simplistic Indian/white, primitive/civilized, traditional/modern dichotomies, asserting that basketball is as much a part of Indigenous culture as any other ritualized behavior (Goldstein 2009; Jaskulski 2014). Moreover, on a few occasions he even alludes to the idea that basketball was an Indian Country product long before it was introduced in boarding schools and even prior to James Naismith's invention of the sport. In "The Only Traffic Signal on the Reservation Doesn't Flash Red Anymore" from Alexie's (1993) seminal short story collection, *The Lone Ranger and Tonto Fistfight in Heaven*, he asserts, "Aristotle Polatkin . . . was shooting jump shots exactly one year before James Naismith supposedly invented basketball" (45). In another short story from the same collection, upon seeing kids playing Rezball, Alexie's narrator declares that basketball "was invented by an Indian long before that Naismith guy ever thought about it" (127). Even Victor's assertion in *Smoke Signals*, a film that Alexie helped write and adapted from one of his short stories, that Geronimo was the greatest basketball player of all time alludes to the potential that basketball originated in Indian Country.[2]

Most conventional (and settler colonial) American narratives would keep the dichotomy intact about Indians having an Indian character give up the "modern" (the sport of basketball) in order to return to a more "traditional" or "real" Indian life. Yet in Alexie's formulation basketball *is the mode* through which he practices an essential part of his Spokane culture, sacrificing something of value to honor the dead. With this story Alexie is not just imagining but is contending that basketball is as much part of Spokane culture as anything else. Indeed, basketball is not wiped from Frank's life once he gives up *playing* ball. Long after his mother is buried, Frank and his father go on to watch as many pro, college, and small-town high school basketball games (in person or on TV) as they can. This becomes their ritualized grieving and healing process.

"Whatever Happened to Frank Snake Church?" continues when Frank's father subsequently passes away. This time Frank feels the drive to resume his basketball career. After wailing in pain and not leaving the house for several days after his father's funeral, Frank finds a basketball in his father's closet—the one his father used to regularly shoot hoops twice a week for much of his adult life. Upon finding the ball, Frank immediately goes to a local court and starts shooting, for the first time in over twenty years. "He's given up this game to honor his mother, and now he was reclaiming it to honor his father" (Alexie 2003, 204). On this part of his journey Frank finds a personal trainer, gets himself in the best shape of his life, and then starts regularly playing and dominating pickup basketball games. However, Frank has a nervous breakdown when an elder from his pickup game confronts him on whether he's really grieved his parents. Frank temporarily becomes a shut-in, regains much of his lost weight, and takes a basketball hiatus. Ultimately, after spending some time in a residential mental health treatment center for his breakdown, Frank enrolls at West Seattle Community College.

It is at the community college where the story concludes. A forty-something Frank goes to the men's head basketball coach, someone who remembers Frank from his high school glory days, and Frank tells him that he wants to try out for the team. The short story climaxes with Frank playing in a five-on-five game with and against the players from the West Seattle Community College team. These players are all half his age and show off their spectacular athleticism in a dunk drill the coach asks them to do to illustrate how outmatched Frank is and the absurdity of his desire to try out for the team. Frank is paired up with a trash-talking point guard who responds to Frank's attempt to keep up with the young ballers, first by verbally clowning him and then by trying to demolish him on the court. Frank struggles at first but then begins to hold his own, scoring some points off his brash young opponent. Soon Frank's team takes the lead due to a lay-up and two deep threes from Frank. But he was hurting all over his body, due to how out of shape he was. Nonetheless, playing in this game, he was as happy as he had been in years. Eventually, Frank makes a move to shake himself free from a brash young point guard so that he can hit the game-winning jump shot, and as he plans to rise up and shoot, his knee buckles and its ligaments explode. Frank falls crumpled to the floor in pain. He realizes his basketball career is finally, definitively over; he rolls over onto his stomach and begins to use the floor as a drum to pound out an honor song with his fist. He chants: "*Mother, Father, way, ya, hi, yo, good-bye*" five times (Alexie 2003, 243; italics in original). Franks finally grieves his parents and recognizes that he is going to be okay, whatever life challenges come to him.

Nearly all the important moments of Frank Snake Church's life are experienced in, around, and through basketball, yet this makes them no less Indigenous. He is able to connect to his family and his family's Indianness by playing basketball with them and for them. Moreover, Alexie illustrates the way Native families can channel the pain and displacement of settler colonial life toward a physical and often joyous release found in a sport such as basketball. This is the physical outlet that allows Frank to experience his emotions and channel them toward the positive expressions of indigeneity such as honoring family.

Similar to Sherman Alexie, Mojave-Pima poet Natalie Diaz acknowledges the import and ubiquity of Rezball in her frank and forthright poetry. Diaz also grew up with basketball as a key feature of her Native life. Indeed, as she put it in an interview with *Indian Country Today*, "Basketball is my core. It made me who I am" (Woodard 2012). Before she began her poetry career, her basketball accomplishments were among her most significant; she played a key role on an Old Dominion University team that made it to the NCAA Championship game, and then she went on to have a professional basketball career in Europe and Asia. Although only a handful of Diaz's literary works feature Rezball, she contends:

The game never left me, meaning I have found in writing what I found in basketball—muscle, momentum, rhythm, tempo, touch, fast, slow, quickness, sweat, noise, body, and to put it plainly, work. I've brought my game to the page. (Diaz 2013)

Her 2012 poem "Two Things You Need Balls to Do: A Miscellany from a Former Professional Basketball Player Turned Poet" is solely dedicated to an elaborate comparison between the two "art" forms. But mainly,

Rezball shows up in her work in more subtle forms as one aspect of her intensely revealing meditations on contemporary Indigenous life. For Diaz, basketball is a key part of the fabric of everyday Indian Country.

In Diaz's most celebrated collection of poems, *When My Brother Was an Aztec* (2012), Rezball only makes one appearance; however, the fashion in which it does is telling. In "Reservation Mary," Diaz imagines a reservation love affair between two Rezballers. Mary Lambert, living on an unnamed reservation, is a basketball prodigy who falls for an unnamed Mojave Indian who comes to her reservation for a "money tournament." After the Mojave Rezballer's team wins the tournament and he wins the top player award, the two occupy the night drinking at the local bar, spending all his winnings, and lovemaking. Subsequently, he stays with her for a while, but then he leaves the town—presumably never to return—and Mary is left to care for their baby, at only age seventeen. The poem simultaneously explores a lifelong passion for basketball, fleeting moments of love/lust, substance abuse, and the lasting effects of in-the-moment decisions. Diaz compassionately and soberly weaves these themes together to produce an artful form of "reservation realism" matched only by Sherman Alexie.

The poem sets Mary's basketball virtuosity against the backdrop of contemporary reservation life. It opens:

> Mary Lambert was born at the Indian hospital on the rez.
> She never missed a 3-pointer in the first thirteen years of her life.
> She started smoking pot in seventh grade, still, never missed
> a 3-pointer, but eventually missed most of her freshman classes
> and finally dropped out of high school. (Diaz 2012, 19)

Diaz deftly contrasts Mary's basketball perfection with her academic dereliction by repeatedly using the word "missed." Diaz does not so much ask us to judge or pity Mary, but rather to see her superhuman basketball skill alongside her human imperfections. The two coexist as a metaphor for the way reservations are not just a place of deficit but of success as well.

Diaz further indigenizes basketball in her description of Mary's lover. She uses Indian Country metaphors to describe his basketball skills: "a smooth-faced Mojave who had a jump shot / smoother than a silver can of commodity shortening and soared / for rebounds like he was made of red-tail hawk feathers" (19). These are symbols of both reservation hardship (low-grade, rationed food) and beauty (natural splendor). Comparing these elements of Indian Country to this skilled Rezballer who wins the tournament's "MVI—Most Valuable Indian" (19)—a telling twist on Most Valuable Player awards—makes commodity food seem as beautiful as a red-tailed hawk in flight. Diaz goes on to describe the MVI's wooing seduction of Mary through further allusions to basketball:

> Afterward, at a little bar on the corner of Indian Route 1,
> where the only people not allowed to drink were dialysis patients,
> he told Mary she was his favorite, his first string,
> that he'd dropped all those buckets for her. He spent his entire cut
> of the tournament winning on her Wild Turkey 'n' Cokes,
> told her he was going to stay the night with her, even though
> it was already morning when they stumbled from the bar. (19)

Through Rezball Diaz holds the mundane together with the sublime. "Reservation Mary" provides us with neither a romanticized nor depressing depiction of reservation life, but rather with the way people find moments of joy within a community outside of American capitalism's obsession with individual success and failure. An individual's prowess, like their basketball skills, exists to produce moments of joy to counterbalance poverty and addiction. But success is not part of a trajectory to overcome hardship, and the reservation is not marked as a place of failure from which to escape. Because the two always exist simultaneously in Indian Country, success is for and in the community, not an escape to or in a space outside of it.

Diaz's "Reservation Mary" also provides implicit observations on gender and basketball in Indian Country. The fact that one of the two Rezball stars in the poem is a woman is significant in so much as the fact that Diaz treats this as a completely normal part of Rezball. A renowned and praised female Rezballer is commonplace in Indian Country. This contrasts with basketball in mainstream America. While basketball is perhaps not marked as a male sport as much as other American sports such as football or baseball, American culture still privileges the men's game over the women's. True, there is a relatively popular professional women's league that along with women's college basketball gets more media attention than nearly any other women's sport. Nonetheless, this media attention and the mainstream valuation of the quality of women's basketball are rarely ever the equivalent press and praise that men's basketball receives. However, as Diaz's personal and professional lives attest, women's basketball is just as important in Indian Country.

Go to any Rezball tournament or high school game in Indian Country and the crowd is just as large and boisterous for the girls' games as they are for the boys', if not more so. Women's basketball is not seen as a degraded form of the men's sport, but rather as equivalent in terms of importance to the community. An equal amount of communal investment of time and energy are spent on female basketball. In ITS basketball, all the teams of coed girls play right along with the boys, sometimes dominating play just as much as their male counterparts. Moreover, players and fans treat the experience of boys and girls playing together as a normal part of community life. Rarely did I hear a single ITS girl or boy comment that this was a problem or something that affected play. This is not to romanticize some idyllic expression of gender equality in Indian Country, but rather to note that what is significant is how insignificant it is to have girls and boys play Rezball together. It is not as if the gendered distinctions disappear (the ITS boys and girls separate for all-star teams, and recently ITS has been experimenting with all girls' teams for the oldest age group), but rather that girls' and women's play is equally appreciated as evidenced by Mary Lambert's skill.

In many Indigenous contexts, it is the girls' team that sustains the most pride for the community in that they are often more likely to make it to and win high school state finals than the boys. Take, for example, the Shiprock High School team from the Navajo Nation. As chronicled in the brilliant documentary *Rocks with Wings* (Derby 2001), the Shiprock girls, in their multiyear effort to win the state championship and overcome their prime rival, Kirkland High School, received communal-wide celebration even when they lost a big game. They were always welcomed home as heroes, in large part because of their success, but specifically because of their success against white reservation border town schools. *Rocks with Wings* illustrates how these contests are frequently seen by Navajo fans as confrontations between themselves and white communities that express significant racial persecution toward Navajos and are part of the long-term settler colonial project that has appropriated and polluted Navajo land and resources. Similar narratives of Rezballers becoming heroines in Native communities are detailed by Larry Colton (2000) for the Crow in Montana and Ian Frazier (2000) among the Pine Ridge Lakota in South Dakota. Moreover, the Schimmel sisters, Shoni and Jude, have become icons beyond their Confederated Tribes of Umatilla Reservation. The national attention they received for their All-American play and NCAA Final Four appearance with the University of Louisville team, the nationally released documentary made about them (*Off the Rez*, Hock 2011), and Shoni's success as a WNBA player (first-round draft pick, two-time All-Star, and All-Star game MVP) have made the Schimmel sisters pan-tribal hardwood heroes. For a while Shoni's jersey was the highest sold in the WNBA, and wherever she played, those games frequently had higher than average attendance. Both of these can be attributed to her fame in Indian Country that caused fans to turn out in droves to support her and revere her as emblematic of Native success. These examples attest to how the skill and success of Rezball heroes stand in for the community as a whole and provide an opportunity to assert pride and resiliency in the face of oppression. The fact that women and girls become respected as strong community heroes, in large part because of their participation in Rezball, is critical in communities that often have high rates of domestic abuse and violence against women. At several points throughout this "Some Days It's a Good Day to Play Basketball" chapter of the book, I explore further the places where gender and Rezball overlap.

Suffice to say for now, adaptively employing and blending multiple kinds of resources that often manipulate and subvert settler cultural, political, and legal categories, Indigenous communities have maintained vibrancy in the face of attempted assimilation and elimination (for broadly similar arguments see, e.g., Vizenor 1994; Deloria 2004; Bruyneel 2007; Rifkin 2009).

Another contemporary Indigenous artist who deploys Rezball in his writing is poet Michael Wasson. Wasson is Nimíipuu (what Europeans have labeled the Nez Perce), and his allusions to Rezball are highly reminiscent of Diaz's and Alexie's literature. For Wasson, Rezball is the backdrop for his recollections about loss and sorrow of his youth. Like Alexie's story of Frank Snake Church, Wasson's (2016) blog poem "Small Mediations" uses basketball imagery as a balance to sickness and death on his Nez Perce Reservation on the Columbia Plateau. Rezball and loss conjoin in his writing as memories blend together. He reminisces how his adolescent-self dealt with experiences of sorrow through playing basketball—one does not seem to exist without the other. Wasson's poem achieves this indigenization of basketball through sensory and visual imagery and linguistic allusions that vividly evoke the rural reservation life from his childhood. The poem opens with the smell and the feel of Nez Perce Rezball:

Crushed in the hands, the scent of pine needles & the smear of sap on the ball. My jump shot comes to me from hours behind my childhood home shooting at the hoop that my long-haired uncles drilled into the face of the pine . . . the ball lies half-discolored. A face I had not touched in years it seems. Flattening. But I pick it up again & arc through the low hanging arms of this skeletal, living tree. (Wasson 2016)

As with most daily activities of his mountainous reservation, pine trees (and their byproducts) loom large over his playing. This opening stanza clearly evokes a sense of place and the uniqueness of basketball at Nez

Perce. Wasson continues to memorialize the reservation life of his youth by including more kin in his remembrances of Rezball:

Inside the house, my great grandmother is dying. I'm 12 years old. I shoot at a rusted rim. A squaring patch of dirt is *the paint*. The gravel & broken down cars hoisted on chopping blocks leading to the HUD house: *the perimeter*. The dilapidated, splitting backboard—literally *a board*—is how I rebound to keep the semi-graspable. I wash my hands before I help her to the restroom.

Wasson delineates the court, of both his Rezball playing youth and his poetic remembrances of it, through familiar markings of worn-out reservation life. As with his great grandmother, there is a sense of deterioration and decay. Yet through it all Wasson and his relatives keep playing and persevering.

His father pours rugged cement to make a small court beside their house. After, my cousin & I take our living room *Fisher-Price* dunks & clutch shots from behind the sage-smelling couch covered in a Pendleton blanket to this *real* court. At least *we* think it is. I'm 9 years old. He lost his older brother last year. We play H-O-R-S-E until our relatives start three-on-three. It's past supper—*hunger* somewhere deep in the open mouth of the rim. *Something* we want to swallow over & over. Before winter I won't see *'ácqa* alive again. I forget how to cry at his funeral. Until after. When his body's not there.

The tragic, and all too common, loss of young life on reservations and the reality of limited material resources are rawly revealed here. Yet Wasson contrasts these challenges with the joy and ingenuity that Rezball channels through himself as a young Nimíipuu boy and his relatives. He plays with the word "hunger" in both a fundamental physical sense and a desire to play basketball nonstop and the way this hunger to play basketball overlaps with a desire to have something better, a rez life without the concerns of material deficit and the physical and spiritual death brought on by extreme poverty.

In addition to writing about his cousins and the pain of their early deaths, Wasson concludes "Small Mediations" with imagery of playing Rezball with his uncle. He does so to articulate an implicit message of continuance and survivance. He speaks of his uncle and the way he constantly played basketball as a youth and still does today in the tribal community center even though he only has one eye. In this stanza he uses Niimiipuutímt (the language of the Nez Perce) words to label where Rezball is played. The use of indigenous language in this section and elsewhere throughout the poem highlights the survivance of Nimíipuu culture in the face of the challenges that he writes about. Wasson concludes with a stanza set in a contemporary space, an elementary school in rural Japan where he now lives. He shoots hoops in the dark in this gym. Against any odds, Rezball is still with him. It is his connection to his reservation childhood, his family, his people, and all that comes with this, and it is a through line in his life that keeps him going. In "Small Meditations," Rezball is entwined with and at the same time a release from the challenges of Indigenous. The reservation of Wasson's upbringing is not merely a memory of deficit, but of perseverance.

Similar to Wasson's "Small Mediations" and Diaz's "Reservation Mary," one of Alexie's (1993) short stories, "The Only Traffic Signal on the Reservation Doesn't Flash Red Anymore," also employs Rezball to develop a sense of reservation realism that balances joy and hope with disappointment. It opens with Victor (one of Alexie's mainstay characters in many of his stories) and his friend Adrian sitting on the porch engaging in a game of Russian roulette. It is not until after Victor chickens out and hands the gun to Adrian, who swallows the barrel and pulls the trigger, that we learn that it is just a "BB" gun. They turn away from this simulated suicidal despair to gaze from Victor's porch at the (non)happenings of a standard day on their reservation. A crew of local teenage, petty hooligans then walks past them on their way to engage in some sort of minor ruckus when Adrian recognizes one of them as Julius Windmaker, who is known to be the best basketball player on the reservation. Here is how Alexie (1993) proceeds to describe the fifteen-year-old Rezball phenom:

> Julius Windmaker was the latest in a long line of reservation basketball heroes, going all the way back to Aristotle Polatkin, who was shooting jumpshots exactly one year before James Naismith supposedly invented basketball . . . [Julius] had that gift, that grace, those fingers like a goddamn medicine man. One time when the tribal school traveled to Spokane to play the white high school team, Julius scored sixty-seven points and the Indians won by forty. (45)

Windmaker is seen as a basketball genius in his own right, but he is also understood in a historical context of all the great Indian basketball players that came before him and will come after. He is not just an individual star but part of a collective.

This is a key way Alexie indigenizes basketball, by discussing it as a part and parcel of the community as a whole—both in a collective and temporal sense. A reservation basketball star is not understood merely as an exceptional individual: he or she represents the community as a whole and is also understood as part of a larger legacy of Rezball that existed before any given standout player and will continue after her or him. For example, chatting about Julius leads Victor and Adrian to "sit in silence and [remember] all of [their] heroes, basketball players from seven generations, all the way back" (52). Rezball standouts are remembered both as a group and in terms of a loosely connected lineage. In Alexie's rendering Rezball heroes have always been a part of reservation life and will always be.

The delight these two Spokane Indian characters have in swapping stories and shooting the shit about Rezball legends acts as a counterbalance to their ensuing depressing revelation that Julius's problems with alcohol seem to have cut his basketball career short. In this way Alexie uses Rezballers, their athletic prowess and success, as a metaphor for reservation life as a whole: in the face of desperate circumstances Native people can still find hope and joy within their community. Here it is crucial to note that the narrative of this success does not take the shape as a way to escape from dire conditions. Basketball is not seen as the ticket out of a troubled community in the way that this narrative is often used for inner-city African American basketball players. Regardless of how viable this "ticket out" narrative actually is or how much people in impoverished African American communities believe in this "ticket out" narrative themselves, it is the narrative countlessly retold by the white American popular media about basketball in urban African American communities. Commenting on the relationship between basketball and Blackness in American society, cultural theorist Todd Boyd (1997) suggests that the "rags-to-riches mythology" of Black inner-city ballers ought to be contextualized in the civil rights era (115). Before civil rights struggles basketball was mostly a white sport, and an outcome of the civil rights era's advances was increased collegiate and professional opportunities for Black athletes. In Boyd's preface to Boyd and Shropshire (2000), he explains this as a Horatio Alger-esque story infused with racial and class struggle: "to me . . . what the league [NBA] is all about: Brothas gettin' paid for their unique contribution to the culture. That's the American Dream ain't it" (xi).

Yago Colás's (2016) theorizations of basketball and Blackness complicates this popular idea and is more critical of the notion of "getting yours." He argues there are several popular myths about basketball (i.e., "The Myth of Amateurs," "The Myth of Blackness," "The Myth of the Right Way," "The Myth of The Man") that all get inflected through race (Colás 2016, 13–15). In most cases these myths work to refract the sport through a lens that legitimizes broader American capitalism and rationalizes the contradiction between the purported unlimited opportunities of American capitalism and the limited number of African Americans who succeed in it. Black (and white) basketball players become emblematic for larger societal behavioral and ethical codes and idealized notions of "on-court" meritocracy are used as a metaphor for "off-court" American race relations and class mobility. For Colás the "ticket out" narrative operates and fails in ways more complicated than merely questioning whether a Black inner-city kid could parlay his skills into a pathway out of his or her impoverished community.

Journalists from dominant media outlets commonly attempt to uncritically translate this African American "ticket out" metaphor to Indian Country. Since the 1980s it seems about every five years an article pops up in popular media about Rezball, usually heralding the high level of skill despite the remoteness and lack of resources (e.g., G. Smith 1991; Abdul-Jabbar and Singular 2000; Colton 2000; Frazier 2000; Goldman 2003; O'Neil 2010; Sauer 2014). These "quinquennial discoveries" of Rezball all seem to rest on the same conclusion: if some of these players are good enough to lead their teams to state championships, why can't they parlay their skill as a ticket out of reservations communities.[3] Of course, inherent to most of these journalistic accounts of Rezball is that the reservation is an impoverished, damaged place that people would want to leave—a deficit from which any "normal" person would jump at the chance to escape.

However, within Indian Country the "ticket out" narrative seems to be used much more sparingly. For example, Lumbee scholar Joseph Oxendine (1988) is one of the few academics to speculate on the complex reasons why very few Native athletes, since the second half of the twentieth century, have even achieved at the college level, let alone the professional. This dearth of collegiate and professional sporting accomplishment is even more stark when we consider how many Native athletes prominently *did* succeed during the first half of the twentieth century. Oxendine preliminarily suggested that the decline in participation beyond the community level could be connected to both internal cultural reasons and changes in mid-twentieth-century Indian education when boarding schools began to de-emphasized athletics. However, even Oxendine suggests that athletes do not leave because of the negative pressure from peers and family not to leave. This analysis strongly implies the "ticket out" narrative, even if Rezballers chose not to redeem that ticket.

In the chapters that follow I turn this question, of why successful Indian ballers don't leave, on its head. I attend to how playing basketball in Indian Country is primarily a community-based activity, not one with an outward focus of how the sport helps Rezballers get off the reservation. In most cases in Indian Country the question of why skilled Rezballers cannot parlay their skill in collegiate or professional arenas is never even asked. Instead, basketball is played to bring pride to the community, to participate in Indigenous communal life, and to be a reservation hero—not a basketball hero in general. A Rezball hero's value and significance is tied to a specific community within a specific context. Rezball heroes are revered more for how their skills entertain the community or represent it well in competition with white teams or other tribes, than for the Rezballer's ability to get paid. Rarely is the narrative that a Rezballer is trying to use his or her skills to escape the reservation.

Alexie addresses the uniqueness of a Rezball hero in "The Only Traffic Signal" by arguing that heroes in Indian Country are venerated for longer and perhaps more intensely, even for doing less, than heroes in the rest of America. He suggests this is so because the hope that they represent is so critical to a reservation community. He submits:

In the outside world, a person can be a hero one second and a nobody the next. Think about it. Do White people remember the names of those guys who dove into that icy river to rescue passengers from that plane wreck a few years back? . . . And, to be honest, I don't remember none of those names either, but a reservation hero is remembered. A reservation hero is forever. In fact, their status grows over the years as the stories are told and retold. (Alexie 1993, 48)

Alexie undergirds this point by having Victor and Adrian reminisce about the near mythical Silas Sirius who made only one play on the court in his entire Rezball career; yet this alone was enough to gain him legendary status on their reservation. Replying to Victor's query if he remembered Silas, Adrian exclaims:

Hell . . . Do I remember? I was there when he grabbed that defensive rebound, took a step, and flew the length of the court, did a full spin in midair, and then dunked that fucking ball. And I don't mean it looked like he flew, or it was so beautiful it was almost like he flew. I mean, he flew, period . . . Shit . . . And he didn't grow no wings.

He just kicked his legs a little. Held that ball like a baby in his hand. And he was smiling. Really. Smiling when he flew. Smiling when he dunked it, smiling when he walked off the court and never came back. Hell, he was still smiling ten years after that. (47)

Silas Sirius is the distillation of a Rezball hero. His feat was so remarkable that even he knew not to ruin its perfection by attempting another play; he ended his Rezball career the instant he completed his dunk and then walked off the court mid-game. Thereby his legacy could live on permanently, unmarred by what might come next. Moreover, as constructed by Alexie, Silas's success lives on, not as something that he benefits from as an individual—through a professional career or marketing opportunities in the world outside the reservation—but rather as a story of pure hope and joy that the entire community relishes vicariously with each retelling.

Alexie concludes the short story by highlighting the ambivalent nature of reservation hope. Hope is a crucial sentiment for reservation communities in its ability to counterbalance the despair that is integral to these communities—as a result of settler trauma. Yet, at the same time, hope is also a precarious sentiment because it can never completely extinguish the damage of settler colonialism. In "The Only Traffic Signal" all the Rezball heroes express this ambivalence. Victor and Adrian realize that Julius Windmaker has succumbed to alcoholism as a year later they discover him passed out on Victor's floor. He is no longer the dominant player he was just the year before. The protagonists, however, do not give into despondency. They cover Julius with a blanket and leave him peacefully where he is lying. Next, they walk out to the porch only to immediately see the next potential Rezball hero walk by—Lucy, a third-grade girl who is so good she plays with the sixth-grade boys. You can feel the ambivalence of Victor's hope as he yearns, "'God, I hope she makes it all the way'" (53), almost as if he is trying to convince himself it can happen. Structurally, though, Alexie not only leaves us with a new hope but also illustrates how the role of the Rezball hero (and hope, joy, and desire) is always an unending resource that confronts despondency and failure, seeking the delight, not the pain, in the community of reservation life.

REZBALL AND DESIRE

The realism and aspiration of this Rezball literature not only works to illustrate the ubiquity and overall significance of basketball in Indian Country, but it also mirrors the decolonizing methodology proffered by many current Indigenous studies academics.[4] Scholars such as Audra Simpson, Eve Tuck, and K. Wayne Yang scrutinize social science research conducted in Indigenous communities. These three, and many others, critique how research has rarely been done with Indigenous peoples' needs and desires in mind and how it treats the production of rational data and knowledge as a worthwhile end in itself, unquestionably able to effect change merely through its existence and circulation in academic and policy-orientated institutions. These Indigenous scholars call for refined methods given the potential damage (in spite of "well intentions") of much of the research done in Indian Country.

Tuck (2009) and Tuck and Yang (2014), in particular, critique research designed to reveal the ills, tribulations, or dysfunction in Indigenous communities. They potently argue against utilizing models that begin with the premise that these communities are damaged. Examining deficits to comprehend disenfranchised communities is far too common in academic discourse, and more critically, it is rarely an accurate or complete depiction of how Indigenous people feel about their communities. A primary focus on the damage done to Indigenous communities treats them as if they are broken or defeated, reifying the racist notion that these communities and the people living in them are dysfunctional. Tuck (2009) calls this "damage-centered" research because it

> looks to historical exploitation, domination, and colonization to explain contemporary brokenness, such as poverty, poor health, and low literacy. Common sense tells us this is a good thing, but

the danger in damage-centered research is that it is a pathologizing approach in which the oppression singularly defines the community. (413)

Notably, Tuck is not trying to nullify the importance of this historical-based work but rather is suggesting that it had a time and a place that has now come and gone. She affirms that contemporary scholars, like herself, are indebted to the revelations of damage-centered work that revealed the horrors of settler colonialism, but at this point it has effected little change and has no real effective connection to the process of transforming the Indigenous communities being studied. She instead calls for more nuanced research that attends to "desire," which she asserts can be far more "generative, engaged, and engorged," noting that "desire is not mere wanting but our informed seeking" (Tuck 2009, 418). In other words, desire-based research not only emphasizes the needs of people being studied and what they actually value, but it also forces the researcher to be more open to the achievements of Indigenous peoples and their aspirations to make Indian Country a healthy space. She notes that "even when communities are broken and conquered, they are so much more than that—so much more that [an] incomplete story is an act of aggression" (416). Critically, Tuck does not think of desire-based research as an antonym or replacement for damage-based work, rather that most social science work has only concentrated on damage and that so much is missed when this is the case. Desire-based research is a more complicated and sophisticated understanding of marginalized communities because it defies clichéd dichotomies such as resistance versus reproduction, structure versus agency, assimilation versus radical separatism, and so forth.

> [Desire-based research] is important because it more closely matches the experiences of people who, at different points in a single day, reproduce, resist, are complicit in, rage against, celebrate, throw up hands/fists/towels, and withdraw and participate in uneven social structure—that is, everybody. (420).

Alexie's, Diaz's, and Wasson's lyricizing of Indian Country, in general, and Rezball, specifically, deals with the unevenness, contradictions, and dynamism by describing hope and longing alongside the endurance of pain and loss. Furthermore, attention to desire is not some Pollyanna denial of pain, nor is it "seeing the bright side of hard times, or even believing that everything happens for a reason" (Tuck and Yang 2014, 231). Rather, what you get with desire-based research and literature are nuanced understandings of Indigenous personhood. As Tuck (2009) so succinctly (and appropriately for our purpose here) puts it: "We can desire to be critically conscious *and* desire new Jordans, even if those desires are conflicting" (420).

An important complement to replacing deficit-based models with desire-based models is an understanding of the role refusal can play in research. Conventionally, refusals are seen as dead ends especially in conventional social interaction; however, Tuck and Yang (2014), following Audra Simpson (2007, 2014), urge us to consider how a refusal in both ethnographic interlocution and in the social science researcher's end product can be generative and humanizing, not an impediment to productive collaboration. The former necessitates the latter, in that through the process of closely attending to the topics that ethnographic consultants choose *not* to talk about and the moments when they *refuse* to engage certain issues and ideas, researchers in Indigenous communities have an obligation in their research to exclude these proscribed issues. Simpson (2007, 2014) notes, in her research with her own Mohawk community, an unwillingness of community members to explicitly discuss some of the challenging and problematic aspects of enacting tribal sovereignty and determining tribal citizenship. In her writing and research, Simpson in turn refuses to air the community's "dirty laundry" and the thorny details of tribal governance. Simpson's choice is made in response to what Tuck and Yang (2014, 225) have described as "settler colonial knowledge" that is "premised on frontiers" and constantly receding limits that conventional social science researchers feel entitled to "transgress" in the name of seeking out new knowledge to contribute to a universal good. To these Indigenous studies scholars, "refusal, and stances of refusal in research, are attempts to place limits on conquest and the colonization of knowledge by marking what is off limits, what is not up for grabs or discussion, what is sacred, and what can't be known" (225).

Hence, Simpson is not ignoring the negative when she refuses to discuss intertribal political tensions in writing up her research. Rather, she is staking a boundary against social science's unquestioned right to discuss and thereby expose the community's deficits and damage. Without heeding these refusals in research, damage and pain become decontextualized from community life and circulate in settler academic and policy discourses in ways that deficits come to define Indigenous communities. Cultural, traditional, and communal resources built in to a community in order to deal with damage and pain are obscured by narratives of dysfunction. Tuck and Yang (2014) assert:

> We are not arguing for silence. Stories are meant to be passed along appropriately, especially among loved ones, but not all of them as social science research. Although such knowledge is often a source of wisdom that informs perspectives in our writing, we do not intend to share them as social science research. It is enough that we know them. (234)

In my work with Rezballers, I have made the conscious choice as a researcher to follow this route of desire-based research and attending to refusal. Avid participation in Rezball can clearly be seen as a response to pain in other parts of Indigenous people's lives, and it has been openly discussed with me as a tool to avoid pain and loss in Indian Country. However, an in-depth chronicle of the minute details of this pain, family dysfunction, or the consequences of bad choices is not necessary to understand the joy of Rezball, nor does the repetitious and ongoing trauma caused by settler colonialism nullify the hope found in Rezball. I have not ignored the pain of Rezballers with whom I have worked, but I refuse to push them to reveal to me the precise challenges in their lives, and I refuse to relate those stories if they happen to confide in me.

Instead, I focus on the joy and hope fashioned from the vast desire in Indian Country to play basketball.

CONCLUSION

The stories of Rezball that I retell in the following chapters, most of which come directly from Rezballers themselves, serve the same function as the lyricizing in Alexie's, Diaz's, and Wasson's works of reservation realism. They all emphasize Indigenous peoples' desire to do more than just survive settler colonialism and their desire to thrive in Indian Country by forging healthy and positive social, cultural, economic, and political relations. After hundreds of hours of fieldwork, interviews, and volunteering, I have made a conscious decision to highlight this desire by focusing on the hope, joy, and fun inherent to Rezball, just as Native folks who participate in Rezball have made a conscious choice of joy and hope instead of despair. This is explicitly not done in a way that ignores the immensely debilitating, ongoing legacy of settler colonialism, but rather an overt attempt to refuse to treat the reservation as a space of deficit. My choice to write this way comes both out of respect for the Rezballers with whom I have worked and who choose the fun and joy of friendly competition and chose to discuss it this way with me. This also includes downplaying, but not ignoring, the hardships in their communities and personal lives as a way to avoid the trap of constructing Indian Country as a damaged space. They live with the ongoing challenges of settler colonialism but desire quotidian moments of happiness and connectedness. Furthermore, my choice to focus on Rezball is a methodological and theory-based decision, seeking to heed the calls of decolonizing research from Indigenous academics that have greatly influenced me, such as Linda Tuhiwai Smith, Audra Simpson, and Eve Tuck and K. Wayne Yang, among many others. The Rezball experiences I relate illustrate the pleasure that American Indians get from playing basketball in spite of any depravity in their community. Like the artistic work of Alexie, Diaz, and Wasson, for these Rezballers the two things can exist side by side.

REZBALL, THE ANTI-FUNERAL   3

The mission statement of Inter Tribal Sports (ITS) reads: "Unifying tribal youth and communities through structured athletic programs while providing necessary resources and developing a strong foundation in culture, leadership and wellness."[1] One of the best expressions of this mission is Saturday "game day." Each week during the ITS basketball season one or two tribal partners offer up their gymnasium for game day; over the course of the one day kids, ages eight to eighteen, from tribes all over Southern California will play games at these chosen gyms.[2] There will be anywhere from two to four games going on at once starting as early as nine in the morning and often ending after six at night. Community members come out in force to support young Indigenous athletes. It is not uncommon for vendors to sell food or jewelry and clothing outside these venues or for nonprofits to come and set up a table, sharing their organization's efforts with the community. These Rezball games have an important unifying effect, as they weekly (re)connect people from all across Southern California's Indigenous nations. During ITS basketball season, Saturday *is* game day.

One unseasonably warm Saturday in February 2016, I attended the ITS games being held at the Pechanga Band of Luiseño Indians' Recreation Center. Approaching this sleek, modern, concrete and granite structure, I am greeted by the smoky scent of roasted corn and vibrant reds and blues of sticky-sweet snow cones from the food vendor out front. Approaching the entrance to the rec center, I am greeted by the phrase *Kwáatilah Hamú'kungawish* etched in the glass door. These are Cham'teela (Luiseño) words—the Indigenous language of this area—and they roughly translate to mean "lobby." Small plaques in Cham'teela can be found all over the walls inside the rec center demarcating different sections and architectural features. This is just a small part of the Pechanga tribe's comprehensive and ubiquitous language renewal program, making the language a common part of everyday life. Rightfully so, the Pechanga people are proud to be one of the most active cultural bearers of all the Payomkawichum (Luiseño bands collectively), as they have one of the most successful language revitalization efforts in all of California. Inside the lobby, kids are darting around playing tag, laughing, or reclining on the several modern-style cushioned benches. Intermixed with this joyful screaming of energetic youth, I begin to hear the high-pitched squeaks of sneakers and thumping of leather balls on hardwood floors.

I enter the cavernous gym to the shiny glare off the perfectly conditioned parquet floors. There are four high-tech digital scoreboards, abundant pull-out bleachers lining three of the four walls, and two massive thirty-by-thirty-foot mesh curtains hanging from the ceiling that divide the gym in half—two full-court games are in midplay on either side of the curtains. The gleaming blond wood floors and sand-colored cinder block walls are accentuated with splashes of purple and yellow—the tribe's adopted colors—throughout the gym. At center court on each side of the curtain the Pechanga tribal seal is painted into the floor displaying massive acorns and a depiction of the mountains that surround Pechanga land. The Luiseño word *wiiwish* is in the center of the tribal seal. *Wiiwish* is the acorn mash made by Payomkawichum people, and it has been the most important staple of their diet for thousands of years. It is literally and figuratively the sustainer and in many ways the center of Pechanga traditional life. Being affixed to the center of the basketball courts, it is also a reminder to all those who play about what sustains life and how important a healthy, active life is.

Amid all the activity of four games, I look to my left and immediately see my friends, the Taylor Sisters, sitting in the bleachers. Misty is a former student of mine, and Brandie has been a great ally to our Department of American Indian Studies and our Native students at SDSU. At this time each of their sons was playing on the ten and under team for the Iipay Nation of Santa Ysabel. Joining them is their mother and Misty's friend, whose son plays for the Mesa Grande Band of Diegueno Mission Indians' eighteen and under team (even though he is a Santa

Ysabel tribal member). Misty's friend stands between the two courts, swiveling his head from side to side, as if he were watching a tennis match, in order to capture all the action.

I greet the Taylor women and join them in bleachers to watch their sons, grandsons, and nephews compete against the Barona tribal team. Family and fans from both tribes cheered on these young Rezballers as they tried to learn the game. Repeatedly players would tentatively dribble down the court and then, upon crossing midcourt, pick up the ball and hold it high above their head, to evade the two or three defenders swarming them. Coaches from each respective community traversed the sideline, patiently offering instruction and encouragement to these aspirants who tried to employ the arms-up, feet-sliding techniques of proper defense while others put every ounce of strength into hurling three-point shots at the rim. These shots went in with surprising frequency, given the under-five-foot frames that launched them. There was little surrender from any of the players on either team. During the game the Taylor family sat with a friend from another tribe whom they had not seen in a while and passed the time catching up on each other's families and friends. Their reconnecting in this small section of bleachers was only one small part of the community bonding occurring on this Saturday at Pechanga gym.

One of the things that makes ITS game day such a significant community event is that rather than each team (at each level) playing a home-away schedule at several different tribal gyms—a schedule that would spread teams out all over Southern California—all teams congregate at one or two tribal gyms. Each game day is a collective event. Earlier in this particular game day at Pechanga, the under-eighteen team from the Soboba Band of Luiseño Indians played against the La Jolla Band of Luiseño Indians, followed by the Pechanga oldest team (in their second game of the day) taking on a team of urban Indians from the City of San Jacinto's Tribal TANF program.[3] Both of these games featured several supporters sitting in the bleachers actively cheering on the players from their tribe's team—often just as vociferously as the Taylor sisters. Fans enthusiastically exclaimed "ohhh" and "ahhh" every time a player blocked a shot or when one player had a breakaway and even attempted a dunk. Cheering often took the sporadic form of common fan phrases directed at a given team, such as "Let's go Pechanga," "Come on La Jolla," or even hollers of "Atta boy" encouragement aimed at specific players by name. In one corner of the gym, a group of eight- to ten-year-old girls from the Viejas Band of Kumeyaay Indians sat in the bleachers chanting organized cheers. These girls were part of the ITS cheerleading program, and they were led by a mother-daughter collaboration who themselves were from Viejas and had been cheerleaders when they were in high school. The addition of this program created a space for more kids, particularly those who may not play basketball, to still have a meaningful role in the vibrant community event that is ITS basketball game day. While all of the fans' support, on one level, was partisan, nothing was directed mean-spiritedly toward opposing teams—the way you might find in the most extreme version of youth sports outside of Indian Country. Rather, Rezballers cheering for their tribes simultaneously reinforces a broader sense of Indigenous community among the fans.

Months later, after basketball season ended, Misty and Brandie reflected with me about these ITS game days. Misty observed how these game days have a positive effect on community wellness. In particular she pointed out that Rezball games are one of the few intra- and intertribal sociocultural gatherings not centered around funerals or other community tragedies that happen all too frequently in Southern California Indian Country. Comparing these two kinds of events, the Taylor sisters note that they both appreciate game day as a regular opportunity to see relatives and friends and catch up on each other's lives and happenings (Brandie and Misty Taylor, interview August 15, 2015). They both are also commonplace, happening multiple times a month, unlike powwows or traditional gatherings that are more annual events. Both are intergenerational commemorations of community life, but ITS game days obviously tend to be more joyful and hopeful. Robby and Alek Tortes, Rezballing brothers from the Rincon Band of Luiseño Indians, also shared with me that when they were young, the most common place for them to be introduced to distant cousins was at funerals (Alek and Robby Tortes, interview, February 2, 2016). However, they say that now the ITS game day is where they connect and bond with extended family. As Misty puts it, there might be little joy without the weekly ITS basketball game day, speculating, "Otherwise we're always at funerals, so I think [the Rezball games] just give us hope" (Misty Taylor, interview). She recognizes that Rezball can be an antidote for reservation despair and bereavement. An "anti-funeral," if you will, that eschews deficit models of Indian Country and is a healthy outlet, not just for the youth playing ball, but for those supporting them in the stands.

While certainly not all funerals are completely bleak events, ITS game day, in contrast, centers around the contemporary vibrancy of the community. Those being celebrated and focused on are the youth, who will be carrying these tribal communities into the future. Moreover, occasionally (and unfortunately at a higher rate than anywhere in the United States outside of Indian Country) these funerals are for teenagers. This provides an even starker comparative with the positive impact ITS is trying to impart on the kids, encouraging healthy living and an outlet to foster physical and mental wellness in the youth of these tribal communities. Indeed, one could easily argue that participation in ITS game day is a key activity that can keep Native youth away from the influences that generally cause the alarmingly high rate of Native deaths before the age of twenty—many of which are suicides. Addressing this high mortality rate and understating its connection to ongoing settler colonialism is crucial for understanding contemporary Indian Country. Equally important is highlighting emergent traditions such as ITS game day that are the vibrant alternative to the intergenerational trauma in these communities.

The way ITS Rezball fosters Native community solidarity in Southern California is a microcosm of how it happens all through Indian Country. Several of my Navajo students (in my American Indian studies classes as SDSU) have shared how avid Rezball fans are in their home communities. The reservation towns of Chinle, Tuba City, and For Defiance, Arizona, and Shiprock, New Mexico, for example, all have arenas large enough to hold 70–90 percent of their towns' residents. High schools in these towns are literally prepared for the whole community to show up because, in fact, they do! Frequently members of these communities line up early, hours before the game, in order to ensure they get a seat for the game. Cheering on the local Rezball team provides a huge rallying point and collective activity for Navajo communities. Once high school basketball season is over, the obsession with Rezball does not stop. Nearly every weekend in the summer there is a tournament in some town in the Navajo Nation. Youth and adult teams travel for miles to play in these Rezball tournaments. Additionally, most of the Navajo national and regional tribal fairs feature Rezball tournaments as one of the many activities alongside parades, powwows, cultural performances and competitions, and rodeos.[4] Rezball is truly an integral part of Navajo communities (see also Powell 2019 for description of Navajo basketball fanaticism).

The same could be said for many tribal communities in the Northern Plains. Alan Klein's 2020 ethnography, *Lakota Hoops*, on basketball at the Pine Ridge Reservation illustrates that Lakota communities' passion for this sport equals what can be found at the Navajo Nation. Earlier than Klein, Gary Smith famously wrote a *Sports Illustrated* article about a 1983 Montana State Championship team from the Crow Reservation. In it, he describes how nearly the entire population of the eastern Montana reservation border town, Hardin, followed the bus carrying the predominantly Crow boys' basketball team to Bozeman to compete in the state championship game. Smith describes the caravan of cars behind the bus extending bumper to bumper for eight miles: "They made the asphalt go away!" (G. Smith 1991). Larry Colton (2000), following the predominantly Crow girls' basketball team from the same high school in Hardin, Montana, observes: "Crows usually rank basketball right up there with oxygen in importance" (23). Thirty-five years after Smith and on the opposite side of the state, Abe Streep (2018) chronicles the 2018 Montana State Championship team from the Flathead Indian Reservation in the *New York Times Magazine*. He witnesses a scene similar to Smith's and details how the entire six hundred residents evacuated their reservation town to head south to Hamilton, Montana, to see their Arlee High School Warriors compete in an away playoff game.

Further east, in South Dakota, there is little difference. The Pine Ridge Reservation, for example, also has a long history of community involvement with Rezball (see Klein 2020). This is perhaps most evident in the Lakota Nation Invitational discussed in chapter 1 but is also illustrated by the local legend of SuAnne Big Crow. In the late 1980s and early 1990s, SuAnne drove the Pine Ridge Lady Thorpes High School basketball team to a series of playoff runs including winning the South Dakota State Championship one year. In *On the Rez* Ian Frazier (2000) relays the local stories told about this time period in Lady Thorpe history and SuAnne's prominent role as the best Rezballer and one of the most respected members of the community as a whole. Frazier collects heroic stories about how the community rallied around SuAnne's poise and presence such that she could bridge factional gaps both in terms of fierce internal rivalries among the Pine Ridge community and in terms of the hostility directed at Lakota people by the surrounding white communities. As for the latter, many tell Frazier of a near-mythic instance when SuAnne and the Lady Thorpes played an intense road game at the gym of a non-Indian, off-reservation, rival high school. Just before the Lady Thorpes entered the court, the white crowd began taunting them: in unison hurling racial epithets and creating a frenzy of anti-Indian passion in order to rattle the Pine Ridge girls. Sensing the uneasiness and fear in her teammates, SuAnne assumed control and led the team onto the court despite being one of the youngest players on the team. Instead of commencing the regular pregame practice of lay-up drills, SuAnne stopped at midcourt, took off her warm-up jacket, and began to use the jacket like a shawl to do a Northern Plains powwow-style fancy dance. Her spinning and twirling at midcourt stopped the hostile crowd dead silent, and soon they began to applaud in admiration. SuAnne is attributed with single-handedly diffusing the tension within her teammates and the opposing crowd, helping the Lady Thorpes go on to win the game (Frazier 2000).

There is some suggestion that this story maybe apocryphal (Klein 2020); however, its factual accuracy is beside the point given that people from Pine Ridge repeatedly tell this story to demark a profound statement of strength, power, and resistance displayed by one of their young tribal members (SuAnne was apparently only fifteen when she did this). Equally, it speaks to the way the Rezball heroes are community heroes in Indian Country. Indeed, when SuAnne led her team to the state championship in 1989, as the team's top scorer and by hitting the championship-clinching, final buzzer–beater shot, Pine Ridge community members gave the Lady Thorpes a hero's welcome. Hundreds of folks from Pine Ridge drove out to meet the team bus and started to follow it, creating an impromptu championship parade of over one hundred cars long. The girls from the team responded by getting on top of their bus and dancing and waving to the cheering crowd (Frazier 2000).

In an ironic and sad twist of fate, just over three years after this championship parade, most of these same cars produced a funeral procession, following the hearse carrying SuAnne's body. Tragically SuAnne died in an interstate car accident in 1992 on her way to a ceremony honoring her as one of the best basketball players in the state that year. Hundreds came to her funeral to honor her community leadership through Rezball. SuAnne's life and death, like Sherman Alexie's fictional Rezball heroes, embodies the duality of despair and hope in Indian Country. Her on- and off-the-court exploits made her a role model for community members. Her sudden death highlighted the challenges of life in impoverished tribal communities. Nonetheless, her legacy lives on as an emblem of hope. Twenty-five years after her passing, she is still heralded as one of the best Rezballers the community has ever seen. Today her influence is memorialized in the Pine Ridge Boys & Girls Club that bears her name and legacy. This rec center and gym is one the key safe spaces on the reservation for kids to congregate after school, participating in all kinds of positive activities—particularly Rezball.

Robby and Alek Tortes come from an athletic family. Their father, Rob Tortes Sr., played all kinds of organized sports growing up on the reservation of the Rincon Band of Luiseño Indians, and, consequently, so did they. The Rincon tribal nation is fifty miles north of San Diego nestled in the Pauma Valley. It was one of the early leaders in this area in utilizing tribal governmental gaming to promote sovereignty and self-determination, and today their community has one of the more successful casinos in Southern California along with a vibrant citizen base. Rob Sr. has seen a lot of change at Rincon throughout his life, but participation in sports has been a constant. He passed this sports enthusiasm down to his four children (three boys and one girl, now ages seventeen to twenty-five), who are constantly either playing or watching basketball, baseball, football, and softball. Robby and Alek look as if they were meant to play basketball—particularly in the low post. Robby, the eldest sibling in the family, is at least six feet eight with giant hands that allow him to palm the ball in the post, back defenders down toward the rim, and keep the ball away from them as he decides to make a deft pass or sink his, nearly impossible-to-block jump hooks. Robby's large, strong frame also suits him perfectly for the banging and rebounding expected of a basketball big man. Despite coming in about three to four inches shorter and two years younger than Robby, Alek has a similar frame with particularly broad shoulders that help him box out and maintain a low post presence. Alek is arguably not quite tall enough to play with his back to the basket in some contexts, but as far as high school and Rezball goes, he strikes an imposing force around the lane, particularly with the deft footwork he possesses for someone of his size. From many years of practice and playing, both young men have learned how to control their large bodies in a way that strikes a fearsome combination of force, speed, and agility.

Sports played such a significant role in the Tortes brothers' upbringing that it often came at the expense of their involvement in and connection to their Native community when they were younger. Robby notes, "We grew up on the reservation, but we were away playing travel ball on weekends." Even when they were home, they "basically just stayed at the house shooting hoops or hitting off a tee" while the other kids their age at Rincon "were out playing in the dirt or riding bikes" (Alek and Robby Tortes, interview). Both he and Alek realize that this compromised relationships with cousins—relationships that are key parts of peer networks in any Indian community. So much so that they often got the sense in junior high and high school that tribal members their age thought of them as more "white" than "Indian." It was not so much that playing sports marked them as "white" as opposed to the "Indians" who participated in more cultural events, but rather the fact that they generally played their sports off the reservation. However, this all swiftly changed during their teenage years once the two started playing Inter Tribal Sport (ITS) basketball. Now Robby and Alek are pillars in their local Indigenous community.

One can clearly see their central role in community life on full display by attending any of the basketball practices they hold for the youth teams they coach, as I did one bitterly cold (by Southern California standards) evening in February 2016. The Rincon reservation's only basketball court is outdoors; nonetheless, despite the chilly nighttime air, nearly twenty boys and girls from the coed ITS eighteen and under basketball teams of the Rincon tribe and the nearby San Pasqual Band of Mission (Ipai) Indians showed up to scrimmage for over an hour and a half under the lights shinning on the concrete court. And it was not just the players who were willing to tolerate the cold. A collection of siblings, cousins, and friends came to hang out and watch the scrimmage. Some of them goofed around outside the perimeter of the chain-link fence that surrounding the court. Others lingered inside the fence, sitting on the ground or bouncing basketballs along the sidelines, calling out to players, shouting encouragement and instructions, or laughingly joining in on some friendly trash talk initiated after someone gets their shot blocked, gets beat off the dribble, or sinks a three. The Tortes family loosely orchestrates this gathering of collective adolescent energy as Robby coaches the Rincon team and Alek the San Pasqual team. Robby's father helps coach the Rincon team, which includes his third son, Noah, who not infrequently glances at his father and brother when on-court actions slow, appealing for empathy and understanding of his on-court decision-making that they have just vocally criticized. Noah's superlative playmaking skills are rarely in question—they are just used as justification for his dad or brother to set higher expectations on him than any other player on the court. Meanwhile, Alek ruefully encourages his players, frequently subbing them in and out, with the affably competitive, satisfied smile of someone who is about to beat his big brother and father. Along the sideline at midcourt between the two brother-coaches is the youngest of the Tortes squad, sister Aliyah, who from time to time asserts coaching and substitution suggestions that so-and-so "isn't playing hard enough" and ought "to be pulled from the game." About thirty yards away sits the family matriarch staying warm inside a pickup truck. Yet this does not stop her from occasionally leaving the cozy vehicle and walking over to the court to share her observations and coaching suggestions with her husband and sons. This is undoubtedly a family affair as a handful of other parents spectate or demonstrate proper defensive stances and court positioning to their children from the sidelines. Rezball is the ritually pragmatic activity that makes this all happen and a key activity through which the Torteses and other Rincon and San Pasqual youth experience community.

Basketball is not just what is helping bring these people together on a random Monday night, but it is what makes the Tortes brothers feel bonded to their Native community and makes them a vital part of it. When not coaching basketball, Robby and Alek work with Native youth at their day jobs. Robby works as a youth coordinator in their tribe's Rincon Recreation Center, and Alek is employed by the neighboring San Pasqual tribe's Educational Center. On a daily basis they are interacting with Indigenous kids as positive role models. Given this employment and their lifelong experience with basketball, it became natural for them to volunteer to be ITS coaches. Their consistent and integral part of these kids' lives inherently promotes a community of wellness and fun simply in the amount of positive time and energy they are expending on these kids. From programing at tribal youth centers to coaching basketball to even being the "shuttle bus" drivers to and from practice, this all illustrates the investment Robby and Alek are willing to put into the youth of their community and the way they implicitly bond with the kids with whom they work.

An equally meaningful way that the Tortes family promotes well-being in the Rincon community is through the basketball tournament that they organize and host during the annual Rincon Fiesta. Held every August, the Rincon Fiesta predates contact with Europeans and was modified during the Mission period to blend traditional practices with the Spanish Christianity forced upon them (see Muñoz 2022). The Rincon Fiesta parallels similar ceremonial events held by several of the other nearby Luiseño and Kumeyaay tribes. It is a weekend-long celebration that traditionally includes culturally specific singing and dancing, food and vendor booths, a rodeo, traditional stick-gambling games, and basketball, softball, and horseshoe tournaments. While softball arguably is more popular than basketball among most San Diego County Natives, the basketball tournament is one of the more highly attended events at the Rincon Fiesta. It usually lasts the full three days, and on some of the days play goes well into the night—not ending until midnight. The number of teams that enter varies from year to year, and while many are composed of players from local tribes, it is not uncommon to have teams come from as far away as Arizona. The final few games of the tournament often draw crowds of over a hundred people, as fans overflow the small set of bleachers adjacent to the court and hang on every inch of the surrounding chain link fence.

This basketball tournament has become an expected part of the Rincon Fiesta and thereby rapidly a new tribal tradition. The fiesta is the annual communal celebration of "Rincon-ness" and all that it means to be a member of the Rincon community in the contemporary world. The fact that basketball is a key part of this celebration illustrates its significance in the definition of contemporary Rincon identity. Moreover, the fiesta is a celebration of survivance and vibrancy of the Rincon people despite several hundred years of settler colonial imposition. As a fast-paced game that is a unique blend of physicality, agility, and creativity, the Rezball tournament reflects the survivance of the Rincon community and provides a venue for people to express their vitality and joy—both as players and spectators.

It is no small thing that the volunteer job of organizing and running the Rincon Fiesta tournament was handed to the Tortes family a few years back. Not only does it signify recognition of their family's knowhow, but it also recognizes their collective reliability. Being handed this responsibility is a sense of pride for Alek and Robby, especially when one considers how far they have come in their connection to their community. They have described to me how, when they were younger, few of their Rincon community peers even knew who they were. They noted that it was not uncommon for them to only engage their cousins and older relatives at funerals and then rarely see them again. But in their late teens they began to play for the Rincon ITS basketball team, where they earned the reputation as committed, hardworking kids. Now they are entrusted with a key annual event that brings the community together. Robby and Alek are no longer merely peripheral members of the tribe but rather central figures in the youth and young adult network of the community and are key coordinators of this annual event that articulates a contemporary expression of what it means to be a Rincon tribal member.

One thing that makes the Rincon Fiesta Rezball tournament particularly fun is the intersecting and crosscutting relationships between the participants. Even though this is Rincon's Fiesta, people from several of the surrounding Luiseño, Cupeño, Cahuilla, Kumeyaay, and Serrano Native communities come to the celebration and participate in events. In addition to being an intertribal event, the basketball tournament also has an intergenerational quality to it as well. Teams are open to all ages, and frequently there will be a team that has players ten years (or more) apart in age. The teams are also intertribal in composition. Many of the teams are comprised of Rezballers who have either played with or against each other (often both) in ITS league play, adult leagues, or pickup games. All of this creates friendly competition, the kind that can only come from people who know each other very well and know each other's games and playing style. What increases the fun even more for events like this is that some of the teams are composed of guys who were the coaches of younger Rezballers playing for other teams. Younger players love to play against their coaches, with the chance to prove that they can beat them, and the coaches play to try to maintain their status and experience over the younger players. Because of all of the mixing and crosscutting of close tribal, familial, and generational relationships, the games at Rincon Fiesta include a healthy amount of good-humored trash talk. This good-natured ribbing increases the sense of community even more by affirming that their relationships are strong enough to tolerate the humor in being teased.

Teasing is a joyous endeavor that helps relieve stress and allows everyone to enjoy themselves even more when playing Rezball. Raymond Torres, a tall, lean, resilient Rezballer in his early twenties from the Pauma Band of Luiseño Indians, echoes these feelings. Raymond almost always had a big grin on his face, laughing and joking with his friends and his Rezball opponents. The better he played, the more he would laugh and joke around with everyone on the court. He would use his long arms to block a shot as the help defender coming across the key or to hoist three-pointers from long range. Raymond was never nasty or rude to his opponents, but when he knew them, his competitive spirit would come out through playful trash talk. He told me this was particularly the case at the Rincon Fiesta or recreation men's league games hosted by several North San Diego County tribes. He noted, "We're all friends but we're really competitive as well. During the game, we'll tell them to 'F-off' with a smile on our face, but we'll give each a [gregarious] 'whassup!'" (Raymond Torres, interview, February 8, 2016). This embodies the camaraderie that sports competition can create.

Poking fun at each is a very common part of the friendly competition found in all levels of sports. Talking (trash) during play is a particularly integral part of basketball, and Rezball is no exception. Now in his early twenties, Connor Flores, who has been playing ITS and pickup ball for a long time, shares with me the frequency of trash talk in Southern California Rezball. Connor has lived on the Pechanga reservation his whole life, and even though it is well known that he is a tribal member, his friends still enjoy teasing him for how "white" he looks. He is far fairer skinned than most of his peers and does not wear his hair long. Instead, his hair is short and parted down the middle with bangs that fall over his forehead. He tells me that when he interacts with non-Indian folks, rarely do any of them recognize him as Native. Alternatively, when he's among his Native friends—playing basketball or just hanging out—they often tease him about looking "white." This is not done in a mean-spirited fashion, but rather is something that actually deepens the bonds of the relationships he maintains with his Native friends. Joking about Connor's appearance signifies how close they all are in that they can tease him about "not being Indian" and get away with it in a manner that would likely be very offensive coming from someone outside of the community. This closeness created by trash talk not only helps Rezballers affirm who is in their Indigenous inner circle but also doubles as a way for them to safely observe and test the boundaries between being Indian and white. In many places in Indian Country, this boundary can be hotly contested and highly politically charged, but joking about it among friends on and off the basketball court is a way for youth to sort out and make sense of otherwise complicated and stressful notions of race, Indianness, and tribal identity.[5]

Connor, for example, speaks of the playful "trash talking" that goes on during ITS and Rezball pickup games and asserts that mean-spirited jabs are hardly ever lobbed at each other. Instead, he sees the playful challenging and teasing as increasing the fun of the game. Often the verbal sparring will continue long past the game. One day when I was helping coach the pan-tribal ITS All-Star team, I witnessed players from the La Jolla Band of Luiseño Indians teasing Connor and his Pechanga teammates about having recently beat them to win the ITS Championship, which is always played on the Pechanga courts because, frankly, they have the nicest facility. The ITS All-Star team also practiced at the Pechanga gym, and at the beginning of practice when everyone was lacing up their shoes and getting ready for practice, a Rezballer from La Jolla jabbed Connor and said, "Feels good to be here, nice to be home. Thanks for taking care of the gym for us" (Connor Flores, interview, October 29, 2014). With this statement he jokingly implied that since they beat Pechanga in the championship on Pechanga's own court, the gym now belongs to the La Jolla players. All the players from both tribes laughed, and when the Pechanga players tried a comeback, the La Jolla players reminded Connor that he missed two free throws at the end of the game that would have prevented Pechanga from losing to La Jolla. Connor was not afraid to acknowledge these misses and sometimes even made self-deprecating jokes about those free throws. He did so in a way that recognizes "yes, you got us, and there is nothing I can really say or do about it, but wait till next year" (Flores, interview). But more significantly, this banter, and Connor's willing participation in it, is the building block of community, for you can only tease someone about this failure if you are certain that your relationship is strong enough that your teasing is not perceived as egotism or harsh criticism, something that would divide the All-Star Team.

It's a random Thursday afternoon in midsummer in 2016, and I am heading back into Pechanga Rec Center, this time to meet with two tribal members in their late teens or early twenties, Ruben Rangel and Gejo Salgado. I met these two the first year I helped coach them on the ITS travel team of summer of 2014. I have visited this recreation complex many times, either as a coach or a spectator, yet each time its architectural beauty impresses me. The tribe has used its governmental gaming resources well to add collective value to the community. It is a two-story building with offices, classrooms, and community meeting rooms upstairs, and below are two large fully decked-out locker rooms, another set of public restrooms, and a pristine foyer with modern concrete and wooden padded benches. Also located downstairs is a fully equipped weight room, a five-lane bowling alley with a full snack bar, and large outdoor pool facility. Yet, the pièce de résistance is a massive, cavernous basketball gym that occupies most of the rec center's space. The courts are in immaculate condition. As I enter on this July day, I see Ruben has arrived early so he could put up some shots. On almost any given day of the week, you can find Ruben at the Pechanga Rec Center, whether lifting weights or "working on his game" on the basketball courts. Today Ruben is working on his midrange pull-up jump shot. When I first see him, he is repeatedly taking two or three dribbles forward and then leaning back slightly as he releases the ball. A fadeaway jumper is important to Ruben's game because he is an undersized point guard. Yet what he lacks in height

Ruben makes up for in strength, grit, and determination. He plays with great body control as he uses his very muscular upper body to create space on lay-ups or to back opponents down in the key. Often during the several practice drills in which I participated while being one of the assistant coaches for the ITS All-Star team, I felt his massive strength as I tried to defend him (we were generally matched up by height, not skills—I have nothing on Ruben!). He would lower a well-placed shoulder into my chest and knock me back or use his strong legs to box me out, or (and I am not too proud to admit it) he would do a crossover dribble and then use his explosive first step to blow past me toward the rim. To Ruben's credit, he tried not to embarrass me . . . too often.

Gejo Salgado, on the other hand, is a unique contrast and complimentary teammate to Ruben. While he might not have the same thick physique or body control, he is a constant whirlwind of energy and movement. One of his playing strengths is that he never stops moving, constantly surprising the other team and earning the respect of his teammates by hustling for loose balls and flying in the key to obtain a defensive rebound or a swift put-back offensive rebound, often made from deceivingly challenging angles. In practice I was also often Gejo's victim as well. He would leap over or sneak past me to dart in, grab a rebound, and put the ball back up quickly before I ever knew what hit me. Gejo has seemingly endless energy on the court.

When Gejo shows up at the gym a little bit after me, he, Ruben, and I sit down on the bleachers that are astride one of the side courts away from the several kids playing a pickup game on the main court. We sit down to chat amid the echoing squeaks of the basketball shoes, the thumps of floor-pounding dribbles, and screams of glee after a good shot or nice move. Ruben hollers at them to turn down the hip-hop that they are listening to so that we can better hear each other in our interview. Without any argument, the kids give him the respect he has earned as one of the better and more dedicated Rezballers of his tribe and immediately turn down the volume of the music.

The basketball courts at the rec center have become a community focal point and a venue to enact the process of maturing in the Pechanga community. This is evidenced by the sheer financial commitment alone that the tribal government has put into its basketball and recreational facilities. While Pechanga does happen to have one the most successful casinos in the country, the fact that the tribe prioritized healthy active living by building the rec center over other ways it could have spent the money is not lost on Ruben and Gejo. The two are very proud of how spectacular the gym and courts are in the Pechanga Recreation Center, both noting to me that the Los Angeles Lakers do an annual preseason practice one day a year on the Pechanga courts. It is a closed practice, open only to tribal members to spectate. Gejo and Ruben have gone to this practice every year, not only to view some of the most famous (and their favorite) sports figures in the world, but also as a way to take communal pride in knowing that one of the most recognizable franchises in all of sports chooses their gym as a place to train. Ruben and Gejo beam at the realization that the same courts where they and their friends play daily are deemed superior enough to meet the Lakers' needs. In fact, Gejo tells me that some of the Lakers have told him that the Pechanga courts are in better shape than the Lakers' regular practice facility in El Segundo, California. Indeed, most of the Pechanga community takes pride in how impressive their gym is and the acknowledgment of such by significant members outside of the community.

Ruben and Gejo also recognize that the elaborate design of and comprehensive services at the rec center are not just an exercise in a grandiose, meaningless display of wealth. As Gejo declares, "I think this is the best investment that Pechanga has ever made for us" (Gejo Salgado, interview, July 16, 2015). He and Ruben acknowledge that at first, when the council was voting on the plan to build it, there were some doubters in the community who felt that the money could be spent more wisely in other ways. Yet Gejo and Ruben notice what a difference the facilities, such as the basketball courts and swimming pool, have made in terms of the physical and mental health in their own lives and the community as a whole. Gejo observes: "I know it helped a lot of kids . . . like help them come in here, get actually fit. 'Cause before [the gym] kids were getting out of shape and then this happened [and] everybody started to be more active" (Salgado, interview). Ruben echoes Gejo's sentiments of physical health when he affirms what the gym has done for his own mental health:

> I can honestly say that when [the rec center] was being built, you know, I was into like smoking and all that stuff . . . there were times, you know, when [the gym wasn't yet] here and I'd be just like, "alright man, let's just go burn, or something," you know something like that.[6] And then once [the gym] got here, I mean we always had the outdoor courts . . . too, but it just made it better being in here . . . so instead I would just be like "Nah, I just gonna go to the rec. Go workout. Go play ball," you know. So it definitely helps out, you know, keep you out of trouble. (Ruben Rangel, interview, July 16, 2015)

Gejo agrees and recalls that he often makes a conscious decision to keep himself away from negative influences by going to the gym instead of just "hanging out." Much like the SuAnne Big Crow Boys & Girls Club on the Pine River Reservation, the Pechanga Recreation Center has become a safe space for tribal youth to hang out instead of doing, as Alek Tortes puts it, "things that they are supposed to be doing" (Alek Tortes, interview).

And Rezball is a key thing that keeps kids and the Pechanga community as a whole on a positive path. The basketball courts in the rec center have become an important space for joy and hope for the Pechanga tribal members and Indigenous folks from the region. On any given day, one can find kids and young adults like Ruben and Gejo enjoying themselves shooting hoops alone, playing half court three on three, or running a full-court pickup game. In addition to these daily activities, every few months the rec center hosts a large community basketball event, whether it is an ITS game day or "All Native +2" benefit tournament to raise money to buy shoes for the ITS All-Star Team.[7] It is rare for the courts not to be abuzz with the activity of people working hard on their game, laughingly talking trash during a pickup game, or the "ohhhs" and "ahhhs" coming from the bleachers provoked by great play on the court. The basketball courts are a key venue to enact the vibrancy of the community. Much like a powwow, they present a space for people to meet up and enjoy local community members that they see every day or reconnect with expanded community members whom they may not have seen in a while. Rezballers, like Gejo and Ruben, use the Pechanga courts to physically embody cultural values and social relations in "a good way" —a way much needed in Indian Country.

REZBALL AND GENDER 4

When American Indians use the word "Rezball," they do so in a way that is far more gender-inclusive than the way the word "basketball" is used outside of Indian Country. "Rezball" is understood to encompass both men and women playing ball without much need for a distinction to be made. In non-Native contexts, by comparison, the term "basketball" is generally unmarked as male and commonly understood to mean the men's game, while female basketball is normatively demarcated with feminine modifiers (i.e., the "NBA" and the "WNBA"; "Final Four" and "Women's Final Four"[1]). This is not to say that Rezball and Indian Country are devoid of sexism or patriarchy. Indeed, several female Rezballers with whom I spoke told me of challenging and empowering experiences that are likely very similar to many women's experiences in sports throughout the United States. Irrespective of these similarities, it is also important to consider the Rezball-specific ways that gender is articulated through basketball. A key reason why men's and boys' basketball in Indian Country is not thought of as the default—from which everything else is an alternative version—is because Indigenous female athletes have played since the beginning of Rezball and have continued to do so up until today. Moreover, girls' and women's Rezball merits the same fervor and support from the community as the male version. I contend that female participation in Rezball is so highly valued because Indigenous communities tend to start with a baseline of gender balance and harmony generally unseen outside of Indian Country, in spite of the settler colonialism efforts to systematically unsettle this balance (see Mihesuah 2003; Goeman and Nez Denetdale 2009; Ross 2009; Risling Baldy 2018). Key practices designed to maintain this gender dynamic are girls' coming-of-age ceremonies (and the traditional stories linked to them) that have existed in Indian Country for hundreds of years. A contemporary parallel practice of this celebration of the importance of girls and women in Indigenous culture is the way powwows equally focus on females as they do males. Rezball is another such contemporary expression of Indigenous people's recognition of the value of gender equality. Girls' Rezball frequently receives the same amount, if not more, attention than boys': this can be illustrated in terms of the size of crowds for girls' games, the intensity of the fans at these games, and ubiquitous participation of girls and women in Rezball.

On the contrary, in mainstream American society and media, women's basketball (at all levels) is normally covered and discussed as if it is inferior to the men's game (see Connell 1987; Cahn 1994; Hargreaves 1994; Kane and Greendorfer 1994; Kane and Lenskyj 1998; Messner 1992; Glick and Fiske 1999; Veri 1999; Messner, Duncan, and Wachs 2001; Shakib and Dunbar 2002; Shakib 2003; Lisec and McDonald 2012). Thankfully this is beginning to change; however, a great deal of academic scholarship has analyzed the history of this discrimination in the forms of: individual treatment from male athletes toward female athletes; biased popular media and cultural portrayals of female basketball players; and the structural forces that limit the development of female basketball. The normative message in America is that female basketball is inferior to the basketball played by males — although there are some very strong signs of the narrative beginning to crack with the growing popularity and media attention given to women's college basketball and the WNBA. But unlike many other sports that are intrinsically coded as masculine — such as football, baseball, and hockey — female participation in basketball possess a more explicit threat to chauvinistic discourses about sport. In this regard basketball parallels soccer and the meteoric rise of the women's game globally. This threat in basketball can be attributed to the rapid growth and prevalence of women's and girls' basketball in the United States. For example, in the last thirty years, basketball has been the most popular organized sport for high school female athletes to play (Cahn 1994; Shakib 2003). Secondly, the women's college game is given significant airtime and discussion in the major sports and conventional media. And lastly, the WNBA is one of the most successful women's team-sport professional leagues ever. However, even given the ubiquitous participation of women in basketball, one can find significant evidence of gender discrimination: girls' high school basketball rarely gets the same attention and adulation of boys' (despite instances of equal success), the women's college basketball season and its concluding tournament are treated as secondary to or an afterthought of the men's season and tournament, and for many years sports media regularly characterized the WNBA as a "watered-down" version of the NBA—sadly for most of its existence the WNBA has been publicly mocked as much as it has been praised. But again, this too is starting to change as it is becoming rarer and rarer to find public skepticism of the value of the WNBA.

These gender dynamics in American basketball have as much, if not more, to do with overall American patriarchal, heterosexual constructions of gender relationships than any objective evaluation of the basketball being played or what qualifies as elite basketball and why. But in the context of Indian Country, where women's roles, accomplishments, and virtues may be reconciled differently than in the rest of mainstream American, girls' and women's basketball might be experienced and valued differently. In places that regularly hold ceremonies for girls when they "come of age" or proclaim girls as official cultural standard-bearers through tribal "princess" competitions or celebrate girls' powwow dancing abilities with much fanfare, it should come as no surprise that basketball played by girls and women is inherently a natural part of Rezball.

Take, for example, the community of the Soboba Band of Luiseño Indians. This tribal nation is nestled up against the foothills of the San Jacinto Mountains, about eight-five miles southeast of Los Angeles. Summer afternoons at Soboba can easily reach triple digits. Smog drifts in from the LA metro area, and when it gets trapped in by the San Jacinto Mountains surrounding the Soboba reservation, it compounds the already normal summer temperatures. These conditions conspire to keep most people of this region indoors. Many of the non-Indian residents from the working-class towns of Perris, Minefee, Hemet, and San Jacinto that surround Soboba, escape the heat and smog by gambling in Soboba's expansive, flashy casino. Many of the Soboba youth, on the other hand, seek refuge from the high temps in their reservation's deluxe rec center and gym. This tribal resource was built from and is sustained by the very revenues produced from those thousands who feed the slots in order to escape the summer heat. One Soboba youth who consistently took advantage of the rec center in her teens was Tehya Marcus. She spent most of her summer days at the gym, perfecting her Rezball game.

The Soboba Rec Center is a hub of community activity and a celebration of Soboba sociocultural life. A trophy case greets visitors upon entrance. It contains photos of the several tribal sports teams that have won various league championships and tournaments in sports such as basketball, softball, baseball, and volleyball. The community as a whole takes pride in the accomplishments of their children, peers, extended kin, and close family members, and the prominent display of success illustrates this tribal pride and marks the rec center as a celebratory space. Additionally, many of the objects and features of the gym are labeled—often with hand-drawn signs—in Luiseño and Cahuilla, the dual languages of the people of Soboba.[2] Not only is this a simple, practical way to teach a language that has a decreasing number of fluent speakers, but it also promotes the notion that culture matters and ought to be a relevant part of daily life. Behind the wall that backs this trophy case is a gym. It is about double the size one might find at an average high school despite the fact that tribal enrollment in total is only about half the size of an average Southern California high school. The gym can accommodate up to four full-sized basketball courts, but generally there is a massive canvas curtain hanging from the chains attached to the thirty-foot ceilings and dividing the gym in half. On one side people play pickup basket games or shoot on one of the four hoops lowered from the rafters. The other side of the gym frequently hosts powwow dance classes where tribal members of all ages learn dance steps or hone their skills for upcoming powwows.

In the summer of 2016, Tehya Marcus was a constant at the rec center, appearing every day to get up shots or play pickup if there was a game going on. Often she would see Jeremy [pseudonym] there shooting and goofing around. Like many teenage boys on the reservation (or off, for that matter), Jeremy liked to tease and goof around with girls his age. When he saw Tehya at the gym, he would try to clown her basketball skills and claim that he was way better than her, mainly because he thought girls could not be good at basketball. He would tell Tehya: "Go back home . . . this is a guy's sport; girls are not supposed to play basketball" (Tehya Marcus, interview, July 20, 2016). This is nothing she had not heard from boys before, so Tehya generally retorted with a simple "Whatever"; "What are you talking about?"; or "Shut up." On one such day, Jeremy replied, "Fine, play me one-on-one, and you won't beat me." (Marcus, interview) So Tehya took up the challenge—first player to five baskets. Tehya dominated Jeremy: draining jump shots when his perimeter defense slacked off or backing him down to the low post when he tried to guard her tight; making spin move lay-ups, fall-away jumpers, or hooks shots he could not block. Equally, she played smothering defense on Jeremy, not letting him get a clean shot. When it was all over and done, Tehya shut Jeremy out, 5–0. Nevertheless, this would not quiet Jeremy. Upset and embarrassed about not being able to back up his words, Jeremy doubled down and chirped, "You won by luck." Tehya had the last word though, sarcastically laughing, "Ya, *okay*, five points to none is luck!" (Marcus, interview). This intergender competition illustrates the extent to which female Rezballers feel just as empowered to compete as the boys.

Another young woman from Soboba, Lexi Lopez, has had experiences while playing Rezball. During the open tryouts for the Soboba's Inter Tribal Sports (ITS) youth coed team, a few of the boys tried to haze her. Among the most vocal was Andre [pseudonym], whom she does consider to be a friend despite his being a perennial trash-talker. Taunting Lexi during one of drills, he snidely remarked, loud enough for all on the court to hear, "Can somebody please get this child off the court?" Not one to easily accept patronizing comments or to shy away from verbal sparring, Lexi responded by mentioning a video clip she keeps on her smartphone—the evidence of them playing against each other. She snapped back, "What are you talking about? I have the video right here. I shot the three in your face, Andre!" When he still persisted to brag about how much better and more dominant he was than her, Lexi was not afraid to get personal in taunting him: "Andre, you're frickin' short too; what are you talking about; you're not even that tall!" (Lexi Lopez, interview July 20, 2016). Lexi was not the only target of the trash talk. Tehya was at the same tryout, and she remembers the other boys making similar comments, such as: "Go easy on her. She's a girl" (Marcus, interview). Nevertheless, as Lexi and Tehya tell me, they enjoy basketball too much to let the boys' petty attempts at dismissing them get in the way of playing the sport they love. They know they have a fundamental claim to play Rezball just as much as anyone in the community, whether they be on the court with girls only or mixing it up with boys.

Indeed, Tehya and Lexi both figured out several strategies to succeed when playing coed Rezball. One was to turn the boys' own bias and ignorance of superiority against them. Frequently the boys they played against were blinded by their chauvinism to an extent that it disrupted their own success. Both Tehya and Lexi suggested to me that they could frequently get steals during coed ITS league games because the boys did not protect the ball as closely when playing against them compared to when they go head-to-head against other boys. Commenting to me, Lexi said, "it's funny because, like, they come down [from a rebound] with the ball, I just grab it [out of their hands]" (Lopez, interview) Tehya giggled in agreement with Lexi and chimed in: "And they don't think you'll grab it [away from them]. They're totally surprised" (Marcus, interview). These young women knew all too well that some boys underestimated them *and* how to take advantage of it when they did. Lexi and Tehya were frequently able to get open jump shots or to drive right past an unsuspecting defender, mainly because some of the boys did not think that girls were good enough to play with such skill. However, Tehya noted that the boys she plays with at Soboba have caught on and were learning that they needed to guard her just as attentively and aggressively as they would any player. Lexi, on the other hand, recalled one time during an ITS league game when she was able to dribble through three guys because none of them thought she had the handles to skillfully navigate their zone defense. On other occasions when she would play body-on-body defense, boys would get annoyed and say things like "What the heck! Why are you all up on me?" Lexi, however, did not take the bait and simply responded by laughing it off and retorting something along the lines of "What are you talking about? I'm just playing good D and boxing out" (Lopez, interview). In this instance the phrase "all up on me" is a double entendre that intensifies the chauvinism even more. It is often used as slang to describe someone trying to aggressively flirt and assert sexual attraction. When used in the context of coed basketball, it acquires a double meaning with the connotation that if a girl plays aggressive defense ("like a boy"), she (a) is not acting feminine; (b) must only be acting that way because she is physically attracted to her opponent, not because she is a tough basketball player; or (c) both. Despite her ability to laugh off this comment, it is still no fun to have to deal with on a regular basis.

Despite these challenges, Lexi and Tehya play coed basketball because they did not feel that Rezball belongs exclusively to the boys and not to them. As they tell me, "Ball is ball"; ultimately, it does not matter if one is playing boys', girls', or coed Rezball—it is all the same (Marcus and Lopez, interview). Indeed, on the whole, community members across Indian Country consistently message to girls that basketball is their sport too, and that Indigenous people are very proud of their female Rezballers. This is not to say that reservation life off the court is immune to patriarchy or sexism, but rather that Lexi and Tehya are just examples of the many Native girls who avidly play Rezball because they believe they belong on the court just as much as anyone. Moreover, despite the petty, snarky, sexist comments that can come from teenage boys testing the powers and limits of their budding masculinity, girls' Rezball is as (if not more) supported by Indigenous communities as boys' Rezball. There are multiple reasons for this, and the degree to which this is the case likely changes from Indigenous community to Indigenous community. But what is important at Soboba is that Lexi and Tehya feel that Rezball is a venue for them to feel a part of and through which to feel connected to their community and family. Indeed, Lexi and Tehya reckon their connection to Rezball is not through a gendered version of the sport, but rather how it connects them to their family of Rezballers.

Like most Indigenous communities, family relationships are particularly important to the Luiseño and Cahuilla people of the Soboba Tribe. These relations are critical to the inner dynamics of their community as they help determine the people's relationship to cultural and material resources, and they create the bonds (and the factions) that define the social and political life of the tribe. Moreover, family relations play an important role in how an individual understands their own personal identity–especially in a community that has a mixed heritage such as Soboba. That is, community members know they are from a Luiseño family or one intermixed with Cahuilla people from Soboba. What is often just as important is what social scientists might call clan or kin relationships. As a way to reckon identity, Soboba community members will often be asked "Who's your family?" or "Who are you related to?" as a way of reckoning an individual's identity (Lopez and Marcus, interview), illustrating what may be most important about an individual is not who they are, per se, but to whom they are related. Lexi and Tehya, for example, share a strong bond not just because both happened to be female Rezballers, but rather because they are female Rezballers who are *cousins*.

Tehya and Lexi are acutely aware of their familial relationship with each other and how they are connected to the rest of their kin: who are their other cousins, their aunts, and their uncles for several generations back. They are also highly cognizant of the Soboba community members who are not a part of their extended family. These family connections do not just indicate where one fits within the genealogical history of the community, but they are also indicative of how a person ought to act and what is of contemporary value for their family. These family connections can also be seen in the way Lexi and Tehya describe their relationships to Rezball. I asked them to tell me about themselves as basketball players, and rather than detailing their own experiences and expertise, they immediately talked about their family members who played ball. These are the people they look up to and hope to emulate.

Lexi and Tehya emphasize their family networks over talking about their own skills as players, the hard work they have put in to become excellent Rezballers (which I insist they are), or even the gendered aspect of their play. They see themselves as part of a specific Soboba family line of Rezballers, irrespective of their own gender, and they see it as their responsibility to uphold this kind of traditional practice of their kin.

Lexi's and Tehya's Rezball lineage starts with a shared grandfather, affectionately referred to as Grandpa "Bebop." Bebop taught them all the game. He had been coaching on the Soboba reservation and nearby San Jacinto High School for over thirty years and rarely missed a game at either location. Even now, although he no longer coaches, he is still a huge fan of the game and goes to as many games as possible. For him it was not just teaching the game of basketball but also being an elder who shows up to support the younger generations of his family and his community—both male and female Rezballers. Bebop also mentored Tehya and Lexi's cousin, Joe Burton. They are very proud to be related to Joe, both because of his athletic accomplishments and his commitment to his Soboba family and community. Joe is a highly skilled Rezballer who has also had a great deal of success outside of Indian Country. He is the only player in the history of Oregon State University men's basketball who has scored at least 1,000 points, grabbed at least 700 rebounds, and made 300 assists. He has played basketball for four different European professional teams. In 2015 Joe won the Statistical Player of the Year Award in the Dutch Professional League, and in 2016 he won the French League's MVP award (Wikipedia n.d.). These accomplishments are impressive for any basketball player, let alone one who grew up on a reservation. However, what Lexi and Tehya admire about Joe is not so much the way he was able to parlay his skill to get a "ticket out" of the reservation.[3] Rather, they respect the fact that Joe maintains his connection to his Indigenous community despite his professional basketball success—how he stays connected to his Rezball roots, continually returning to Soboba and supporting younger Rezballers.

Lexi and Tehya consider Joe a prime influence on their own basketball playing lives. He is about fifteen years older than Lexi and Tehya, and as long as they can remember playing themselves, they can remember watching Joe play Rezball. He was a source of pride for the community as a whole and specifically for Lexi and Tehya's family. Even more important to them are the times when Joe returned back to the reservation and went to watch their games. In this sense Joe picked up Bebop's tradition of attending games to support one's family and community. In a similar vein, Tehya told me that before she started to play basketball her younger sister was only interested in softball, and now that Tehya plays Rezball, her younger sister cannot stop dribbling a ball. Tehya is proud to be this kind of positive influence on her younger sibling. Evidently, Bebop and Joe are not the only family or tribal members with whom Lexi and Tehya have a bond; however, they have a particular affinity with these two older relatives (and each other) because they all share a love for Rezball. They all share a nearly visceral affinity because they all play Rezball in the same gyms, experience the same highs of winning and the same frustrations of losing. Rezball ties them together.

Playing Rezball not only connects Lexi and Tehya to each other and their kin at Soboba but also connects them to thousands of Indigenous women who have come before them. There is a long and extensive tradition of Indigenous women playing basketball. Girls and women have long been an integral part of what has come to be understood as Rezball (see Cummins, Anderson, and Briggs 2005; Peavy and Smith 2005, 2008; Diaz 2013; Schimmel 2015). This Native female participation in basketball should be viewed against the backdrop of American female participation in the sport in general. Since the game's origins in the last decade of the nineteenth century, women have been playing basketball. However, as Susan Cahn (1994) documents, along with female participation in basketball often came significant gendered tensions. In the late nineteenth century and the first quarter of the twentieth century, social reformers (mostly male) encouraged physical fitness for women, and basketball was often considered a great sport to meet this end. Nevertheless, many reformers, male and female alike, also believed that James Naismith's rules for basketball were too strenuous and dangerous for women and sought to create adaptations that were purported to "better serve" the female physique and sensibility (Cahn 1994). Various adjustments to the conventional five-a-side rules were suggested, such as having at least twelve (and up to twenty or thirty!) girls or women on the floor all at once. Moreover, unlike the way boys and men played, it was suggested that for girls and women the physical contact and constant running would place too significant a strain on their "female endurance." Therefore, rules were proposed to prohibit women from contesting an opponent's shot or to constrain female players to specifically demarcated zones of the court based on their position—thereby being "saved" from having to run up and down the court. Up until the 1950s, many of these stifling rules were implemented all throughout the United States in recreation leagues at the high school and collegiate levels. In several instances the sport was banned completely if women would not accept the modifications to the rules (Cahn 1994). Yet, these rule adjustments did not happen without debate and controversy. Many teams, leagues, and states refused to implement the modifications, instead opting to play the same way the boys and men did.

Working against these fitness "reformers" was the fact that women and girls had already played and become avid fans of the original version of basketball before the adaptations were suggested. Most players did not want to slow the game down or limit physical contact (Cahn 1994); indeed, these aspects of the game were a draw for women who might otherwise be suppressed into heteronormative, male-dominated American society. Ultimately the female ballers won out as today nearly all the fundamental rules of the game have remained universal for both male and female basketball.[4] While these "female rules modifications" have almost completely disappeared from the game, a two-tiered perception of the game has not. Sohalia Shakib and Michael D. Dunbar (2002) show that among high school players, girls and boys are thought to be playing two different versions of basketball. Moreover, as Lexi and Tehya have often found, most boys, and some girls, deem the men's game to be the superior version. The conventional, biased view from the earlier twentieth century that women are biologically obliged to play the game in an inferior way has not faded from the discourses that surround basketball. However, due to other factors in Indian Country, it can be argued that Rezball is more progressive than basketball played elsewhere. Some of this likely has to do with gender and cultural norms in Indian Country. Equally important is the fact that, from the beginning, Indigenous women's participation in basketball was marked as much, if not more so, by race than it was by gender.

Linda Peavy and Ursula Smith (2005, 2008) have compiled the most extensive history of the racializing and gendering of Native women's basketball. They weave a detailed account of the discourses that circulated around a historically important all-Native basketball team, the Fort Shaw Government Industrial Indian Boarding School girls' basketball team. This boarding school was established in 1892—coincidentally, just one year after James Naismith developed the game of basketball. Within ten years, the boarding school's superintendent, Fred Campbell, established basketball as a recreational activity and confidence builder for both his male and female students (Peavy and Smith 2005). Soon the girls' team, which Campbell coached, was dominating nearly all of its regional competition in and around the Northern Rockies, including playing and beating a few boys' teams. In 1904 they starred at the Louisiana Purchase Exposition, also known as the St. Louis World's Fair, not losing a single game. They played against all comers from high schools and state colleges, beating them with superior skill, speed, and strength (Peavy and Smith 2008). Despite their success, Fort Shaw players could not escape getting caught up in the national debate about the format and rules most appropriate for the "fairer sex" to play basketball. Moreover, in addition to this gender discussion, the Fort Shaw team was also wrapped up in an even larger conversation about race in America: if and how Indians could be assimilated into the growing and modernizing U.S. nation-state.

Fred Campbell's dual position of school superintendent and girls' basketball coach obliged him to engage in discourses on both gender and race. As for the former, like many other coaches west of the Mississippi (Cahn 1994, Peavy and Smith 2005), Coach Campbell was not persuaded by conservative-minded fitness reformers who advocated that girls play a less strenuous version of the game. Instead, Campbell believed that the fast-paced and physical nature of basketball was as good for the girls as it was for the boys (Peavy and Smith 2005, 2008). In terms of racial discourse, Superintendent Campbell sought to use basketball to fulfill the settler colonial project of "civilizing" Indians. Like many other "educators" who installed sports programs in Indian boarding schools (see Bloom 2000, Deloria 2004), Campbell hoped that playing a game based on rules, order, and sportsmanship could help the girls of Fort Shaw learn how to manage their "primitive," corporeal instincts and channel them toward positive values of honor and discipline (Peavy and Smith 2008). The ultimate imperial goal of the entire boarding school system was forced assimilation of Native peoples, starting with the youth as a form of cultural reeducation (see Lomawaima 1994). Boarding schools were a key part of a larger settler colonial project to eliminate any Indigenous claims of separateness that could undercut emerging American nationalism and the growing nation-state's consolidation of land and geopolitical space (see Rifkin 2009).

The St. Louis World's Fair played an integral part of this budding geopolitical nationalism, as it was designed to commemorate the centennial of the Louisiana Purchase — one of the largest annexations of Native land base into U.S. governmental possession. The Fort Shaw girls' basketball team was invited to join some 150 other Indian boarding schools that attended from across the West to participate in an exhibit named the "Model Indian School" (Peavy and Smith 2005, 2008). This exhibit was a working reproduction of a boarding school meant to illustrate exactly how these institutions purported to convert Indians into "productive" members of society, even if full citizenship was not thought to be an achievable (or desirable) goal. Thousands of visitors came daily to watch Native youth receive academic lessons and industrial training, complete chores, perform traditional and cultural arts, and, in the case of the Fort Shaw girls, exercise via intra-squad basketball games. As with the other activities housed in the "Model Indian School," superintendent and coach Campbell hoped displaying the girls' basketball skills would illustrate how "savagery" could be contained and channeled toward what was deemed proper "civilized" behavior. He sought to demonstrate this further by having the Fort Shaw team play not just against themselves but against white teams as well. For full effect this needed to happen outside of the "Model Indian School," and Campbell and his players had desires to compete in the larger sports complex at the center of the St. Louis Fair. This venue was prized because, later that summer, it would be hosting the third Modern Olympiad. However, he and the girls were up against the same forces that sought to limit girls' participation in basketball throughout the rest of the country. The man in charge of athletics at the fair was strongly concerned about the appropriateness of girls playing sports in public, in front of mixed-gendered audiences (Peavy and Smith 2008). Nonetheless, after much persuasion, the Fort Shaw team did play in the main arena, where they swiftly and forcefully beat the Missouri State Girls Championship team. This victory (along with a few others they played in other Missouri locales) earned them much press and fanfare and a large trophy awarded by the fair organizers, declaring the Fort Shaw team basketball "World Champions." While the success clearly meant a lot to the individual Native young women who comprised the team (Peavy and Smith 2005, 2008), it also contributed to larger societal discourses intersecting race and gender apparent in such locales as the Louisiana Purchase Exposition, government-sponsored boarding schools, and institutions mandating settler colonial policies at the turn of the twentieth century.

To a large extent, the willingness of the world's fair organizers to include the Fort Shaw team in such a high-profile venue was due to the team's promotional value to the fair as a whole (Peavy and Smith 2008). Similarly, to the popularity of the "Model Indian School," the growing notoriety of the Fort Shaw team brought many paying fairgoers to come see their practices and exhibition games. The team's popularity can, in large part, be attributed to the fact that, at that time, girls who played basketball *and* were Indian were a novelty. This is precisely the phenomena Philip J. Deloria (2004) discusses in his exploration of white America's fascination with "Indians in unexpected places." The mere existence of the Fort Shaw girls' team ran counter to early twentieth-century white society's conventional notions of Indianness: that Indians were not and could never be modern citizens. On top of that, the girls' exceptional skill at this modern game is what made them so interesting to fair visitors. Deloria (2004) calls these instances, when Indians' cultural productions contradict normative expectations of Indianness, "Indians in unexpected places." What's more, he asks us to consider if these apparent contradictions can be transformative or are merely anomalies, that is, exceptions that ultimately just prove the conventional belief that Indians are inferior to white folks. The latter seems to apply to the Fort Shaw Indian basketball players. Given the overall settler colonial bravado of the 1904 Louisiana Purchase Exposition and the social Darwinism and scientific racism inherent to all world's fairs of this era, it is hard to see the girls' athletic performances as something that subverted the normative views of most fairgoers. However, if we look at it from a more individualized perspective, it is easy to see how the experience might have transformed the Native athletes' lives and that of their descendants.

Peavy and Smith (2008) argue that despite the Fort Shaw basketball team's short existence (the school closed down in 1910 and the team along with it), for the ten to fifteen Native girls who were on the team, playing basketball was a foundational life experience. They traveled all over the western United States, received mostly adulation, and bonded with Indigenous women their age at a time of tremendous upheaval and uncertainty for tribal communities. Moreover, Peavy and Smith (2008) also note how many of the female descendants of these original Fort Shaw Rezballers look up to them and actively seek to keep their legacy alive, honoring them by telling their story every chance they get. Despite how their athletic performances might have circulated in white media of the time—as a novelty or material for the racist puns of newspaper headlines—to many Native folks, the Fort Shaw Girls Basketball team exemplifies bravery, talent, and exuberance at a time when it was not easy for Native women to express those characteristics, and when the venues for them to do so were extremely limited.

The agency of these women is particularly important when we consider the extent to which boarding schools were a place that promoted settler patriarchy and heteronormativity (Morgensen 2011; Rifkin 2011; A. Smith 2015). Above all else, boarding schools were places of extreme conformity. Indigenous youth from diverse cultures and languages were thrust together in order to erase the social patterns in which they would normally engage — particularly the transmission of cultural knowledge that community elders would pass on to Native youth as they grew and reached puberty. Instead, boarding schools had regimented military-style living conditions and strict daily schedules. This disrupted the way Indigenous youth would otherwise relate to one another, to seasonal and life-stage time, and to their land. The missionaries and military officials who ran the schools would repress anything that did not fit within a predominantly Protestant model of social and gender relations.

The promotion of girls' basketball at the Fort Shaw Boarding School represents a noteworthy exception to this settler colonial gender conformity. While the leaders at Fort Shaw likely saw basketball as an additional means to foster order and discipline in these Indigenous girls, many of the individual girls who played basketball experienced their participation as an outlet for individual self-expression and an exploration of nonsettler ways of being a woman and relating to men. Basketball was a way for these Native girls to experiment with their full potential—their physical and mental capabilities that extended beyond the boarding school education and its confinement to domestic labor and "feminine" arts.

Tehya and Lexi are the inheritors of the legacy of the Fort Shaw girls' basketball team and the many Native women Rezballers who came after them. Today Rezball still provides opportunities for Indigenous girls and women to express themselves. Like the girls from Fort Shaw, Tehya and Lexi also must navigate similar complex fields of gender relations while playing Rezball, as detailed above. Additionally, like the Fort Shaw girls, they are at a stage in their lives where their Indigenous community and the general American society expect them to begin to take on the responsibility of adulthood. Significantly, this is also an age that many scholars of female athletics find to be a critical juncture for girls' participation in organized sports. In their middle to early teens, many girls across the United States begin to quit playing sports. The reasons for this tend to be complicated and interrelated, but many researchers suspect it has to do with how puberty in girls brings on a different set of societal expectations and cultural pressures than it does for boys.

For example, Colette Dowling has surveyed academic research on the relationship between sports and gendered notions of strength, physicality, and embodiment. From this data she concludes:

> By the time [girls] are eleven, twelve, and thirteen, female children in our society are plucked from the world of childhood in a way that is harsh and abrupt. . . . Society's focus on female sexual characteristics—a glaring, virtually voyeuristic focus—has made girls excruciatingly self-conscious. Internalizing the view of them presented by a male-biased culture, they learn to overvalue their external selves. The body becomes a fetish, one they are obsessed with in the same objectifying way the culture is. (Dowling 2000, 116)

This internalizing of societal notions of how female bodies should look and move impacts the way girls see themselves in relation to athletics. The "tomboy" look and attitude that may have been cute or tolerated prepuberty becomes increasingly frowned upon as girls move into their teen years. There is little doubt that over the last half century there has been a dramatic expansion in notions of beauty, of body type, and of the various forms gender can take in America; however, despite this broadening of the sense of what counts as female beauty, puberty still brings a significant decline in a girl's participation in sport. Dowling (2000) notes:

> Two out of three girls in the United States don't participate in school athletics . . . and only half take high school phys ed classes. Trained to halt the development of their bodies at puberty because of the culture prescription against females being strong, girls weaken themselves unnaturally. In adolescence most stop using their bodies and start using appearance for whatever power they're going to exert in the world. The majority of girls in high school are interested

in a different kind of body culture [that is more readily connected with conventional notions of femininity]. (57)

This phenomenon of girls dropping out of sports during their puberty years is certainly not unknown in Indian Country. Take, for example, the Inter Tribal Sports in Southern California. All ages of ITS basketball are coed. Go to any ITS league game days, and you will find the "7 and under" and "11 and under" teams with nearly as many girls as boys playing. But at the "14 and under" and "18 and under" games, there are far fewer girls on the court.[5] At the younger ages, it is not uncommon to see girls dominate the play, but this is rarer as they get older. As female Rezballers get older, they tend to turn to their junior high or high school teams that are girls only.

Nonetheless, individual female Rezballers or teams of Rezballer girls receive tremendous amounts of support from their communities, something that appears quite different from the national norm of how girls' sports are valued.[6] In most reservations communities, girls' high school games have as many (if not more) fans filling the stands for the games as the boys' teams do. What is strikingly different when attending a girls' high school game from a reservation community as opposed to most elsewhere in the United States is the fervor and intensity that Native fans invest in their teams.

This community support and participation is so significant that sometimes it is the girls who do not play basketball who can feel left out of the energy and joy that the Indigenous community invests in basketball. Take, for example, Raini Tesam-Reading; she grew up on the Viejas Reservation, about fifteen miles east of downtown San Diego. Like the Pechanga and Soboba tribes that are within an hour's drive, the Viejas community decided to use its significant gaming revenues to build a beautiful rec center with a large, multicourt basketball gym as its centerpiece. Arguably, this is the nicest gym and rec center among the nine tribes of south San Diego County—so much so that it is often the centralized location for ITS's game days down in the southern part of San Diego Indian Country. Compared to the neighboring tribes, the

Viejas gym is the largest and has the most amenities, making it the perfect place to host the volume of games that need to happen on an ITS game day. Additionally, adjacent to Viejas's gym is a softball field complex. Among Southern California tribes, softball is also immensely popular with women and men—as much as basketball, if not more. For all of Raini's life, she has witnessed the way that a significant portion of community life at Viejas revolves around basketball and softball games. And while for some of the time, she participated on the sidelines as a cheerleader at basketball games, Raini admits that her lack of real interest in playing basketball or softball often made her feel alienated from community life. She recollected to me:

> I have this distinct memory of [always] being at the rec center by myself and waiting to be picked up [by her mom after the school bus from the off-reservation school dropped her at the rec center] . . . and everyone else was showing up for the softball game or basketball practice, and *everybody* was there. I mean it's huge. Everybody on the Rez, would go and watch the softball or basketball games, regardless of who's playing, whenever it is. And, like, the snack bar will be open. There will be people everywhere. The parking lot will be filled. People will be coming the from other reservations, and I would just be on my way home. [*she giggles*]. "Uh, I'm gonna go read or something" [*she says facetiously and self-mockingly*]. (Raini Tesam-Reading, interview, December 14, 2017)

What is interesting here is that her lack of participation in sports made her feel left out of the community. Ironically, in communities outside of Indian Country, teenage girls are often made to feel aberrant for continuing to play sports past puberty, not for nonparticipating.

Lastly, it is worth noting one more telling example of how Rezball can function as a subversion of settler heteronormativity. Mvskogee novelist and literary critic Craig Womack was one of the leading voices in what's often known as American Indian literary nationalism—a literary criticism movement centering tribal modes of interpretation over postcolonial and postmodern methodologies that Womack (1999) developed in conversation with other Native literary scholars such as Jace Weaver, Robert Allen Warrior, and Greg Sarris. Womack's 2001 novel *Drowning in the Fire* is widely regarded as "one of the first novels to situate a gay Native character as its central protagonist" (Tatonetti 2003, 95). Womack does so to claim space for queer Indigenous folks both in contemporary and historic Mvskogee communities as a resistance to the settler attempts to erase diversity and complexity in Indigenous cultures. As Mark Rifkin (2008) puts it, "the novel foregrounds homoeroticism among Creek people in the early and late twentieth century in ways that emphasize how identification with straightness is enmeshed in the continuing legacy of the civilization program and allotment" (444). The novel features the perspective of multiple characters over a one-hundred-year period. Two of the main contemporary characters are Josh and Jimmy; their love affair prominently features Jimmy's athletic prowess as a Rezballer. Like Natalie Diaz's character in "Reservation Mary" (mentioned in chapter 2) who falls for a star player, a key part of Josh's attraction to Jimmy is his basketball skill. And although most of the analysis of this novel circulates around Indigenous sexuality, identity, and sovereignty (see Tatonetti 2007; Rifkin 2008), we should not overlook Womack's intentional inclusion of Rezball in such a significant novel.

Not unlike Raini Tee-Sam's story, Josh's character understands what makes him different from the other kids in his community through basketball and athletics. Yet, in the case of Womack's novel, this is overlap onto Josh's distinct sexuality and perceived lack of masculinity. When being mocked for his inability to play in a game of pickup Rezball, Josh admits:

I felt sick . . . Nothing panicked me more than being thrown a basketball and the transformation when the ball landed in my hands. The moment when everything that comes next matters so much. Should I keep it? Get rid of it as soon as possible? Lop it over the sidelines like a live grenade in order to save myself? . . . I would stand there thinking, "Please, please don't past the ball to me," unlike my other teammates running around the court begging for it, pleading for their chance to shine. (Womack 2001, 67)

It was this supreme confidence of Jimmy's—his wanting to shine on the court—that Josh found so attractive. Ultimately, Jimmy returns Josh's affection, and they become lovers for a time. Here Womack is queering the standard American trope that the male high school sports stars get the girls because of their overt physicality and bold masculinity.

In this novel basketball acts as the backdrop for everyday life in Indian Country, just a normative feature of the community. It also acts as the locus of Josh's attraction to Jimmy. Hence this queering of boys' basketball reinforces the notion that Rezball is not gendered in Indian Country the same way it is outside of it. For example, in a key scene after Jimmy and Josh make love in Jimmy's room, surrounded by NBA posters on the wall and stray Air Jordan shoes the floor, they are lying in bed talking about their childhood and how Jimmy always tried to get Josh to play basketball with him despite his diminished skills. Josh admits his hesitancy and youthful anxiety that his poor basketball skills betrayed his queerness before he was ready to reveal it to the world. Jimmy lovingly assuages this trepidation, claiming that when he played with Josh those were the best games of his life. Jimmy refutes the need to connect basketball skill to a conventional settler notion of masculinity or even equating skill with fun. That is, Jimmy just loved playing Rezball with his friends even if they weren't good; being in community is what mattered. Through Jimmy's love for Rezball (in any form or any skill level, free from a masculinist bias), Womack articulates why I believe girls' Rezball is commensurate to boys' Rezball. Community bonding is valued over elite competition; hence, the distinction between girls' or women's and boys' or men's basketball is not as stark as outside of Indian Country.

Again though, as I have said repeatedly throughout this chapter, general American normative notions of gender and sports are rapidly changing. In terms of basketball, this might be seen most clearly in the way NBA superstar players are now supporting WNBA players, showing up courtside to watch and vociferously cheer them on, thereby calling into serious question the argument about the inferiority of the women's game—if NBA players enjoy the product on the court, one would wonder how anyone else could question the quality of the basketball. College and WNBA players are certainly receiving far more attention in the media and public sphere, though this has yet to translate to anything comparable with NBA salaries and endorsement money. Former ESPN sports reporter Kate Fagan has recently noted that "basketball culture is fluid, often genderless" (Fagan, Bryant, and Haberstroh 2021). While this is becoming increasingly true for Americans at large, one could argue that it has always been true for Rezball. Sure, individual's sexist remarks and attitudes seep into Rezball, like anything else, but on a systematic level Rezball has always been and continues to be a safe, fun, and healthy space for Indigenous women to feel respected, honored, and valued in their communities.

In 1982 Rodney Mullen pulled off the first ollie from flat ground in an organized skate competition. An "ollie" is trick where the skater performs a fluid seesaw-like motion making the nose (front) of the board pop up by pushing down with their back foot on the board's tail (back) and then, in rapid succession, pushing the nose down with their front foot to pop up the board's tail, with the result of getting all four wheels off the ground at the same time.[1] The move is meant to simulate the kind of vertical air (or height off the ground) that riders get from the momentum of skating in swimming pools or that a large half-pipe provides to launch the skater into the air. Mullen figured out how to instead get air from flat ground (progressing from a one- to three-foot-high mini ramp and to straight from the ground). This intuitive but rather simple move revolutionized skateboarding by making it possible to do tricks from the ground or low heights and thereby initiating a panoply of new maneuvers based off the ollie, unlocking infinite realms of where skateboarding could be practiced and creating dramatically new ways athletes could relate to space and the built environment surrounding them (Borden 2001). Around the time the ollie was invented, popular skateboarding was beginning to lose its national attention, and participation that had peaked in the United States in the mid- to late 1970s was dwindling. However, the popularization of the move soon ushered in the age of street skating, which by the early 1990s made the sport a global phenomenon, a tremendously popular youth activity worldwide that did not require elaborate and massive concrete skateparks or wooden half-pikes. This transformation initiated by the ollie aided in the unprecedented financial success of the sport since the 1990s.

This ollie revolution began about the same time I was starting Horace A. Ensign Junior High school in the Southern California beach town where I grew up. Given my city's surf and beach culture, skateboarding had never really waned in popularity like it did after the 1970s in most parts of the country. Even if people stopped pool skating in my city, at the very least skateboards remained a fun, cool, and popular way to get around town. But with ramp and street skating taking off in the mid-1980s, skateboarding reached a new level of cool beyond the laid-back, counterculture, sidewalk surfing vibe from the 1960s to emphasizing rebellion, grit, and "hardcore-ness." These latter characteristics, of course, are the exact same qualities that are valorized by junior high boys trying to make sense of masculinity. Nearly everyone in my town was wearing skate clothing (along with surf wear)—particularly Vision Street Wear or Bones Brigade—to access a gritty coolness, even at the risk of being called a "poser" if they could not actually skate very well. I was one of those posers. I had a hand-me-down Jeff Philips model Sims board with the artwork of his name aggressively busting through black concrete. I almost exclusively used my Philips for transportation for distances shorter than a bike ride. I could maintain my balance at most speeds and do the most basic tricks like a tick-tac, but I maxed out at the lowest of low ollies—and that was on the rarest of occasions when I actually pulled off the trick by staying on it after pushing the nose back down.

Through much of high school, I rarely skated, and it was not until I went to New York City for college in the early 1990s that I returned to my skateboard. Something about being across the country away from the Pacific Ocean provoked a desire to reemphasize my California-ness. I got a more modern "popsicle" shape board with lips on the tail and nose, and I began skating around campus, to and from class, as much as I could. But even this return to skating made it more apparent to me that I was not a "real" skater and certainly not a street skater. I was very comfortable cruising around on the board because the stance—feet parallel, knees slightly bent to absorb the shock of cracks and bumps in the road—was similar enough to surfing—the sport I was always far better at. However, at this time in my life, ollies were simply out of the question (and kick flips?!—forget about it!). I began to realize how many of my classmates, who grew up far from an ocean, dove into skating and could do far more tricks than I. It was from these classmates that I began to better understand the way avid skaters look at the built environment differently than nonskaters. Unlike me, who mostly skated to get that feel similar to surfing, an experienced skater's mind frame viewed the manmade world from a perspective of how to repurpose architecture in order to pull off a skateboarding trick. They paid attention to the mundane and saw beyond the constructed functions of built environments. Encountering these more authentic skaters, I realize this was not how I viewed things in relationship to the board.

For graduate school I came back to the Pacific Coast and kept up skateboarding for transportation, but in terms of a hobby, I was more interested in returning to the pastime of my youth, surfing, rather than attempting to (re)learn any real skate tricks. Being in Southern California made it a bit easier to keep up with many aspects of skate culture mainly because of a roommate's subscription to *Slap* magazine.[2] A few years after graduate school, I took a tenure-track position in American Indian studies in the city of San Diego, a mecca of surf and skate culture. It came as no surprise to me that many of my students at San Diego State University (SDSU) are hardcore surfers and/or skaters, and so once again I was immersed in board culture. I still tended to pay more attention to surfing than skating, but nonetheless both are ever present here in San Diego.

After teaching at SDSU for a few years, a chance occurrence melded my outside-the-classroom interest in board culture with my academic interest in the various ways Indigeneity thrives by combining the historic and traditional with the contemporary. This fusion of my personal and academic interests was prompted by two settler students in my "American Indians through Film & Television" class. For the final assignment in this class, I allow students to make their own short film, as an alternative to writing a paper, about any topic of their choice pertaining to American Indian history and life. One semester two avid skater students worked together to make a film about a skate pool in the backyard of an abandoned house on the Pala Reservation—located about forty-five miles northeast of SDSU. This DIY (do-it-yourself) skate spot had become legendary in the underground San Diego skate scene, in large part because it was not too far from the Northern San Diego County towns of Encinitas, Carlsbad, and Del Mar, themselves hotbeds of board culture within the larger mecca of San Diego County.[3] My two students knew of the legend of this "Pala pool," both from word of mouth and occasional references to the pool in skate magazines—especially a popular DC Shoes print ad that featured renowned skater Danny Way.[4] In order to make their film, they researched and then visited this "secret" skate spot. Additionally, they visited the tribal skate park that was subsequently built, as a part of the Pala Tribal Governmental and Recreation Complex, after the Pala pool was closed down.

This project prompted my students to further research throughout Indian Country, outside of San Diego, where they stumbled onto a significant skate subculture in American Indian communities. It was from their final assignment for my class that I learned how ubiquitous skating was in Indian Country. I knew skating existed in Indian Country because I knew nearly all aspects of mass American youth culture have found a way into the most relatively isolated locales of Native communities. Yet this student film opened my eyes to just how common Native-run skate companies and tribally sponsored skate parks are. So much so, that it provoked this book project exploring basketball and skateboarding in Indian Country.

Skating helps build community in Indian Country in many of the similar ways that Rezball does. It helps bring Indigenous people, particularly youth, together through a shared love of a positive activity. Similarly, skating is also a sport that can build self-confidence in Indigenous practitioners. This section of the book covers the many aspects of skateboarding in Indian Country that parallel basketball, and it also highlights many of the unique elements of skating that synchronize with Indigenous values, such as relationship to place and space, artistic and symbolic expression, narrative, and mentoring relationships.

In June 2009 the Smithsonian National Museum of the American Indian opened an exhibit called "Ramp It Up: Skateboard Culture in Native

America." After being on display at the Washington DC-based museum for several months, the exhibit eventually traveled to ten different locations throughout the United States—five of which were tribal-run cultural centers, and the other five were in locations that have a high concentration of American Indians in the regional areas. Additionally, Native skateboarding exhibits similar to "Ramp It Up" have been hosted in the Heard Museum of Phoenix and the Museum of Northern Arizona in Flagstaff. All of these exhibitions had certain historical components but were mainly meant to promote contemporary Indigenous culture. One aspect particularly unique to the "Ramp It Up" show was that, in addition to the display of skate decks and photos, many exhibit spaces allowed curators to construct half-pipe ramps in the museum. Hence, Indigenous skaters were enlisted to come put on skate expositions inside of the museum, expressing the lived aspect of Native skate culture right alongside the historical displays of decks and wall text. This was immensely impactful in demonstrating the vibrancy of Indigenous culture, an Ingenious way to combat the overdetermined museum discourses that conventionally treat Indians as people of the past.

Skating is an excellent mode to articulate a dense set of meanings about contemporary American Indian culture. The skateboards themselves provide an artistic palate for visual and iconic representations.[5] Native-owned skate companies use the graphic section, always coated onto the underside of a skate deck, to represent Indigenous and tribal history and culture and to confront stereotypical images of Indianness appropriated and exploited by mainstream culture in general and sometimes in skate culture specifically. This Native artistic expression negotiated through combinations of traditional symbols and colors, historic photographs, or Native language celebrates the thrivance of Indigenous culture. The act itself of skating channels physical energy and particularly vigorous body movements toward an Indigenous expression of presentness and an ongoing relationship with local terrain and place. Engagement with skate culture also provides a venue for storytelling about legendary skaters and their exploits. Lastly, participating in skating is an activity that specifically engages a sense of history, tradition, and improvisation; skaters try to accomplish tricks they have seen other skaters, both their peers and elders, execute in a way that adds their own personal style to the riding of a board on four wheels. Skaters provide vocal encouragement to each other as they attempt tricks. This in turn creates a safe atmosphere for personal growth through a combination of trial and error and positive guidance from respected community members. Hence, skating aligns well with a conventionally Indigenous mode of learning that combines mentorship with individualized experimentation or access to knowledge that comes from personal development and introspection.

"Ramp It Up" elaborated on some of the cultural aspects of skating in Indian communities but mostly from an artistic or symbolic perspective, that is, by providing context for the various Indigenous-themed graphics on these Native-made skateboard decks. The exhibit predominantly focused on the history of skating in Indian Country. And as "Ramp It Up" illustrates, although skating certainly existed on reservations before the advent of street skating, it grew exponentially in Indian Country once street style became popular. This most likely can be attributed to the fact that from the mid-1960s to the mid-1980s, most tribal communities did not have the resources to build concrete skate parks or large wooden half-pipes that were the dominant venues for skating during this time period. Moreover (with the obvious exception of the Pala pool mentioned above) very few tribal communities had homes with swimming pools, let alone drained swimming pools, which were a Shangri-la for the underground guerilla skaters of the 1970s and early 1980s. However, the advent of the ollie made it possible for skaters to do tricks on small ramps and then basically any aspect of a human-made environment. This transformed skating from a more Southern California, regional phenomenon to a global one—including American Indian communities. With street style, skating could be performed virtually anywhere. During the same time of this innovation in skateboarding, it was common for many Native folks in the United States to travel back and forth or live between reservations and urban areas. When they spent time in urban areas, many Natives (mostly youth) began to pick up the hobby of skating and then subsequently brought this pastime back with them to the reservation or reservation border towns. Street skating then spread throughout Indian Country just as it also was catching on in the rest of the world.

At its most basic level, street skating is about altering one's relationship to their surroundings—to place and space in general (Borden 2001). Skaters manipulate their built environment in ways that rewrite the functionality of human-made place and human-manipulated space. What I have found most noteworthy from spending time with skaters is the way that they see the world differently than a nonskater. Avid skaters view steps, benches, stairs, hand railings, concrete slabs, drainage ditches, curbs, and so on with an eye for how a board with four wheels will interact with these features. The intended function at the fabrication of these human-made features is really secondary for skaters. Instead, they comprehend surfaces, slopes, and angles of built environments that others take for granted or just flat out ignore because of their ordinary nature. This attention to the details of the space around them parallels Indigenous relationships to place. Indigenous relationships to place and ecology are encoded in Native language, ceremony, economy, and history in ways that are not common to industrial capitalist society. Therefore, when an Indian street skates, they may be engaging in more than just a skater's creative and often rebellious response to fabricated public space, but engaging isomorphically in Indigenous decolonial discourses as well. In this sense, I would argue that Native skating has more radically transformative potential than either (most forms of) non-Indigenous skating or Rezball.

In a certain sense, skateboarding is a highly artistic sport both in the way that it manipulates space and architecture and in the purely improvisational aspect of attempting and pulling off tricks (Borden 2001). There are also aesthetic elements to the subculture of skateboarding that can be seen as important markers of belonging in skate culture, such as clothing, branding, stickers, and, to a certain extent, graffiti art, especially when painted on top of or in conjunction with a skate spot. Furthermore, notwithstanding team uniforms, few sports have equipment that lends itself to such an explicit canvas for graphic expression as the underside of a skateboard (Waterhouse and Penhallow 2006). It is incredibly rare to see someone skating a deck that is merely blank wood on the bottom instead of an elaborate and symbolic design.

Skate decks uniquely combine art, design, and function. For example, because of functionality, the artistic components must be on the bottom or underside of a skateboard. This can be attributed to the necessity of grip tape on the top of a deck. The grip tape—predominantly black in color, although sometimes clear or multicolored or marked up with chalk—is a thin layer of what is essentially sandpaper. It has adhesive on one side to stick to the top of the board and a gritty surface on the other side so that the rider's feet can grip the board. Hence, when in the act of skateboarding, skaters rarely actually see their board's artistic design, nor does anyone who might be watching them skate—except for quick glimpses when the board is flipped and manipulated through the air. Most frequently these designs are seen in the skater's poses that fill the pauses between attempting tricks: skaters generally stand with the underside of their board facing outward; that is, with the wheels facing away from their body because that is the best preparatory posture by which a skater can quickly drop their board on its wheels, hop on, and skate away. Despite the underside of the board not being seen in the act of skating, a skater knows what is on the bottom of their board and that the design matters even though it is not always visible. The laminated images on the bottom of the deck are a critical part of skate culture as they comprise key individual and collective expressions (Borden 2019). Skaters actively engage in the art because the deck artwork is as much an important part of the process of selecting a board as are the technical specs such as length and width. Moreover, some skaters paint or use indelible markers to draw on the bottom of a board themselves. Skaters will identity preferred graphic designs and will often save up to buy certain decks or brands based on the bottom-side design. Additionally, among skaters there is frequent and lively conversation about deck art, which indexes complex combinations of aesthetics, coolness, rebellion, brand loyalty, humor, trendiness, and countless other discourses (Cliver 2004; Waterhouse and Penhalow 2006; Carayol 2014). What's more, because of functionality, the art is understood to be ephemeral despite its importance. Most tricks end up scratching the bottom of a board, marring, modifying, and ultimately destroying the underside graphics. Paradoxically, as much as the art matters, so too does its erasure because this signifies that a board is actively being used for tricks, thus lending a sense of authenticity to its rider.

While this kind of legitimacy keenly matters to many skaters, there has been a movement within the contemporary art world to give primacy to unsullied decks and curate them for gallery showings. These unmarred decks hanging on white walls are an assertion that the design and graphics have semiotic and artistic meaning, yet in most cases the ones hanging in galleries do not confer the same credibility as boards that are actually used. Moreover, while some gallery shows might feature functional boards that are part of a limited production run that become repurposed for gallery display (not to be used), others feature one-of-a-kind hand paintings on decks that are never intended for use in the first place. The wall-hung skateboard, whether in a gallery or a private home (like the many I have on my walls), sets up a seemingly contradictory dynamic where some view the deck as valuable for artistic appreciation and others cynically question the authenticity of a nonfunctioning object other than as decor. This is a tension that mostly exists between skaters concerned with authenticity and the broader American contemporary art scene that began to exhibit skateboards as aesthetic pieces of appreciation sometime in the mid-1990s. This tension is an important backdrop to understanding the artistic expression on skateboards made for and by Indigenous folks.[6]

I contend that skateboarding became common in Indian Country as it was also becoming a global sport in the 1980s and 1990s. However, despite this growth of skaters in Indian County, it was not until the first decade of the 2000s, when Native skaters (who may have started skating in the 1980s and 1990s) became young adults, that Indians began creating their own skate decks and graphic designs, organizing skate tournaments for their own communities, and even developing their own skate companies. Akimel O'odham scholar David Martinez (2013) contextualizes these

Native skate innovations in the early 2000s as part of a larger, fifty-year cultural trajectory in Indian country that sought to undermine "the obsolete cliché of American Indians struggling between 'two worlds' (the Indian and white)" (375). Instead, Martinez argues, Native youth "are a part of globalized, high-tech universe, in which all peoples are compelled to live in, including tribal nations" (375). Viewed from this perspective, skateboarding is just one of the many contemporary subcultures with which Indians engage and can indigenize by employing multimedia and technology to make meaning about Indigenous resistance, vibrancy, and joy. Native skateboarding is a particularly significant part of this larger indigenizing movement, given that mainstream skate culture, like many forms of popular culture, has a history of non-Indians coopting Indianness in order to signify a rebellious cool. Many white pop culture style makers, including Vans (the quintessential skate company), have appropriated feathered headdresses, spear points, and other imagery to sell their gear. In Native skateboard artists and skate companies, Martinez (2013) recognizes what he calls "creative sovereignty," that is, "the extraordinary phenomenon of Indigenous artists being the producers of pop culture, as opposed to being merely consumers of non-Indian 'merch'" (378). Thereby, Native skaters reclaim Indigenous imagery and reinterpreted skate culture, as a whole, through a Native lens and in a tribal context.

In addition to the artistic and creative outlet that skating provides for Indigenous communities, it also becomes a contemporary pathway for mentorship, for Native youth to develop a sense of commitment to oneself and one's community, and to channel frustrations of reservation life into healing and joy. As was discussed earlier with Rezball, the traumatic effects of settler colonialism have created a disproportionate amount of degradation and despair on many American Indian reservations as compared to many other places in the United States. However, at the same time it is important to not disproportionately focus on despair and desolation when considering Indigenous communities (Tuck and Yang 2014). To do so obscures the cultural strength, joy, and wellness that are products of this resiliency. As I argue in the early part of this book, Rezball is a venue for this health and happiness, and I now contend that so too is Native skateboarding culture. Many Native youth use skating therapeutically to take their minds off challenges in their lives, to experience the accomplishment of mastering a trick, or to enjoy the fundamental camaraderie of a skate session with friends.

More so than Rezball, skateboarding aligns with many Indigenous cultural notions of mentorship and skill learning. Historically, Native cultures are commonly structured such that in the transition to adulthood, Native youth are advised by elders in their family (often an aunt or an uncle) or an important member in the community as a whole (often someone particularly respected for their experience and specialized knowledge). Novices would observe elders, learn a skill from them, spend time alone to hone their own skills, and then return to elders in order to demonstrate their achievement of a skill or body of knowledge. Skating fits this valued pattern in many ways. First, skaters observe a peer or someone older than them pull off a trick. Admiring this trick, a skater will spend countless hours repeatedly attempting the trick until they can consistently perform it themselves. Skaters often practice a given trick in solitude or relative seclusion, such as in front of their house. Other times they will practice the tricks at public skate parks or a "spot" (a semisecret place or part of a built environment shared by a smallish crew of skaters who are "in the know" about this spot). Working on a trick in front of one's peers has the benefit of receiving positive encouragement to complete a trick and garnering advice on minor adjustments needed to complete a trick.

Moreover, unlike team sports that tend to promote more competition for limited opportunities on a team, skateboarders frequently provide a great deal of mutual support for each other. Except for professional competitions, skating is not a zero-sum activity where one participant's success likely means failure or less success for another participant, as it does for athletes competing for a spot on a team or for playing time. In fact, many skaters have a strong oppositional identity whereby participating in skating is seen as a way to reject the intense competition of other American sports (see Yochim 2009). As a general rule, skaters push each other in mutually reinforcing and beneficial ways to pull off the next trick that might push the limits of the sport as a whole, rather than just be interpreted as individual success. Indeed, in observing the way skaters support each other and are genuinely thrilled when a peer pulls off a remarkable trick—from the most casual of skate sessions among friends to the highest level of professional, international competition—it is hard not to think that skaters believe they all win when someone succeeds in pushing the sport farther. Of course, this is not to suggest that everyone gets along perfectly with each other and that there is not some form of competition. However, similar to what can be found in many Native communities, people tend to support each other's success, even in spite of the proverbial "crabs-pulling-the-one-achiever-back-down-in-the-barrel-with-others" that occasionally manifests. I argue this spirit of mutual support is another key aspect of skateboarding that synchronizes well with values of American Indian mentorship and personal development.

In particular, it is worth noting the way this value of mentorship maps onto intergenerational relationships: elders are thought to have wisdom that youth respect and seek to learn from, *and*, thereby, elders have the responsibility to share this wisdom with youth. In several American Indian communities in which I have spent time, older skaters often fulfill mentoring roles to younger skaters, trying to help them better develop their skating skills. Many times these mentors are also the people creating Indigenous-based skate companies and skate teams. I offer the label of "skate elders" for these tribally based central figures as a way to acknowledge the crucial role these "skate elders" play in mentoring youth (and to show how they are looked up to by young Native skaters). This mentorship takes the form of not just how to do tricks, but also how to be compassionately productive members of their communities. Ironically, in this sense skateboarding becomes not about rebelling against conventional values so much as it is about fun and acceptance into a community of love and support. The following chapters in this section explore how this happens by looking at how Native skaters manipulate space, express artistic creativity, and develop fellowship with older members of their communities.

Artist, influencer, social worker, Apache cultural educator, Indigenous businessman, skater, OG. Douglas Miles Sr. has done many things in his life for his Nde Nation (San Carlos Apache), but perhaps the last moniker, OG (original gangster) describes him best. When it comes to skateboarding in Indian Country, few have a greater claim to being an OG than Doug. Of course, OG is a metaphorical term. I am not using it not to connote the violent, fear-based leadership seen in organized crime, but rather as part of the hip-hop vernacular to signify the kind of respect accrued by someone who has been a part of an industry or movement since the beginning and has been influential all along the way. And OG is certainly part of Doug's own linguistic and artistic idiom. He is tremendously well versed in popular culture, often mixing references to hip-hop, jazz, funk, R&B, mafia movies, and so on into his art and the multiple conversations he and I have had and in his social media posts. However, "OG" is not a phrase Doug would use to describe himself. He has such a deep understanding of the term that he would not self-apply it. I, on the other hand, would absolutely label Doug an OG. I believe it is a perfect description for him because few have been a part of the Native skate scene for longer or more consistently than Doug, and few are as well known in the scene. Moreover, he is one of the first to create a Native skate company (Apache Skateboards), has several thousands of followers on Facebook and Instagram, is frequently invited to exhibit his art, and for a while even had a collaborative partnership with Volcom, one of the larger surf and skate lifestyle clothing brands in the country. He is a legend of Native skating—hence, an OG.

For most of Doug's fifty-plus years alive, he has been a permanent fixture in the skate culture of his Apache community (San Carlos Reservation), of Arizona and the rest of the Southwest, and of Indian Country as a whole. His impact is pervasive, but it manifests most in his artistic articulation of skate culture and his influence on the more recent generation of Native skaters. Doug uses any kind of medium he can get his hands on—painting, film, spray-paint murals, skateboard decks, clothing, graphic design, or social media—to express what he believes it means to be San Carlos Apache in the contemporary world. He envisions art and expression as broadly possible, free of boundaries. It's this freedom and versatility that has drawn Doug to skateboarding, in which "you can be as free and creative as you want to be, and I wanted to be a part of that," as he puts it to me (Doug Miles, interview, February 13, 2016). Doug also relates that he was drawn to skateboarding culture because it "has all the overlapping, creative endeavors too, around it: fashion and clothing and hardware and hardgoods and soft goods and film, graphic design and art and fine art, and so I found a lot of ways to be creative just by making skateboards" (Miles, interview). Doug appreciates the expansive creativity and possibility of skateboarding, allowing him to make a career as an artist and cement his legendary status. To be clear, I use the term "legendary" here not to hyperbolize the importance of Doug Miles and Apache Skateboards, but rather to articulate his significance to the origins and the story of Native skate culture. Indeed, storytelling is critically important to both Native cultures *and* skate cultures. Native skate culture, consequently, needs legends of its own, and Doug Miles is among them. Throughout the next few chapters, I narrate stories about him and other legends of Native skate culture.

NARRATING SKATING

Like most people whose culture originates in orality, storytelling is fundamental to American Indian communities. Cherokee writer and cultural critic Thomas King has succinctly summarized hundreds of years and volumes of scholarship on Native oral culture, stating, "The truth about stories is that that's all we are" (King 2008, 2). King repeatedly annunciates this maxim in his seminal book, *The Truth about Stories*, in order to explain the primacy of storytelling for Indigenous peoples. In so doing, King asserts that despite how some might contrast stories to more "concrete" facts, the former have the same value as the latter, even if narrative's value is not quantifiable in the same way that "facts" are thought to be measurable and repeatable. Moreover, origins, identity, and meaning or knowledge come from stories even if stories are not always logical, rational, consistent, or complete (King 2008).

Storytelling is similarly a valuable part of skate culture. Among their friends, skaters often verbally narrate detailed accounts of a particularly spectacular trick they witnessed or they themselves pulled off. Like Native storytelling, skate stories establish the origins of a trick, valorize the skill and eccentricity of individual skaters, or forge the shared values of outsiderness, fearlessness, or coolness in skate culture. The exploits of the best skaters become the material of legends, and while these legends maybe susceptible to the occasional exaggeration or hyperbole, they are also easily repackaged for continual retellings of the unbelievable trick a prodigy pulled off or the whimsy of young free-spirited skaters' shenanigans. As far as skateboarding stories go, few have more allure than that of "Dogtown" and the "Z-Boys" skate team. Arguably, the story of this skate crew is the origins of the trope of the "rebellious outsider" that has come to epitomize skaters in general (see also Bucklew and Kamper 2025). The Dogtown skaters were far from the first to put wheels on a plank of wood and cruise around on concrete and asphalt, but the Z-Boys' modern approach to skating and nonconformist attitude were key to solidifying the popular imagination of skateboarding that still holds today.[1] The Z-Boys represent the beginning of the modern ethos of skateboarding. Before them, skateboarding was mainly viewed as a novelty, a wholesomely fun way for preteens and teens to get around beach communities when they weren't surfing; after the Z-Boys, skating took on a whole new set of meanings. While the Z-Boys were not the only ones to skate aggressively in the 1970s or necessarily even the first to skate vertically in drained swimming pools, their story amounts to the origin story of modern skating as much as Rodney Mullen's story is the origin of street skating (see Louison 2011).

This crew of young skaters, named for their mentors' surf company, Jeff Ho Surfboards and Zephyr Productions, all came from the neighborhood spanning the border between Santa Monica and Venice Beach, California, known as "Dogtown." The story goes that about ten teenage boys and at least one girl who lived in and around Dogtown were avid surfers who hung around the Zephyr shop when they were not surfing. At this point in the early 1970s, skateboarding's 1960's novelty popularity was on the wane with most American youth, except for surfer kids who were looking to keep their board-riding stoke going when they were not in the water. Rather than primarily using a skateboard for transportation as the generation before them had done, the Dogtown kids sought out hills and embankments to gain more speed and better simulate wave riding. As a city with a long reputation for paving over its topography and natural waterways, Los Angeles had a treasure trove of places to which one could dryland-surf on four wheels. Moreover, this incipient crew of surfer-skaters was heavily influenced by stylistic changes in surfing—a sport that itself, in the early 1970s, was going through a relative lull in popularity and experiencing mutations. Surf culture was becoming less of a laidback, Bohemian activity as the boards became shorter and smaller, allowing a new breed of surfers to attack the waves with more aggression than was characteristic of the previous longboard surfing of the 1950s and 1960s. In particular, Hawai'ian Kanaka Maoli surfer Larry Bertlemann heavily influenced the Dogtown surfers with his low gravity, crouching stance, aggressive cutbacks, and early attempts at cutting up the face of the wave to then launch off it like a jump ramp in order to "get air." Additionally, the newly developed polyurethane skate wheels, which replaced the clay-based ones, allowed the Dogtown surfers to imitate Bertlemann's style by power sliding across the pavement. This approach to skating was unlike anything most skateboarders were doing at the time. The more the Dogtown kids hung around the Zephyr shop (many of whom did so because they were sponsored to surf for Zephyr Productions), the more the shop owners—Jeff Ho, Skip Engblom, and Craig Stecyk—encouraged them to push the limits of this skateboarding. Eventually they established a Zephyr skate team to go along with the surf team—hence, the founding of the "Z-Boys." But as is frequently the case with countercultural movements, there is not a precise accounting of who actually were the original members of the Zephyr skate team. Many of the people hanging around the shop became "official" team members, often proudly articulated by wearing their team shirts around Dogtown, and others hung around with team riders or were only briefly on the team. The most common way to identify the original team riders is to list those who competed for the Zephyr team at the 1975 Del Mar Nationals skateboard competition: Shogu Kubo, Bob Biniak, Nathan Pratt, Stacey Peralta, Jim Muir, Allen Sarbo, Chris Cahil, Tony Alva, Wentzle Ruml IV, Peggy Oki, Jay Adams, and Paul Constantineau (Stecyk and Friedman 2000).

Once the Zephyr team was formed, Ho, Engblom, and Stecyk sought to promote their style to the world outside of the enclave of Dogtown. The Z-Boys entered contests and began shocking everyone with their style, winning many trophies but, more significantly, gaining mass notoriety for completely disrupting what people understood as skateboarding. The Z-Boys' rise in popularity was central to what would ultimately be skateboarding's resurgence through the 1980s. The most radical and audacious of the Z-Boys became some of the leading faces of this resurgence, skaters such as Tony Alva, Stacey Peralta, Jay Adams, Shogo Kobu, Wenzel Ruml, Bob Biniak, and Nathan Pratt. These skaters, along with others who were not necessarily part of the Dogtown crew but were surely influenced by them, continued to evolve their skating as they sought grander and grander concrete versions of waves. In addition to riding down hilly streets and the two- to four-foot embankments they found on local school playgrounds, many of the Z-Boys started skating in emptied or abandoned swimming pools. Swimming pools are in an inordinate abundance in Los Angeles, and it just so happens that during the Z-Boys rise to prominence in the mid- to late1970s, there was a drought hitting Southern California. This drought was so significant that many homeowners drained or did not refill their evaporating pools. These empty pools became the prototype for manufactured skateparks that popped up all over the United States in the 1980s because of the way they provided the perfect surface and contours for skaters trying to get ever higher and more vertical.

The Z-Boys became infamous for skating in these pools and thereby helped initiate a skating revolution that relied on verticality. The more these skaters pushed the limits, the further they pushed the trajectory of sport until the mid-1980s, when skating vertical (or "vert") became the signature way to skate. However, it was not just these skaters' skills and willingness to push skating's limits that gained them fame (and in many cases significant money and sponsorships); equally important to their popularity were the stories being told about them. Much of the credit for this narrative of the nonconforming, outsider skateboarders can go to Craig Stecyk, an artist, writer, and photographer who brought the gonzo journalism popularized by Hunter S. Thompson to the world of skateboarding. Stecyk was part of the original collaboration that created the Zephyr Skate Team, and he, in many ways, forged the reputation of the Z-Boys by conducting gonzo journalism among them in Dogtown, documenting their style and promoting their rise to fame. He produced several photojournalistic articles for *SkateBoarder Magazine* from 1975 to 1979, chronicling the Z-Boys crews' skate sessions, profiling many team members, and even interviewing some of them so they could be represented by their own words (these articles are republished in Stecyk and Friedman 2019).

It is Stecyk's depictions that coded the Z-Boys as a gritty, potentially dangerous, vanguard group of skaters who had a devil-may-care attitude to their skating and much of their life in general. He portrayed them as heavily influenced by underground Chicano/a/x, "cholo," or "Lowrider" culture of Santa Monica and Venice Beach—a culture that has been a significant part of Los Angeles since at least the 1940s. This association helped further develop the Z-Boys' antiestablishment authenticity and create an outcast vibe that has been a dominant part of skate culture ever since, even despite the extent to which skateboarding has become a massive corporate enterprise generating hundreds of millions of dollars annually. What is important to note is that this narrative was cultivated by Stecyk and then the skaters themselves. Some of the key skaters from the team increased their popularity throughout the 1980s as they controlled their own skate companies and skate teams. This legend of Dogtown has been passed down mainly by word of mouth until the early 2000s, when it was given new life. Original Z-Boys team member Stacy Peralta canonized the narrative by directing a very popular documentary about the crew and then writing and helping produce a feature-length film about the story that received a great amount of attention as well. By the release of these two movies (*Dogtown and the Z-Boys* [Peralta 2001] and *Lords of Dogtown* [Hardwicke 2005]), the notion of the nonconformist, rebellious skater had long been the most prominent trope of skateboarding, reiterated thousands of times over in thousands of different ways, but Peralta's films revived the origin story as skateboarder as an outsider.

It should come as no surprise that the most prolific and comprehensive narration of the Dogtown legend is Peralta's documentary film.[2] Like surfing, photography and video have always been critical mediums for narrating skateboarding. This materialized in the form of several different magazines dedicated to skating created and capitalized on skating's early popularity. Many publications were short-lived, some distributed nationally with high glossy images. Some were gritty, underground zines that were handmade and circulated only as far as they could be handed out or as widespread as the creators' mailing list, yet their visual imagery was key to all of this narrating of skating (Weyland 2002). Moreover, with the technological revolutions of audiovisual equipment of the last twenty years, visual narratives of skateboarding became even more prolific and personal. Louison (2011) argues that while videos of skateboarding existed earlier, it was Stacy Peralta's *Bones Brigade* VHS release in 1984 that fully initiated video as the predominant format for telling a story about skating. Beginning in the 1990s when home video equipment became increasingly affordable, smaller and lighter, and higher quality, skaters could film themselves and their friends. And with the advent of the Go-Pro camera (which is small and highly durable and requires no focusing and almost no aiming) in the early 2000s and then video capability on cell and smart phones, videos of skating became even more ubiquitous.

Finally, the revolution was complete with the proliferation of the internet (in the late 1990s) and of social media platforms (in the 2010s) such that anyone could make a video of themselves and their friends skating, edit it, and post it for mass audiences. Hence, the visual narration of skating, complete with depictions of dramatic spills and falls and the ancillary antics of skaters, has become almost as central to skating as doing the tricks themselves. These recent technologies democratized that narrating of skateboarding and skate legend making. In so doing, it has increasing allowed Indigenous skaters to tell their own stories of skateboarding and increased their audiences to a potentially infinite number.

LEGENDS OF RESERVATION SKATING

It should be self-evident why youth growing up in tribal communities or within Indigenous cultures might identify with being considered an outsider and subsequently cultivate that outsiderness as a badge of rebellion in ways similar too or perhaps even influenced by what the legendary Z-Boys did. However, whereas the Z-Boys were mainly rebelling against their class position or even just mainstream versions of sport, leisure, and art, Indigenous skaters are inherently confronting settler colonialism and the limitations it forces on Indigenous peoples. In the United States these limitations have manifested in many ways: on space and ecology through the reservation system, on cultural creativity and growth through the forced assimilation and boarding school system, and on career options through the metastasizing expansion of Western capitalism. There are all kinds of responses found in Indian Country to these limitations. Skateboarding is just one. But it is one that, by the 1990s when skateboarding really begins to spread in Indian Country, is easily an adaptable venue for rebelling against norms of space, storytelling, and art.

Similar to the mythology of Dogtown and the Z-Boys, Indian Country has its own skate legends. Doug is one for sure, and there are others as well who began creating Native skate companies in their own communities around the same time as Doug or who were influenced by the work he was doing and followed his lead. Whether following Doug's lead or independently coming up with the idea themselves, in the early 2000s several Native men, most of whom had grown up skating, created their own brands as a way of combining their love for skateboarding and the pride of their tribal heritage. These Native skaters created either skate teams, skate companies, nonprofit skating organizations, or some combination of the three: Jim "Murph" Murphy and Andy Kessler established Wounded Skateboards, later to be joined by Walt Pourier (Ogalala Lakota), creator of the Stronghold Foundation; Todd Harder (Mvscogee Creek) founded Native Skates; and Dustinn Craig (White Mountain Apache/Navajo) created Four Wheels War Pony.[3] This diverse group of OG Native skaters were from several different places in Indian Country, and all had different life experiences. On a handful of instances, their projects converged or overlapped, and occasionally some of them even collaborated with each other. But perhaps their most significant convergence was their collective participation in a Native skate festival and competition held at the Los Altos Skatepark in Albuquerque, New Mexico, known as the All Nations Skate Jam (ANSJ). Lifelong skater Todd Harder established the event in 2006, and it has been held every year since, always scheduled to correspond with the Gathering of Nations Powwow in Albuquerque.

Harder, a screen printer, graphic designer, and skater, has lived most of his life in Michigan despite being born in Oklahoma on the land of his tribal community. A product of the Urban Relocation Program, he grew up skateboarding in the Detroit area throughout the late 1970s and all of the 1980s, heavily influenced by the Dogtown crew and then the Bones Brigade (who were in many ways the inheritors of the Z-Boys' popularity). Todd's enthusiasm for skating and the art and culture that came along with it led him to his career in design and screen printing. As he grew a successful business, some of it catering to clients outside of Indian Country and some aimed directly at tribal folks, he began to think about ways he could contribute meaningfully to Indigenous communities. With the suggestion of his then girlfriend, he decided to make skateboards and skate gear that would appeal to Native youth, and then came the big idea of a pan-tribal skate event. Harder's stroke of genius was to hold the skate jam the same weekend as the powwow, so that it would coincide with a time when Native folks from all over Indian Country converged in one location. Moreover, he was also motivated out of sympathy for the smaller population of Native kids who were dragged to Gathering along with their family despite being skaters, not powwow dancers or drummers. It started off as a moderate-sized event, but within in a few years, it blew up (likely aided by the rise of social media). An additional boost to the event was Todd's ability to connect with the Vans Shoes Company and get them not only to sponsor the event but also to convince Steve Van Doreen (one of the founding brothers of the company) to attend the event. Once Van Doreen saw the popularity and importance of the ANSJ, he began to come annually, bringing the company's massive touring bus loaded with Vans gear to give away, free food to grill up for the skaters, and often professional skateboarders who ride for Vans to come along to sign autographs for the kids and do skate demos. On more than one occasion original Z-Boy Tony Alva headlined the event as well.

By the fourth annual ANSJ, all five of the progenitors of skate culture in Indian Country (Todd, Doug, Jim, Walt, and Dustinn) showed up. These OG Native skaters shared a commitment to the wellness and happiness of Native youth and to the idea that skateboarding and its culture could promote this joy, even if they rarely all saw eye to eye on how to go about doing it. This ANSJ was likely the only time these five legends were all jammed together in the same space at the same time, and it is probably safe to say that space and time could not hold all of their energy. They went their separate ways after, but they all still utilize skate culture as a positive outlet for the youth of their own communities and Indian Country in general, deploying skating's artistic, athletic, and emotional energy to help Indigenous youth express themselves and their Indigenous identities.

Like Todd, these skaters were all of the same generation that was influenced by Dogtown's aggressive approach to skating and its rebellious attitude. Much of the skating's nonconformist subculture, as concretized in the Z-Boys ethos, is based around a class rebellion that implicitly critiques American capitalist and puritanical values. There is much to make of whether skating is a subculture that actually reinforces some of the sustaining and peripheral values of late capitalism such as sexism, racism, and xenophobia; see Beal (1995, 1996) and Yochim (2009) for how this plays out in skating; see Comer (2010), Lawler (2011), Olive (2016), and Olive, Roy, and Wheaton (2018) for an analogous example in surfing. However, when skateboarding is put in a settler colonial context, it can provide Indians with a countercultural venue to implicitly and explicitly critique the racialized capitalism of American settler colonialism.

ENVISIONING REBELLIOUSNESS IN INDIGENOUS SKATE CULTURE

One thing that these legends of Indigenous skateboarding have in common is the way they marshal the varied visual expressions of skating to produce tribal-based critiques of settler colonialism. They all have indigenized skateboarding in ways that had never been seen before. Tropes of race and culture are certainly not new to skateboarding visuals. From the 1980s until today, it is not uncommon for skate companies to use racialized visual imagery in a way that attempts to promote countercultural rebellion. Companies such as Vans and Element have used images of head-dressed, Plains warriors on shirts or the bottoms of decks. Many other skate companies rely on the images of and references to Chicano/a/x street culture to signify toughness. Moreover, it is very common to hear the sonic rebellion of hip-hop culture's music and slang at skate jams and sessions. While there certainly are skaters of color, white teens predominate the demographic of skating, and this kind of racialized imagery in the hands of white teens, seeking to intensify their identification with rebelling against mainstream culture, often smacks of cultural appropriation. However, when produced by Native designers, artists, and skaters and connected to specific tribal contexts (rather than generalized Noble Savagery), indigenized imagery in skate culture is far more powerful and far less appropriative. As I argue above, storytelling in skate culture is highly visual in nature, and many Native skaters employ deck art, clothing, video edits, and social media to narrate their uniquely Indigenous stories of skating.

The most readily apparent form of visual narration of Indigenous culture in skating is the deck art. Most deck art is on the bottom side of the deck, although occasionally designs can be created on the grip tape on top of the deck. To do this, skaters either drawn right on to the grip tape using colored chalk or paint pens or produce a design through the use of negative space by cutting out sections of the grip tape to reveal the wood board below and thereby creating patterns and designs of top of the board. However, most skateboard art is on the underside of the deck. Within the subculture of skating in general, there is a long and deep history of deck art being a key form of expression so that it should be no surprise that this is also the palette that Native skaters have used. Skateboard deck art was originally used to promote the brand of the board maker and the sponsored skater who rode for the brand. Images were meant to reflect something about the skater's personality, reputation, or identity. In the 1990s decks became more elaborate and symbolic of a statement that a skater or skate company wanted to make about themselves — even if that statement often became a spirally out-of-control (almost in a Dadaist sense) attempt to be as offensive as possible as a means of illustrating the extremity of a skater's nonconformity or rebelliousness. Many decks through the 1990s and early 2000s could easily and rightly be accused of misogyny, insensitivity, heresy, or prejudice (Louison 2011), but plenty of decks have a positive imagery as well, and this tends to be the case for Indigenous-run skate companies, where the deck art is a way to promote cultural pride and Native engagement with the modern world.

Most Apache Skateboards decks, designed by Doug Miles, have very stylized images of traditional Apache male warriors or contemporary Apache women giving of a similar warrior vibe of strength and confidence. While being a clearly distinct style of Doug's own, this imagery is heavily influenced by anime and graffiti art. Doug is a prominent aerosol-paint muralist often commissioned for permanent public murals or for temporary gallery installations, and his skateboards frequently are the scaled-down version of his murals and installations. This spray-paint technique harkens to the underground graffiti artists who were a part of early hip-hop culture in late 1970s New York that then exploded all over the world in the following decades. Doug's anime approach to line and form and his frequent refiguring of well-known brands reference his interest in pop art. Doug's combination of anime, pop art, and graffiti, all forms that are generally made in response to and rejection of "high art," alludes to his rebellion of form. Additionally, choosing "warrior" men and women as the most common subject also works to promote a Native-themed resistance. Historic or traditional Apache warriors are often thought to be among the most resistant to Western expansion and white American capitalism—long evading and holding out against American white supremacy and forced assimilation. For Doug these images are a sign of the strength and resilience of Apache people like himself. The images boldly return the gaze of their audience with steely eyes or sometimes the barrel of a gun. Moreover, it is not just the subject of the Apache warrior or the strong-faced woman with flowing dark hair that announces resistance to conformity, but the composition that generally has his figures staring outward from the art, making a bold statement by directly engaging the viewer. Miles also plays with the idea of warrior and "otherness" with a set of boards that combine Apache warrior imagery with Japanese Samurai warrior imagery, Italian American Mafioso imagery, or Chicano/a/x "cholo" imagery. This imagery falls in line with his pop art influence in a way that makes Apache peoples and culture traditional, global, and modern all at once. It narrates a story of Native people's ability to simultaneously hold onto the past and live in the present. It rejects the idea that Indians are people of the past who cannot keep up with modern global world. And his art questions the origins and originality of warrior culture.

Doug's recent and most explicit politically messaged deck directly confronts the ubiquity of U.S. settler colonialism. It has a clean white background with a historic photographic image of Apache leaders superimposed over an anime graphic of an Apache warrior's skull with a traditional headband and hairstyle. Bold, all-caps black type on the nose of the board states, "You're Skating," and on the tail the text declares, "On Native Land." The board makes the proclamation that anywhere one chooses to stake in the United States is on Indigenous land and, mostly likely, stolen land. The deck art forces any viewer (or rider) to confront this fact and contemplate the technologies and discourses of settler colonialism that obscure historical facts about land "ownership." This is particularly relevant to skateboarding when we consider its own challenge of normative uses of land, space, and the built environment (see chapter 5). Doug's decks ask skateboarders who rebel against conventional land usage to realize that their activities may also overwrite Indigenous space—hence "Skating On Native Land" as opposed to a declaration of merely "living on" or "using" Native land. In essence, this Apache Skateboards deck art refuses to conform to presupposed notions, justifications, and rationalizations of American boundaries and land use.

Also Apache (but from White Mountain, not San Carlos), Dustinn Craig, with his creation of Four Wheel War Pony Skateboards, is heavily influenced by Apache traditions and history. Dustinn's imagery is a bit more varied than Doug's, but he calls upon similar ideas. Dustinn uses Apache warrior imagery and occasionally does so with his own animated stylized version, but Dustinn also uses more symbolic rather than figurative representations of culture. Dustinn's work has a unifying motif throughout all of his deck art and graphics. The theme is clearly displayed in the name of the skate team and brand, the notion of four. This number is key to Apache epistemology as many aspects of life and nature are thought to be composed of four parts. Consistent throughout all of Dustinn's skateboard-related art is the recurring symbol of four crossed arrows. These do not take the shape of a weaponized arrow, but rather a block-designed arrow with points on either end, which intersect to make the shape akin to a compass rose (Image 3).

These four-way tipped, linked arrows emblemize the interrelatedness of all forces. Dustinn repeats the concept of four by always putting this symbol in even space across a row of four of them. He talks about the

FIG. 1. 4 Wheel War Pony deck designed by Dustinn Craig. Author's collection. Photo: Matthew Fowler.

Apache numerology around four as having many overlapping kinds of significance: four sacred mountains that surround and demarcate the tribe's territory; four stages in an individual's life (birth, adolescence, adulthood, and death); four directions; four wheels on a skateboard. This repetition of four intrinsically links Four Wheel War Pony to Apache culture. As discussed in the next chapter, this linkage is crucial for Dustinn as one of the main goals of his skate team is to reconnect Apache youth to their culture.

Similarly, Delvan Polelonema is trying to do this with his Hopi-based skate company and team, Naqwatsveni Skateboarding. Delvan is from the village of Munqupi (Moenkopi) in western Arizona. The name of the company and team is a Hopi word that translates to the notion of "harmonious friendship." Clearly, in choosing this Hopi word, Delvan seeks to engage Hopi culture and connect youthful Hopi skaters to their language and culture. For English speakers, the Hopi language can be very challenging to read and to pronounce, especially the longer words; however, this does not stop Delvan from frequently using Hopi words in his marketing, asserting the value of Indigenous languages. Choosing to name his company a word that most people would struggle to say is a unique decision, but it illustrates his commitment to his community and this concept.

Delvan has a similar commitment to Hopi art and design. All of his decks and clothing have elaborately designed Hopi art: abstract images of color and pattern. The Naqwatsveni Skateboarding logo appears the most on Delvan's apparel. It is two crescent shapes facing each other, with the one on the right shifted downward so that the two crescents do not make a completed circle, but rather more of an interlocking design where the top of the right crescent points into the left crescent's center, and the bottom of the left crescent points into the right crescent. Delvan tells me that this symbol is centuries old, and for Hopis, it represents balanced and harmonious relationships, peace, and unity. Indeed, this symbol is associated with the word *naqwatsveni*, hence the name of Delvan's skate company. What is more, each of the crescents are filled in with designs and colors that represent different aspects of Hopi culture and community.

FIG. 2. Naqwatsveni Skateboarding deck designed by Kuwanhepya (Derrance Elmer) and Delvan Polelonema. Author's collection. Photo: Matthew Fowler.

In my conversations with Delvan, he emphasized how important skateboarding was to his life, and he wanted to share it with fellow Hopis (and beyond) in a way that connects to culturally consistent notions of harmonious relationships. As he notes:

> Skateboarding connects with everything, music, art, just anything. It's just free . . . I want to inspire others, not just Hopi kids, but everyone else to start skating cause, I don't know, it's just, it's a fun thing to do. I mean ya, it's scary and everything, but I just want to have an impact on other kids. Mainly my culture to have them just get out and try skateboarding. (Delvan Polelonema, interview, February 12, 2016)

Furthermore, Delvan feels that skating is important for his community because it

> helps you build your confidence, helps you with depression just eases your mind because you're more focused on the tricks and doing them and creating new tricks . . . It helps you be fearless . . . and it helps build character. (Polelonema, interview)

Delvan seeks to share skateboarding with Hopi youth because he believes it develops positive character traits and promotes these strengths among the youth in his community as part of a *naqwatsveni* of building friendly, harmonious relationships with fellow Hopis. Indeed, Delvan so thoroughly views his life and work through this notion that he tells me he considers his skateboard one of his closest friends:

> [My board has] always been there for me through the good and bad. Like if I had bad days I would just get on my board and go out and let it all out. Because you're free with your board and out with your friends. Your friends motivate you . . . Just you and your board. Your board is always with you no matter what, no matter what situation. (Polelonema, interview)

Skateboarding is a stress release for Delvan and a way to bond with others. In this way Delvan sees skateboarding as fulfilling a key Hopi value, and he does all he can to share that opportunity with Hopi youth.

For Naqwatsveni Skateboards, this is not just accomplished by creating a positive, active outlet for youth, but also through the process that Delvan uses to decide on deck art. Early on Delvan recognized that graphic design was not his strong suit, but he was able to turn this into a positive as he decided that he would put a call out to Hopi artists to help design the logo and deck art as a way to try to bring more attention to the skill and beauty of contemporary Hopi artists. This was a bold statement of Indigenous agency: steadfastly deciding to exclusively use Hopi art on his boards. Delvan received a lot of advice and even some financial support from the larger skate community outside of Indian Country, including big name professionals such as Pierre-Luc Gagnon and Jake Brown. Nearly everyone in the skate industry suggested that he use professional graphic designers for his deck art and logo, yet Delvan was adamant that Naqwatsveni Skateboards embrace the notion of *naqwatsveni* and be about community and friendship. This would ensure that Naqwatsveni Skateboards was not just another skateboard company, but rather would be a specifically Hopi endeavor.

One of Delvan's goals from the beginning has been to use skateboarding's influence to empower artists from his community. For the first official design of Naqwatsveni Skateboards he called upon his younger brother Justin to create the artwork. Then he began to include other Hopi artists in order to shine attention on their talent. Ultimately he had seven Hopi artists designing boards for Naqwatsveni. This truly is an incredible feat, given how small the Hopi community is. Even more impressively, five of his seven collaborating artists—Justin Polelonema, Derrance Elmer, Muy Honani, Tyler Kelhoyouma, and Adrian Jenson—are all from the village of Munqupi, which has under a thousand inhabitants. Only Nate Benoist and Otis Naasavti are not from this village, but they still are Hopi, hailing from Polacca and Second Mesa, respectively.[4] Delvan, the artists with whom he works, and the skaters on his team are all part of a younger generation of Hopi. They are mostly in their twenties, with one of his team's skaters being younger than fifteen years old. Skaters such as Eugene Barney and Aliyah Whiterock have been with him for years, even though they are still quite young today. Despite this youth and their interest in youthful pursuits, such as skateboarding, they consciously bridge the contemporary moment and Hopi artistic and linguistic traditions that almost stand outside of settler time.

Moreover, Delvan has been able to expand his skate brand's reach beyond his community in a way that uses skateboarding to promote Hopi values and culture. Delvan received a lot of advice and even support from the larger skate community outside of Indian Country, including well-known professionals such as Brandon Turner and Jake Brown. Naqwatsveni reached a high enough profile that professional skaters Jake and Brandon reached out to Delvan to see if they could collaborate. In 2016 Jake and Brandon helped Delvan host a skate competition at the skatepark in Tuba City. The relationship became even stronger as they helped mentor further. One culmination of this effort is the Hopi skateboarding podcast Delvan created—of course, called "Naqwatsveni (Friendship)." The pod has twenty episodes, including one featuring Jake Brown. Delvan's innovative and creative mind continually works to promote a skateboarding brand built on a Hopi lifestyle, family, and culture.

Other Indigenous skate companies chose to promote cultural narratives that are more pan-Indian in nature. Todd Harder, for example, emphasized a Red Power narrative for the bottom side of the most significant deck that his company, Native Skates, has produced. Red Power is the Native activist movement of the late 1960s and early 1970s. As with other grassroots, radical, identity-based rights movements of this time period, those involved in Red Power sought greater civil rights for those identifying as American Indian. However, in addition to the individual-based civil rights, Red Power activists also fought for collective, land-based rights such as protection of sacred sites, access to traditional hunting grounds and fishing ways, and increased jurisdiction over land in general (see P. C. Smith and Warrior 1997; Cobb and Fowler 2007). One touchstone of this collective action was the occupation of Alcatraz. In late 1969 Native folks from California and beyond descended upon Alcatraz Island in the middle of San Francisco Bay to annex the empty land (the federal prison had been closed for more than five years) in order create a Native community center for the Bay Area. For nineteen months activists occupied this land and commandeered it on behalf of all Indigenous peoples in the United States. This occupation was a key moment in a revival of American Indian agency and political assertiveness. Todd picked up on the vibrancy of this event and paid homage to it through deck art consisting of a photographic collage of images from the occupation and reproduction of the graffiti that still remains on structures inside and outside the decommissioned prison.

During the nineteen months habitation of Alcatraz, the "Indians of All Tribes"—as the occupiers came to call themselves—distinctly reclaimed the land as an Indigenous space and place. The most explicit form of this reclamation was the way the occupiers tagged all over the island with such phrases as: "You are on Indian land," "Indian Land," "Indian Property," "Red Power," "Custer had it coming," "This Land is My Land," "Dept. of Indians, Bureau of White Affairs," and "Taken by Oakes."[5] This graffiti could be found all over: the exterior walls of the building, over-writing the preexisting text on the penitentiary signage, inside the cells that acted as rooms, and on the main water tower. For his skateboard design, Todd mixed together black-and-white photographic images of these tags with archival photos of the island, the protesters or occupiers doing various daily activities, and the teepee set up in one of the yards. Layered on top of these images is red type, reproductions of the graffitied slogans, and Indigenous-themed images occupiers drew on the walls. Todd actively used this deck to educate Native youth he would meet at powwows when selling Native Skates gear. I elaborate more on this in the next chapter, but Todd would ask kids who approached his booth if they knew what the images were from; if they did, he would give them a free deck, but if not, he would tell them to go educate themselves and come back and tell him about it for a free deck.

Few things emblemize twentieth-century Native resistance more than the 1973 Wounded Knee armed standoff and the 1969–70 occupation

FIG. 3. Native Skates "Alcatraz" deck designed by Todd Harder. Smithsonian National Museum of American History.

of Alcatraz. Referencing this latter event through deck art, Todd is not only helping teach contemporary history to Native youth, but he is also memorializing Native power and resistance. Skateboarding is a perfect venue for promoting rebellion from the norm. In this case Todd is not using vulgarity and profanity, as many mainstream skate graphics do, but rather is lionizing rebellion against settler colonialism. He calls upon skaters already with countercultural inclinations in order to educate others about Native history. Also, the images he uses capture the gritty, industrial nature of an abandoned concrete and steel prison, referencing the seedy environs that skaters are certainly no strangers to as they frequently reuse structures made for something else or no longer in use. Moreover, this Native Skates graphic compels all viewers of the deck not only to think about American history but also to do so in a critical and radical fashion, making heroes of Red Power activists.

Another Indigenous skate company that calls on rebellious indigeneity is Wounded Knee Skateboard Manufacturing & Propaganda. Wounded Knee Skateboards is the joint brainchild of Jim "Murph" Murphy and Andy Kessler, founders, and Walter Pourier (Oglala Lakota), creative director. Beginning with the company's name, Jim and Walt are drawing on the resistant spirit of Northern Plains Indians who fought relentlessly to defend their homeland from settler colonialism. Wounded Knee, the place, is often described as a "hamlet." It is located on the Pine Ridge Reservation about twenty miles northeast of the town Pine Ridge, the eponymous capital of the reservation. The hamlet Wounded Knee and the creek the hamlet is named after are an English translation of a Lakota phrase recalling a warrior injured at this spot. In Lakota the phrase refers to an event specific to Lakota traditional legends; however, in English the term provokes a dual reference of two key moments in U.S. settler colonialism and westward expansion. In 1890 over three hundred mostly unarmed elderly men, women, and children were massacred with Gatling guns by U.S. Calvary who then proceeded to mutilate the dead bodies in order to take body parts as hideously morbid "trophies." White imperial narratives mark this as the symbolic "closing" of the West and the end of the "Indian Wars," a narrative that masks the grotesque, savage, and inhuman events of the massacre.

In 1973 the activists of the American Indian Movement occupied the hamlet as a protest against the corrupt and dictatorial administration of an FBI-supported tribal chairman, Dick Wilson. This led to a seventy-one-day armed standoff as activists took over the hamlet of Wounded Knee in protest of Wilson's administration. The Red Power protesters had only hunting rifles and handguns for protection while the tribal government, federal agents, and the U.S. National Guard countered the occupation with automatic weapons, armored personnel carriers, grenade launchers, and F-16 fighter jet air support. Indigenous narratives mark this event as the height of Red Power: a courageous resistance to settler colonialism by a couple hundred activists challenging the full force of the federal government.

Naming the company Wounded Knee Skateboards, Murph, Kessler, and Walt are clearly calling on the power, gravity, and significance of these two events. Similarly, the deck art on all Wound Knee Skateboards references this dual political and cultural significance of Wounded Knee. The most explicitly didactic board art, designed by Jim Pearson, displays five white outline maps of the United States lined up in a row horizontally on top of an all-black background. Under each map is a date: 1491, 1850, 1865, 1880, 1990. The map of 1491 is all completely black on the inside of the white boarder. Then, each map gets progressively more white space filled in on the map as they move chronically left to right. The last map is almost all white with a handful of (mostly small) black blotches that represent tribal nation reservations as of 1990. On this last map, printed in black type is the word "unjust," and along the top rail is the phrase "a north american progression of land loss" in red type. Along the bottom rail is the name of the company in red and white with the company logo in red as well. Obviously, this board is meant to educate and remind any viewer how much land was stolen from Indigenous communities and how quickly it happened. This is a relatively simple but highly potent message that challenges the settler narrative justifying the American nationalism and clearly declares that land was stolen, not made manifest

FIG. 4. Wounded Knee Skateboards "Land Loss" deck designed by John Pearson. Author's collection. Photo: Matthew Fowler.

to white Americans through the predetermined fate of divine destiny or natural progress.

Other Wounded Knee Skateboards deck art portrays nineteenth-century Lakota history and culture with images that index Lakota leaders and Lakota epistemology. These decks all pertain to a Lakota past, but they are designed in such a way that give them a modern feel in order to make them appealing to contemporary skateboard devotees. The decks were designed by either Jim Pearson or Walt. Interestingly they share some similarity with grassroots or guerilla art that Shepard Fairey began in the mid-1990s. Fairey's early Obey Giant campaigns were a highly influential part of underground skate culture, and ultimately Fairey created a skate clothing company called Obey. In 2011, after Wounded Knee Skateboards had a strong reputation, Fairey was commissioned to create a poster for a national campaign of street art to protect tribal treaty rights called "Honor the Treaties." A key part of this campaign was a mural that Fairey created titled "The Black Hills are Not for Sale," referring to Pine Ridge and other Lakota communities' unwillingness to take restitution money from the federal government for its unlawful annexation of the Black Hills. To this day the money is still sitting in a federal trust, untouched by Lakotas despite the extreme poverty at Pine Ridge. The tribal governments have refused to take this money because claiming the money accepts the transaction that alienated the Lakotas from the Black Hills, thereby legitimizing the settler colonialism of this land sacred to the Lakotas.

It is the power of theses contemporary and historic actions of resistance that Wounded Knee Skateboards pays homage to and draws upon to marry the guerilla marketing, counterculture rebellion of skateboarding with the grassroots resistance of the Lakota people. For example, another one of Jim Pearson's decks is centered with the image of a headdress-wearing warrior on horseback, in a pose of exaltation: arms spread wide, chest puffed up, and head tilted back. Emanating from his body are alternating yellow and red graphic depictions of beams of light. The name of the company sits under the warrior in a white and yellow font standing out against an all-black background that fills in down to the bottom of the board. In between the brand name and the warrior image are the words in red, "IT IS A GOOD DAY TO DIE," a phrase that Lakota warriors such as Crazy Horse were reported to say before entering battle, acknowledging both the danger of battle and their willingness to fulfill the cultural role of warrior and defender. This phrase has particular salience in connection with imperial westward expansion, as it is meant to valorize young Lakota men willing to die to protect their family, community, and land. Indeed, on the top of this skate deck are the words—arched under the nose end of the board and above the Wounded Knee Skateboards "four directions" logo—"No Surrender Tashunka-Witko." The English words memorialize this idea of defending one's community at the risk of death, and the Lakota words are the Indigenous name for "Crazy Horse." Clearly this deck is drawing on the mythology and martyrdom of the Oglala warrior who used his purported super-human powers to defend the Black Hills along with

FIG. 5. Wounded Knee Skateboards "It's a Good Day to Die" deck designed by John Pearson. Author's collection. Photo: Matthew Fowler.

Sitting Bull and others until he was assassinated in 1877. Other decks memorialize Crazy Horse and his compatriots, Sitting Bull and Black Elk, with images of their faces in red, black, and yellow on the underside of the boards. These are the heroes of the Oglala Lakota rebellion against nineteenth-century U.S. settler colonialism, as counterculture as you can get, taking of up arms and willing to die resisting the established powers to protect their own culture.

Finally, three other decks in the Wounded Knee Skateboard catalog have sacred animals on them such as eagles and a white buffalo. Rays of energy and power emanate in varying ways from the depictions of these animals. Again, Pearson, Murphy, and Pourier are taking historic images and bringing them into the present as a way to connect culture and power to Indigenous youth. One last interesting piece of deck art that somewhat reverses this order is an image of a strong warrior standing upright with his chest puffed out in black and white outline against the backdrop of an all-red deck. This tattooed (with the Wounded Knee Skateboards logo) and warpainted imposing figure has a mohawk haircut and carries a peace pipe. Whether this is a traditional or contemporary figure remains ambivalent, but what is telling are the words on the deck, "we were punk first." This message traces late twentieth-century counterculture rebellion through skateboarding and underground music back to Lakota warrior traditions. Hence, Wounded Knee Skateboards merges the now with the immemorial.

As with the work of their fellow OG skaters Todd Harder, Dustinn Craig, and Doug Miles, there is a lot more to Jim Murphy's and Walt Pourier's work than just that artistic component. For sure, the underside of a skateboard deck is an excellent palate to express the nonconformity of skateboarding through graphic design. But what really makes these five men unique is how they nurture the actual practice of skateboarding. They have all embraced a mentoring role for the youth of their communities, promoting the joy, fun, and dedication that is inherent to skateboarding. In the last thirty-some years, several artists—from both outside and within Indian Country—have used the unique shape of a skateboard for their art.[6] What sets these OGs apart is rather than merely using a skateboard to display art and culture, they use skateboarding to stimulate the values of their home cultures. Given the trauma and chaos wrought on Indigenous communities by settler colonialism, enjoyment and commitment to community are themselves acts of nonconformist rebellion. Fostering this opportunity for joy and hope in the youth of their communities, Doug, Dustinn, Todd, Jim, and Walt are more than just OGs; they enact the role of elders helping guide those coming up behind them toward positivity that can come from Indigenous values and toward active wellness that comes from skateboarding. In the next chapter, I explore what it is that makes these OG skaters what I call skate elders.

In terms of American (and global) sports, skateboarding is a relatively new sport. The idea of a "skateboard" did not become popularized until the 1960s, and street skating, which is the most widespread form today, really did not become ubiquitous until the late 1980s, early 1990s. Due to this recency, there are not as many skaters over the age of fifty as there are under the age of thirty, hence putting a limit to how much skateboarding can foster the kind and depth of intergenerational connections we might find with other sports such as baseball, football, or even soccer and surfing. Nonetheless, there is still a growing cadre of over-forty-five-year-old skaters who have been skating since they were teens. Moreover, as the sport increases in age, so too will its participants.

Paul O'Connor (2018) has already taken a glimpse as this through research on what he calls "middle-aged skateboarders" (927). O'Connor recognizes that some of the most influential professional skaters of the 1980s and 1990s still continue to skate (in exhibitions or even competition) despite their age. Amateur middle-aged skaters who, when they were young, emulated these ageing pros (such as Tony Hawk and Steve Cabellero) have now realized that they can keep skating, just as the idols of their youth have done. O'Connor (2018) asserts, "rather than being peripheral in skateboard culture . . . middle-aged skateboarders occupy notable positions within the skateboard industry and within local skateboard scenes and communities" (926). That is, despite the fact that skateboarding is normatively coded as a hobby of adolescence, O'Connor's research illustrates that within skateboarding culture, the middle-aged skaters with whom he worked actually maintain what he calls "temporal capital" (927). Within O'Connor's framing, this temporal capital manifests as respect from the current youth skaters for the middle-aged skaters' connection to an earlier era of skateboarding. There is now enough longevity in skateboarding for there to be what appears to the younger generation as an "old school" style of skateboarding, and thereby middle-aged skateboarders who started to skate during this "old school" time now have a sense of cultural legitimacy and authenticity.

O'Connor relates an account from one of the Australian skaters he interviewed who was once riding in an elevator dressed for the business meeting he was on his way to while also holding his skateboard under his arm. Upon seeing this stylistic disjuncture, a middle-aged peer, also riding in the elevator, mockingly asked, "'Aren't you a bit too old for that?,'" to which the middle-aged skater reportedly replied, "'Every tribe has it's elders'" (O'Connor 2018, 934). Setting aside the settler colonial problematics of a middle-aged, white Australian man co-opting the words "tribe" and "elder," this skater's retort nicely captures the concept of an older skater who has a knowledge and a skill set that could be deployed to mentor younger skaters.[1] Yet, on balance, O'Connor's (2018) article does not really delve into the idea of intergenerational mentoring through skateboarding. Perhaps this is because intergenerational mentoring tends to be far more covert in white communities than it is in other communities, such as Indigenous ones. The value of elder leadership is inherent to Indigenous cultures; hence, when something like skateboarding is indigenized, it is also likely to be overtly folded into Indigenous practices of intergeneration relationships. This comparison is certainly more evident when we consider the way skateboarding is often rendered in dominant culture, as an antagonism between generations: the proverbial rebellious teen skater railing at society's traditional norms by performing daredevil tricks versus the distinguished older pedestrian casting disparaging looks or shaking a clenched fist at the hell-raising kids. These tropes of old versus young are played out in skateboarding media, mainstream media, and even city council chambers as public laws delimiting skateboarding are debated (see Irvine and Taysom 1998; Woolley and Johns 2001; Beal and Wilson 2004; Lombard 2010; Beal et al. 2017). However, even this near-clichéd tension between old and young has begun to thaw in the last ten to fifteen years as skateboarding has become more mainstream and as the positive health outcomes of skating have become more apparent (see Howell 2005; Atencio, Beal, and Wilson 2009; Lombard 2010; Thorpe and Rinehart 2012; Atencio et al. 2018; O'Connor 2018; Corwin et al. 2019). This is significant progress, but there is still a lot to be worked out in terms of figuring out how to make skateboarding a part of a community's culture, where skateparks and skate spots can fit into city planning, and skateboarders' willingness to take part in a "sanctioned" activity (see Wheaton and Beal 2003; Howell 2005; Chiu 2009). In terms of Indian Country, it would be false (and, frankly, bigoted romanticism) to say that there is no intergeneration tension. Moreover, there are, of course, many people in Indigenous communities who are not fans of skateboarding and likely share the same skepticism of this youthful endeavor as can be found outside of Indian Country. That being said, like what's been happening in several other places globally, there are plenty of bright spots of intergeneration collaboration in Indian Country among older community members and younger skaters.

Take, for example, these three Indigenous folks who were intimately involved in establishing skateparks in tribal communities: Louise Yellowman, Chris Nieto, and Louie Gong. As a Navajo Nation elder from Tuba City, Arizona, in the western part of the reservation, Louise has been a longtime stalwart in the community. She grew up very traditionally sheepherding, speaking Diné, and participating in many ceremonies. Once she graduated from high school, she was one of the few of her generation to leave the reservation for her bachelor's and master's degrees; she returned to teach at the local high school and then decided to run for public office in order to advocate for her community (Suetopka Thayer 2008). Rather than working at the tribal governmental level, Louise decided she could have a greater impact being on the Coconino County Board of Supervisors. Upon being elected she worked on several projects, but none was more impactful than in 2003 when she listened to her grandson and his friends call for a dedicated place to skateboard in their part of the reservation without having to drive over an hour to other regional skateparks (Louise Yellowman, interview, February 17, 2016). Louise worked five long years to make this skate park a reality, and it opened to great community fanfare in 2008. This park is still heavily used to this day and is a center feature of the small town of Tuba City, a place that, although small, has a high youth population with two high schools that draw many rural students from villages around Tuba City. This large presence of youth is in part why Louise felt this project was so important (Yellowman, interview). What is significant here is that Louise's generation never grew up with skateboarding, and she is the age of people who at worst disdain skateboarding and at best have zero frame of reference for understanding its culture and draw for youth. However, Louise was adamant that wishes of the younger generation be respected, even if she did not have direct experience with the sport itself. She worked tirelessly to push the project through local governance and do the additional fundraising that needed to happen in order to make this dream a reality. This kind of intergenerational respect and responsibility is far from the norm outside of Indian Country.

Another advocate for Indigenous youth who skateboard is Chris Nieto. Chris is a member of the Pala Band of Mission Indians in Southern California. Chris has been very active all his life, but until his teenage brother-in-law introduced him to skateboarding, he was mostly involved in softball, football, martial arts, and motocross.[2] Chris's younger brother-in-law was part of a small crew of Pala skaters who were regulars at the Pala pool (see chapter 5). This underground skate spot was an abandoned house on the reservation with two emptied swimming pools. For the Pala skaters this was a significant treat because several Southern California professional skaters would discretely visit this spot, and the Pala kids would get to watch and skate with guys they'd see in magazines. Not only did this let these kids feel like they were in on an important secret, but it gave them a unique sense of pride that outsiders found value in *their* reservation (Chris Nieto, interview, May 15, 2012). Reservations are frequently marked as spaces of deprivation or at least limited only to a casino as a space of value. Chris soon began to join his brother-in-law and friends at the Pala pool and used its notoriety as a jumping-off point to create a skate brand called Remnant Skateboards. Chris mainly created this brand and company to support this teenage group of Pala skaters. Although Chris himself was not much older than them (in his late twenties), he recognized that creating a skate brand and crew would feed these kids' passion and support them to make healthy life choices (Neito, interview). Soon he began to mentor them further when they decided they wanted to lobby the Pala Tribal Council to build them a skatepark. The tribe's concerns about liability led them to have the pools at the abandoned house filled in and to encourage tribal police to intervene when kids skated in other spots on the reservation, such as the casino parking lot and the tribal government complex. Chris encouraged them to organize and use the tribal governmental structures to their advantage, creating a plan for a tribal skatepark, rallying community support, and making a convincing presentation to the tribal council. The result of Chris's efforts in mentoring these youth to advocate for themselves resulted in the construction of one of the best skateparks in all of Southern California. This skatepark is still the pride of the Pala Recreation Center and a place where Indigenous and non-Indigenous skaters, alike, pilgrimage.

A similar series of events occurred at the Port Gamble S'klallam Tribe's reservation on Olympic Peninsula. In the early 2010s the S'klallam Tribal Council created a youth program called SWAG (S'klallam Working and Giving). A main goal of this program was to get youth more involved in the community support and decision-making (with a long-term goal of developing internal leadership) by providing an avenue for S'klallam teenagers to come up with their own community improvement projects. In 2012 the teens involved in SWAG came up with a plan to build a park that would include a skatepark and outdoor basketball court. They produced a formal written proposal that they used to pitch the idea to Port Gamble S'klallam Tribal Council and outside grant funders. Soon they were awarded a grant from the Sheckler Foundation (started by world champion street skateboarder Ryan Sheckler) through its "Be the Change" grant competition. This team of SWAG youth advocates, all in their late teens, was a combination of kids who grew up skateboarding and those who did not but admired the skaters (Brandon Hailsey, interview, August 16, 2017). Their dedication to their community impressed not only the older generation of tribal leaders on the council but the non-tribal decision-makers as well. At the grand opening of the park, tribal councilman Kyle Carpenter applauded the SWAG youth for what they accomplished, noting that the location where the park was built was once known as "the place," a spot where thirty years earlier many tribal youths would go party—resulting in all kinds of unhealthy activity and consequences. Councilman Carpenter declared, "Now you have turned it into a drug-and alcohol-free park," echoing the community's sentiment of gratitude and praise for SWAG's effort to counteract addiction and unhealthy inactivity on the reservation (Seymour 2014, par. 2).

SWAG youth conceived of the skatepark as a comprehensive, intergeneration intervention into the health and wellness of the S'Klallam community. Their appeal to the tribal council to revamp a space of partying into a space of wellness gave an opportunity for the generation above them to reconcile their past with the future health of the community. This sense of healing is made clear by all the older community members who attended the skatepark's opening, even though they would never actually use it (see Seymour 2014; Halsey, interview). Additionally, these SWAG team members also look forward to the generation coming up behind. An explicit part of their proposal was to use the skatepark to offer skate camps run by SWAG members to younger kids in the community—these skate camps still happen to this day. Brandon Halsey, a tribal member who was part of SWAG, got very involved in the development of the skatepark and ended up becoming a counselor for the skate camp. One of the things that Brandon is proudest of when he considers his involvement with the skatepark is the fact that "the whole park is a safe space . . . [and] it is meant for wellness for the whole community" (Halsey, interview).

Another way the skatepark bound the S'Klallam community together across generations was the way it tied the relatively recent youth culture of skateboarding to the enduring culture of the S'Klallam people. The most material example was the artistic design of the skatepark, which integrates S'Klallam cultural symbols into the physical construction design. To accomplish this the tribe reached out to Seattle-based Nooksack artist, educator, and activist Louie Gong. Louie was a perfect choice for this project in that he had long been a part of the intersection between skate culture and Indigenous culture. He and Rico Wurl were some of the first artists to put Northwest Coast Indigenous art on skate decks. Louie also gained acclaim for drawing and painting his interpretations of this design style on Vans and Converse shoes. Louie was brought in to help design what would be painted on the concrete that the S'Klallam youth would be skating on. Painting the actual surface that skateboarders roll across not only explicitly marks the space as Indigenous (regardless of the activity going on), but it also is an ever-present reminder of the community's cultural values and the way they are expressed by representations of animals and the natural world.

Brandon was thrilled that he and the other SWAG youth got to work with Louie (Halsey, interview). The SWAG youth had a few initial conversations with him about what the design could be, and then Louie came out and stenciled a design on the concrete. What's more, as with most of Louie's art, the community is a central part of the work, so once the image outlines were done, Louie taught the SWAG youth how to do the painting and worked with them to accomplish a fantastic display of culture and beauty. The painting features an eagle, an orca, a school of fish, wave images, and a profile of elders wearing traditional regalia in a canoe. These images are meant to represent strength, growth, and community. Additionally, in more than one place is painted the Klallam word *txwa*, which is a play on the Sheckler Foundation's moniker "Be the Change." In the Klallam language (a Salish dialect) it means "becoming new" (Seymour 2014, par. 8). This term emphasizes both the transformation of the spot on which the skatepark sits and the importance of growth both on communal and individual levels. If you visit the skatepark today, most of the paint has worn off through use, but there are still several places where one can see the remnants of the overall design. Brandon tells me that they knew from the beginning that the artwork would not last, but rather it was the act of the SWAG youth getting to put their imprint on the park that mattered and the engagement and learning with Louie Gong, who acted as an artistic mentor for this project. Again, Louie was perfect for this, considering how much of his art is about bringing Coastal Salish (and other Indigenous designs) into the present by decorating contemporary items in a way that values Indigenous culture and educates about the meaning of the symbology, beyond merely the aesthetics.[3] In this instance what the youth already value, skateboarding, is merged with the values of their ancestors in a way that mentors the youth in how to "become new" and maintain tradition.

In chapter 6 I describe a certain generation of Indian Country–based skaters that I have called the "OGs" of Indigenous skateboarding. As I note, although they have occasionally collaborated with each other, they do not always see things the same way. On the whole, all five of them share the same zeal for skateboarding and the same dedication to prosperity and happiness of Indigenous youth, and they all firmly believe in employing skateboarding to achieve the latter. While I would say it is rare for them to work at cross-purposes or in conflict with each other, it also has become almost as rare for them to have worked collaboratively beyond the one All Nations Skate Jam when they were all together. Perhaps this a byproduct of their shared countercultural ethos that might coincide with proclivities toward individuality and working on one's own. This is not to say that these OGs are loners who isolate themselves from people; in fact they are all strongly engaged in their own communities and even more so engaged with the youth of their communities. Or, maybe put another way, it would be naive to assume that these guys would necessarily work together just because they all happen to be Native. One of the bigger myths non-Native folks have about Indian Country that there is a uniformity in Indigenous culture or that Indians inherently share a solidarity and all work together. More often than not, every Indigenous community does things in their own way and difference and distinction is respected rather than thought of as something that needs to be overcome.[4] Yet despite their differences from each other, I believe these five skaters are uniquely distinguishable from the other skaters in Indian Country. I argue that this distinction lies in the fact that Doug, Dustinn, Todd, Jim, and Walt are not just skaters who put Native art and imagery on the bottom of a deck, but rather they immerse themselves in skate culture as a way to connect to the generation coming up behind them. This allows them to both stay connected to the subculture and sport they love and to the Indigenous youth around them who are becoming just as avid skateboarders as these OGs were when they were growing up. All five of these men recognize that skating is a vehicle to connect with these kids and to engage the youth in the value of their own Indigenous culture through skateboarding. In this regard the OGs who create skate brands, teams, and events, all in conjunction with Indigenous cultures and arts, are more than just fellow skaters but are also cultural mentors to the youth of their community.

In acknowledging the phenomenal community work of these five, it is equally critical to acknowledge that they are all cisgender men. This overrepresentation of cis men is not unique to the subculture of skateboarding, nor is it completely foreign to Indian Country. The historical conventions of most Indigenous communities have far more space for female and queer, trans, nonbinary equity than the customs of skateboarding, although both have plenty of room to improve. The good news is that just as Indian Country as a whole has been engaged in the decolonizing work of disposing of the gender inequalities produced by settler colonialism, so too are there many bright spots where skateboarding is shedding its sexist past. There is always work to be done, and as I illustrate below, skateboarding in Indian Country is a potential nexus where progress in gender equality can flourish as a central part of joyful futures.

The subculture of skateboarding has long manifested what, at a minimum, could be described as masculinist bias and, at maximum, flat-out sexism in its worst forms. There are many paradoxes that surround gender inequity in skateboarding. First and foremost, U.S. skaters who consider themselves rebels refusing to conform to society's normative conventions often do the exact opposite when it comes to America's sexist, homophobic, and transphobic norms. In most cases the rebelliousness of skateboarders subsided when it came to resisting the norms of gender and sexuality (e.g., Beal 1996, 2013; Kelly, Pomerantz, and Currie 2005; Atencio, Beal, and Wilson 2009; Yochim 2009; MacKay and Dallaire 2012). This paradox can be seen from the very beginning even among the legendarily countercultural Dogtown skaters. Despite the relatively progressive fact that a female skater, Peggy Oki, was an original Z-Boy, the skate crew as a whole did little to tear down patriarchy. Not only did many of the Dogtown skaters often filter their aggressive style through hypermasculine displays of identities both on and off the board, but at least one proudly acknowledged assaulting a gay couple (see Borden 2019). Since the days of Dogtown there have been many steps forward (but never without some steps backward) in skateboarding doing a better job of including female and queer (and more recently trans) skaters. Even more important are the moments where female and queer skaters have utilized the countercultural ethos of skating to make their own path of creativity, athleticism, and community despite and irrespective of what any male skater might say, do, or think of as "real" skateboarding (Kelly, Pomerantz, and Currie 2005; MacKay and Dallaire; 2012; Beal 2013).

In their own way these five OG Naive skaters I discuss have also sought to be inclusive of female skaters and promote equity, either through brand sponsors of female skaters, including female skaters on their team, or having females- and girls-only sessions as part of their skate jams. I believe this is the case because at their core what matters most to these OG Native skaters is intergenerational mentoring.

Intergenerational relationships are highly integral to Indigenous communities where the conventional expectation is that knowledge is passed down from older people to younger, beyond merely the parent-child relationship. This contrasts the tendencies in Western cultures where a great deal of knowledge and cultural transition is meant to happen from parent to child—promoting the primacy and almost exclusivity of the nuclear family–or in institutionalized educational settings—promoting industrial capitalism hyper-division of labor. However, in Indigenous cultures, "elders," people in the community who are to be respected because of their knowledge and experience, pass on culture through mentoring youth even if they are not connected by direct heredity.

Similarly, skateboarders frequently hang out with the "adopted" community of those they skate with or happen to be at the same skate spot. Skaters often learn tricks and the habits of skate culture from fellow skaters. It is much less likely that these fellow skaters are their parents; rather, they are a kind of fictive kin based around networks of shared commitment to skateboarding. Given these similar forms of intergenerational cultural transmission, I have coined the (admittedly imperfect) term of "skate elder" to describe these OGs who use skateboarding to mentor the youth of their communities. In much the same way conventional Native community "elders" are respected throughout the community for their experience and knowledge and take on the responsibility of mentoring youth in the community, these OG Native skaters do the same with the skater kids they mentor. Hence, I have chosen to call them skate elders.[5]

NATIVE SKATES

A fundamental illustration of what I mean by "skate elder" can be found in the story I relayed in the last chapter about Todd Harder's Native Skates "Alcatraz" deck. Before establishing his own skate brand, Todd worked as a screen printer and would set up a booth at powwows, often selling shirts that he had self-printed. Being a skater, he also took notice of all the Native kids he would see in the community with beat-up boards that were on their last legs. Around 2003, he decided to do something about this dearth of new decks and skate equipment. First, he used his contacts in the California skate industry to get donated decks that he could pass out to Native skater kids in need of new gear.[6] But then he had the idea to put some Indigenous imagery on the decks that he was giving away, in addition to mainstream decks he had been gifting kids. From this he began to make his own skate gear with the idea that for every two boards he sold he would give one free to a Native kid. For the first decks he made, he put a graphic image of a medicine wheel on the bottom. Kids would come by his powwow booth and marvel at them, as they proved to be a good conversation starter for Todd to talk about skateboarding with them in general and about the specific relevance of the medicine wheel to many Indigenous communities. At first Todd did not even realize the full value in these Native-themed decks (and the conversations about them) and how much they could mean to a Native kid interested in skateboarding. It was not until his girlfriend pointed out to him how meaningful these conversations were and how connecting with Native teenagers was far easier for Todd than it was for most people: he was "reaching kids that most people have a hard time reaching" (Todd Harder, interview April 30, 2017). Her comment inspired Todd to think more intentionally about what a powerful vehicle for Indigenous cultural transmission a skateboard deck could be.

As a child of the 1970s and 1980s obsessed with skateboarding, Todd grew up fawning over the photos of the Z-Boys and Bones Brigade crews in skateboard magazines. Equally, growing up an Indian kid during this time period meant hearing tales of radical Indigenous civil rights activists. He so admired those in the Red Power movement that he decided to use a skate deck as a way to pay homage to the occupation of Alcatraz. In chapter 6 I describe the deck and the way its graphics comprise a collage of images and graffiti from the occupation. Independent of their Native historical significance, these images of graffiti, concrete, and protest gave the deck a gritty-cool vibe common to many skateboards in the 1990s (see Cliver 2004). And one Native kid in particular was really drawn to the board. Todd told me the story this way:

> I had one little guy, one little skater that used to skate for us, and he wanted that deck bad, I had just come out with it. And I said, "What do you know about Alcatraz?" He goes, "I don't know, I don't know nothing I just want that board, it looks cool." And I go "Well, you're not getting that board until you know something about Alcatraz, about the occupation of Alcatraz." So that was like on a Saturday at a powwow, and Sunday he came back and goes "I want that board." "Well, what do you know about Alcatraz," and he starts "Well, in

1969 the Indians of All Nations started the occupation, and they were college students and the occupation lasted . . ." [With a big smile on his face, Todd declares,] "Alright you got it! But now when anyone sees your board you tell all the people and your friends what *you* learned about Alcatraz." (Harder, interview)

Experiences like this are transformative, not only for the youth with whom he connects, but for Todd as well. They helped Todd realize that although he has no formal or Western institutional training in educating, he has a knack for reaching Native kids where they are at and then expanding their worldview from there.

Interactions such as these led Todd to think bigger than just the localized skate brand he created called Native Skates—to think bigger and develop the All Nations Skate Jam (ANSJ). The ANSJ allowed him, and other skaters he knew (both Indigenous and non-Indigenous), to reach a much larger audience of Native youth. From his screen printing and graphic design work Todd had connections at Vans, Inc., and from his lifelong involvement in skateboarding he was friends with several skaters who were currently or at one time professionals. He was able to leverage this network to get the financial support and credibility he needed to pull off a Native skate contest, and the ANSJ is still thriving today. It is an annual event with one to two full days of skating and multilevel "fun" competition and prizes; several booths for Indigenous artist and skate brands to sell their wares; Native garage and punk bands playing live shows; and a Vans tour bus bringing food to share, gear to give away, and current and retired professional skaters to sign autographs and do skate demonstrations. Perhaps the most significant regular guest is Tony Alva, a living legend in the skate world who seems very at home among Indigenous skaters. He is so comfortable with this community that as recently as 2017 he used it as a venue to mention his recent revelation that one of his grandmothers was likely Hopi.

I have attended the ANSJ three times (2014, 2105, 2017), and each time it was a spectacular experience. There is always a hive of activity with hundreds of kids skating in the open jam sessions between the competitive runs—completely filling the Los Altos skatepark in east Albuquerque. It is a wonder anyone can move around and that more kids don't get hurt from running into each other. The majority of attendees are from the many Native communities in the Southwest and the reservations that surround Albuquerque or from the city itself, but many also drive from very long distances to be a part of the event, such as Denver and the Dakotas. Todd and his family make the twenty-four-hour drive every year from Detroit, and one year I met folks from various Pacific Northwest tribal communities that made the equally long drive from the Olympic Peninsula. The energy at the event is remarkable. Everyone is excited to be there to connect with friends, be around other Indigenous like themselves, and support each other's attempts to pull off increasingly radical tricks. Todd sees the event as both a way for Native kids to feed their hunger for skating and to have fun with peers from other tribal communities.

Todd also sees skateboarding as a way to illustrate life and the variety of life trajectories that could be open to these Indigenous youth. Todd did not go to college, but he does recognize the value of college and the importance of promoting education in Indian Country. However, at the same time he is keenly aware that, as in his case, college may not be the right (or even viable) option for many of the kids with whom he connects. As an alternative Todd envisions the ANSJ as a way to expose kids to career options that do not necessarily require college—the many professions peripheral to skateboarding. Many skaters have creative and artistic sensibilities that can be channeled toward graphic design, marketing, or event planning. These are fields that are critical to the skateboarding industry, and a skater who develops one of these skills, along with the familiarity with the industry and the networking that comes with hanging out with skaters, could forge a career without going to college. Todd is well aware of the starkly low statistics of Native kids that go to college, and he applauds the effort to fix this, but this is not his expertise or even what he sees as his battle necessarily. He has astutely remarked to me, given that he did not go to college, it is difficult for him to be advocating such a route. He would rather leave that to those with college experience. "All you educated people are working on that," Todd teased me with a playful smile (Harder, interview). It's not that he sees college and the efforts to get Native kids there as a waste of time, or that he wants to give up on these kids. Rather he is a realist who wants to help provide solutions for those who do not want to choose a college life. Skateboarding, as a whole, provides an interesting model: many who have well-paying jobs and careers in the global skate industry never went to college but instead immersed themselves in the industry of skating as they were growing up.

Far from promoting the notion of a "dropout" or "burnout" skater, Todd takes it upon himself to mentor Indigenous skaters for potential careers. He likes to broaden the minds and goals of young Native skaters who tend to only think about getting good enough to earn sponsorships and to go pro, like many of their skate idols from outside of Indian Country. In relatively casual conversations with these young Native skaters, Todd will often drop in the question, "What's higher than pro?" He poses the question to them almost as if it was a riddle and then uses it to expand on a larger idea for the kids to contemplate.

> They can't answer it . . . [so I repeat it] and go, "Well, what's higher than being pro?" [They'll reply,] "I don't know." I go, "Well, let's pick another sport. Let's pick basketball, ya know, who's higher than LeBron? The guy that signs his check! [That's who!] He signs his checks, so somebody has an account [that] they can pay a check of LeBron's [salary]." I go, "So, company owners are higher than pros." I go, "So you can have a goal of a company owner . . . who doesn't necessarily have to have very good skateboard skills." (Harder, interview)

These kinds of exchanges that Todd has with younger Native skaters are a key place where I see the parallel with more traditional forms of mentoring. Rather than providing a didactic seminar on "how to build a career," Todd asks questions and provides an example (NBA star LeBron James) that he knows are relatable to the generation below him.

He plants the seed of a thought and then encourages these teenagers to expand in their own way. This subtle mentoring fits with Indigenous mentoring that frequently takes the shape of guidance balanced with leaving room for individual exploration and expression. Granted, this example of mentoring is about a particularly capitalistic way of thinking about the world—striving to be a corporate owner who is the highest boss—and therefore might contradict more conventional notions of elder wisdom. But, of course, tradition always adapts to meet the needs of the present, and Todd is far from the only one in Indian Country promoting economic self-sufficiency as a key component to Native success. Ultimately, Todd encourages Native skaters to think within the realm of their own experiences and use that as their strengths to help them create productive lives for themselves. This wisdom prioritizes Native skaters and the social ecologies in which they thrive as their own source of strength and character, not something they need to receive and learn from outside of Indian Country.

In addition to the career-preparatory skills skateboard culture can provide, Todd also urges Native skater kids to see the lessons they learn from skating as translatable to their life in general. For example, he shared with me about an ongoing relationship he has with an incredibly gifted Native skater who was beginning to have contest success and was being offered various sponsorships. Despite (or perhaps because of) the success this skater was having, they began to develop a serious alcohol problem and struggle with addiction. The skater was genuinely worried that this addiction might ruin their budding career and trusted Todd as a mentor with whom to share this fear and vulnerability. Todd, of course, acknowledged to the skater that they should seek out a mental health professional to deal with addiction, but Todd also provided this young adult with mentoring guidance so that they could have the strength to seek this help. The skater confessed to Todd about how they wanted to quit drinking, but how hard it was to do so. Todd's advice to this skater's plea for help was to use skateboarding as a metaphor to help this skater see the inner strength they had.

[I said to the skater], "Hey, is there any trick that you can't do? You can do every trick, right?" and [the skater] goes, "Ya, for sure." And I go, "You can, can't you?! How do you do that, you know? Do you just do them?" "No." "What do you do?" and [the skater] goes, "Well, I just put my mind to it and keep working on it." I go, "Just turn it into a trick, but you got to do the trick every day . . . just don't drink for today, and then start again. You have to distance yourself from those people that keep you from being able to do the trick. If you were out here skating and there was always someone standing right in the way of where you wanted to do your trick, you'd go somewhere else and do your trick. You can't just stay here and keep trying to do that trick when that same person is an obstacle—you won't fucking do it." (Harder, interview)

In order to support and mentor this extremely talented skater who was struggling with life, Todd was able to marshal their mutual skate culture, language, and experience toward formulating a plan to overcome addiction. Todd asserts that just by being a skater "we're learning a great life lesson . . . on how to achieve something. You know, if you're gonna get to the most complicated flip trick, you gotta learn kickflips first" (Harder, interview).

Without skateboarding, Todd would likely not have much interaction with Native youth, especially given that he does not live in a tribal community per se. But because skateboarding brings them together (physically and metaphorically), he has the occasion to help these kids see that they actually have the tools within themselves—their skateboarding proves this—to tackle life's challenges. This is an incredibly valuable message for any young person facing the challenges of growing up and figuring out what it means to become an "adult." However, when considering Indigenous youth there is also a doubling effect produced by the daily obstacles that come from settler colonialism—the ongoing institutionalized oppression that seeks to eliminate the notion of "Indigenous" by trying to sever peoples' innate connections to land, and in the few remaining places where Indigenous peoples' bonds have remained immovable and inseverable, settler society seeks to exploit, denigrate, and starve the land in order to undermine any value of remaining connected to it. Given this ever-present settler colonial context, skateboarding in Indian Country can be a powerful way to stay connected to land, place, and self—all things that are important to becoming an adult member of an Indigenous community (let alone an adult member of humanity in general).

DESIRE-BASED RESEARCH AND SPACES OF HOPE

What sets apart those that I call skate elders is their conscious sense of the challenges of growing up in Indian Country, their recognition that skateboarding has been a valuable resource in their own lives to smooth out these challenges, and their commitment to providing resources so that those younger than them can take advantage of skateboarding in the same way. Skate elders often articulate this role and value of skateboarding in a kind of ongoing tension between promoting skateboarding explicitly as an "anti-drug" or "suicide prevention" activity and more implicitly as just a fun thing to do that may also advance wellness. The former positions skateboarding as a positive alternative or response to social plagues in Indian Country, while the latter conceives of skateboarding more as just something that people like to do because it is fun and desirable, but it also happens to promote personal strength and community building—both of which can be powerful enemies of oppression. In many ways this tension maps onto Eve Tuck's and K. Wayne Yang's (2014) insistence against treating reservations (and other marginalized communities) as spaces of deficit and their proscription against damage-based narratives. The main thrust of their argument is about, and directed toward, social science research(ers)—like me. Tuck and Yang (2014) reveal how social science research carries a Western Enlightenment legacy that formulates theories of practice and change based on a flawed logic: documenting damage, pain, and humiliation in oppressed communities will reveal inequities and therefore motivate support for the remedying of and restitution for these inequities. In some instances this model has worked, although generally in a limited way. Moreover, even when this model successfully provokes change, Tuck and Yang assert that it still dehumanizes research subjects. Drawing on Tuck's earlier work (2009), Tuck and Yang (2014) observe that "'won' reparations rarely become reality, and that in many cases, communities are left with a narrative that tells them that they are broken" (227). Deficit models create a dynamic wherein marginalized peoples are only recognized by (and for) their suffering, as Tuck and Yang (2014) incisively and pithily put it: "*You are in pain, therefore you are*" (228).

There is zero dispute that hardship and challenges exist in Indian Country and likely on a scale more significant than most other places in America, but moving the focus away from deficiency and toward empowerment, joy, and wellness is far more likely to bring about real change that is healing and humanizing. A key to this healing and humanizing is acknowledging "refusals" in research. Here Tuck and Yang (2014) rely on the transformative work of Indigenous anthropologist Audra Simpson (2007, 2014), who attends to the silences in her ethnographic research within her own Mohawk community—that is, the refusals of her consultants to answer certain questions or elaborate on certain topics. Moments of a research subject's intentional silence and a researcher's acknowledgment of these refusals represent a transformative comprehension of the humanity of oppressed peoples by allowing them to maintain the privacy and dignity that any human being would expect. Tuck and Yang (2014) note not only that refusals are critical strategies for ethnographic "Others" to forestall interrogation, but also that it is the duty of anyone who works in minoritized communities to refuse to engage in the sensationalism of pain and damage. Instead they argue for a "desire-based" research that attends to the hope and joys that marginalized and oppressed peoples generate by marshaling their past experiences and localized knowledge toward a more fulfilling future (Tuck and Yang 2014, 231). They attest:

This is not about seeing the bright side of hard times, or even believing that everything happens for a reason. Utilizing a desire-based

framework is about working inside a more complex and dynamic
understanding of what one, or a community, comes to know in (a)
lived life. (231)

I contend that skate elders do this organically. They refuse to see their
communities as solely damaged and instead frequently promote, sustain,
and feed the desire found in their communities no matter what form
it comes in, whether that be skateboarding, art, music, dance, fashion,
design, and so on.

Take, for example, Todd's comment teasing me as an entrenched member (a professor and departmental chair of American Indian studies)
of institutionalized higher education. He joked that "all you educated
people" are working on getting Native kids into college but since the
numbers are still so low, we are barely doing better than him, who is
not doing anything explicit in this regard. His ribbing me alludes to
the massive and long-term challenge of connecting Indigenous folks
to college degrees. But rather than dwell on that deficit, Todd seeks
to nurture the desire Native youth have for skateboarding and skate
culture by mentoring them in ways to make a meaningful profession
and life out of skateboarding. Todd acknowledges not everyone can or
needs to go to college, but he refuses to accept someone not going to
college as a defeat.

STRONGHOLD SOCIETY AND WOUNDED KNEE SKATEBOARDS

Walt Pourier established a nonprofit, the Stronghold Society, to engage
in similar tactics to support Native youth through skateboarding and
other forms of artistic, athletic, and cultural expression. Stronghold
Society was designed in collaboration with Jim Murphy and Wounded
Knee Skateboards, a handful of other nonprofit organizations, and a few
corporate partners. Walt's original motivation was to provide resources
to his home community, the Pine Ridge Reservation, but he also sought
to reach beyond into other reservations and large urban Indian populations such as his adopted home of Denver, Colorado. The Stronghold

Society orchestrated the construction of two skateparks on the Pine Ridge Reservation (at Pine Ridge and Manderson-White Horse Creek, South Dakota), and it hosts skate contests in both Denver and Pine Ridge. As elaborated in its mission statement, the Stronghold Society's goal is

> to inspire confidence, creativity, hope, and ambition for the youth of Native communities and non-Native communities through empowerment, arts programs, skateboarding and athletic activities while encouraging youth to take action to live a healthy life in mind, body, and spirit; this is our LIVE LIFE CALL TO ACTION CAMPAIGN. (Stronghold Society n.d.)

This is clearly a desire-based agenda working to help the grassroots Native skate scene both on and off the reservation flourish. I have been to the skate jams in both Denver and Pine Ridge, and they are tremendously popular and celebratory, drawing hundreds of skaters and fans alike for these one-day events. Walt conceives these skate contests as highly collaborative and community-building. Hosting them both in the heart of a reservation and in a strong urban Indian community such as Denver fosters connections between on- and off-reservation Indigenous skaters, many of whom do not get much of a chance to interact otherwise. Indeed, that these events are gatherings in specific locations matters; this is why Walt chose to call the foundation Stronghold Society. As their website states, a "stronghold is a place where a community regroups, a place to stand your ground and together face all of life's challenges" (Stronghold Society n.d.). Pine Ridge, despite the "reservation" being a product of settler colonialism, has been consistently used by Ogalala Lakotas as a stronghold in recent and distant historic times. The gathering of Native people in one spot of an urban center, no matter how temporary, can also be conceived of as a stronghold. One of Walt's main missions is to get Native youth to recognize that a skate park or spot can be their stronghold to build the power, energy, and confidence to thrive in the contemporary settler world.

When Pine Ridge skaters come to Denver, they get to meet and skate with Native folks from Denver and Albuquerque and can thereby see how expansive Indian Country is beyond their reservations.[7] By the same token, when urban (and often non-Lakota) Indian kids come to the contest in Pine Ridge, they get reconnect with the depth of tradition and open spaces that are more prominent in a place like Pine Ridge than cityscapes. When urban Indian kids visit Pine Ridge, everyone around them is Indigenous, unlike the way they are minoritized, even in cities with larger pan-Indian populations like Denver. Walt and Jim have dubbed these skate jams "ONE Gathering Skate for Life," and they make an effort to hold one a year in each location (although they are not always able to pull off two a year). In Denver skaters come down from Pine Ridge and other Northern Plains communities and travel from many southwestern urban and reservation-based Indigenous communities. It has a vibe similar to a small university or regional community-based powwow with about ten to fifteen booths set up to sell frybread, jewelry, or skate gear or to promote urban-based community programming, such as resources for Indigenous-specific health care, advocacy organizations, or substance abuse programs. Heavy metal, punk, and hip-hop are alternatively blasted from a DJ's speakers as Native youth swam the skatepark in a flurry of activity, getting runs in during the "Free Skate" sessions that are between the "Contest" sessions, when only a few skateboarders at a time skate for the audience of everyone else lining the edges of the park, standing two deep or sitting, hanging their legs over the edge of the bowl. This one-day event is a joyful opportunity to strengthen local and pan-Indian communities, to connect with old friends, to make new ones, and to fulfill the desire to just skate.

While the Denver contest tends to be a stand-alone event, the ONE Gathering Skate for Life at Pine Ridge is part of a much larger community celebration. It is generally held in early August the same weekend as the Ogalala Lakota National Wacipi & Fair (a four-day event including a massive powwow, a parade through town, a rodeo, several cultural activities, and the athletic events and competitions).[8] Unlike the Denver event, where the skate jam is the only thing going on, the ONE Gathering is a smaller part of a much larger community festival. Nonetheless, the event certainly does not get lost in the shuffle. Many skaters attend the event, and many community members come and watch while they are taking a break from the other events going on. The ONE Gathering and the larger Wacipi & Fair are celebrations of Lakota vibrancy and thrivance and undoubtedly are desire-based events. However, the ONE Gathering and the Stronghold Society as a whole are also implicitly established to confront teenage suicide. Tragically suicide has reach epidemic proportions on several reservations — particularly Pine Ridge. The subtitles of the ONE Gathering, "Skate for Life," and the Stronghold Society, "Live Life Call to Action Campaign," are clear references meant to counteract suicidal thinking and the importance of choosing life over death. Yet the Stronghold Society rarely describes its programs as "suicide prevention," instead choosing a rhetorical and activist strategy that revolves around Native youth's desire to skate and have fun, not the potential deficits surrounding these kids.

Suicide, substance abuse, and domestic violence are deep intergenerational traumas in Indian Country and are more ubiquitous than in almost any other U.S. community. However, most skate elders endeavor to see beyond this damage. That is, just because these things happen disproportionately in Indian Country does not mean that Native folks have to disproportionately focus on damage. Rather, they happen disproportionately in Indian Country as a direct and ongoing result of settler colonialism, and addressing this root cause through decolonial acts and reinfusing Indigenous values throughout all aspects of a community is the path to healing and wellness (e.g., Jacob 2013; Million 2013; L. B. Simpson 2013; Risling Baldy 2018). These indigenizing and decolonial acts are grounded in and prioritize hope, joy, and desire. It means not succumbing to despair or fetishizing damage but rather humanizing trauma beyond statistical measures.

APACHE SKATEBOARDS

One example of this approach is the work Doug Miles does with Apache Skateboards. Apache Skateboards is more than just the decks he designs; rather it is an artistic movement promoting the strength of Nde and

Indigenous people in general, through murals, public art, film, social media, music, and skate competitions. One part of this creative movement is a film called *Awakening* that Doug and his son, Douglas Miles Jr., made at the request of the Northern Ute tribal community of Fort Duchesne. The film features Doug Jr., someone who is already recognized through the Native skate community for his dominant skill and style, playing a character struggling with suicidal thoughts alongside a handful of other Fort Duchesne community members acting in the film. *Awakening* has a minimalist and powerful feel, as the fifteen-minute-long movie is about a young Native man who is struggling with his strong feelings and his mental health. We see this young man skateboarding to the house of a friend, who empathizes with the skater by sharing his own battle with depression; then he asserts that suicide is not a viable answer and encourages the skater to seek counseling. Next Doug Jr. skates to the tribal counseling services and has a brief talk with a counselor, who affirms her willingness to help. Evidently she means this not just for Doug Jr.'s character but for anyone in the community. *Awakening* crescendos—both plot-wise and musically—with the skater going straight from the counseling office to the tribal skatepark that is smattered with small snowy patches. He picks up a little bit of snow, looks at it, rubs it between his fingers, and then proceeds to pull off several ollie and kickflip tricks around the skatepark. The film ends with testimonials from community members who have lost family members at a young age to depression and suicide.

Awakening is not trying to naively present solutions to easily resolve the complexity of the problem, nor does it sensationalize trauma or heroize those coping with mental health challenges. Through Doug Jr.'s character and several Fort Duchesne community members, *Awakening* openly acknowledges that mental health on this reservation is a reality for all in the community and thereby humanizes the "epidemic of suicide" in Indian Country as something much more than a public health statistic. Importantly skateboarding is not presented as suicide prevention, per se. For sure skating represents hope and release, but that is only one part of the panoply of experiences and emotions in a community such as Fort Duchesne or San Carlos, where the Miles family lives. This is a far more humanizing way to talk about trauma as something that lives alongside the moments and experiences of joy, not the sole thing that defines reservation communities as permanently damaged.

Indeed, this ambivalence of despair and joy in the same space is something that Doug Miles Sr. thinks a lot about. He has a very sophisticated and nuanced understanding of this ambivalence that also aligns with academic notions of refusal and desire. In our conversations Doug and I talked a lot about how some want to portray skateboarding as an anti-drug or a solution to substance abuse or even a life-saving activity. He does not deny the extent to which skateboarding can be considered a coping mechanism; however, he is, understandably, strongly concerned when this becomes the dominant narrative about skateboarding in Indian Country, and there is a risk, then, of it becoming just another version of poverty and trauma "porn." He maintains:

There are people right now saying that "oh skateboarding is saving Native American kids from depression, alcohol" and I've heard Native people say that "oh I don't know where I'd be without skateboarding." So, I get that, but I think that it totally takes away from something . . . that is the extremely important ethereal aspect of skateboarding itself, which is: it's fun, it's about freedom of expression, there's a lot of creativity in it. (Doug Miles, interview, February 13, 2016)

Doug worries that Native skaters' agency and creativity is obscured by the notion that skating is an intentional strategy to cope with depression. He asserts that, while there are ancillary stress relief and harm reduction benefits that can come along with skateboarding, coping has very little to do with why people start skating. Instead, it is about creativity, a desire-based motivation. Doug observes:

I don't think that's why my kids ended up skating, cause that's never been the angle I ever wanted to put out about Apache Skateboards, like ya, "Well, I helped these kids save themselves through skate-boarding." I think that's rather pompous and that's not only pomp-ous I think it's misleading . . . I refuse to pigeonhole what we do and what we've done in that category, because Apache Skateboards, I say, "is not a quote, let's save the Indians with skateboarding, unquote organization." It never has been and never will be, but that doesn't mean that we don't want help, that doesn't mean we don't need help, that doesn't mean that I'm not cool with allies or ally-ship that's from off the rez, that doesn't mean that at all. I'm just saying that I think [when you] continually hammer away [on skateboarding as a solution to social ills] you keep painting the res-ervation as a negative space. Skateboarding is not about negative space, it's about the reinvention of space, it's about the reclaiming of space, it's about the taking over of space, it's about turning the space of anywhere you're skating into your very own. And in that process, you become one with the space, not in that stereotypical dreamlike Native-American-one-with-nature, but the reality of it is, skateboarders become one with the physical surroundings by reinventing to it. (Miles, interview)

Treating skateboarding primarily as a coping mechanism denies the cre-ativity, ingenuity, and innovation of skateboarding. Moreover, like many forms of art, pain and trauma can be highly generative of creativity, not creativity's death knell. Conceiving of Indian Country as predominantly damaged spaces overwrites how joy, hope, creativity, *and* pain and trau-ma can all be part of the same human experience. Just as in the short film *Awakening*, made with his son, Doug Sr. refuses simplistic solutions with unambiguous answers that would limit complexity and beauty. This is the kind of sophisticated wisdom characteristic of a community elder.

The respect that Doug Sr. garners from younger Native skaters is very self-evident when you see him interact with them in public. It is not just with his own children that he maintains a mentoring relationship, but also with many young skaters from his own San Carlos community and many other young Diné (Navajo), Akimel O'otham (Gila River Pima), and

Tohono O'odham skaters. Doug helped build the small skatepark in San Carlos and often hangs out there helping film, photograph, and host events for local skaters. Every time I have seen him at a public event, whether at an art gallery or a skatepark, young Native skateboarders come say hello and pay their respect by dapping him up. There is little doubt that many Indigenous skaters look up to him and see him as a mentor—even if he himself is not actually skating with them.

4 WHEEL WAR PONY

Many of these same Indigenous skaters from the Southwest (and beyond) that connect with Doug also equally look up to another Apache skate elder, Dustinn Craig. Dustinn hails from the White Mountain Apache and Navajo Nation communities. Simultaneous to the beginnings of Miles's Apache Skateboards, Dustinn created another Indigenous skateboarding brand, 4 Wheel War Pony Skateboards, that is also about so much more than just skateboarding, such as art, anime, Indigenous culture, film-making, decolonizing practices, and more. Dustinn learned the value of creativity and a multivariate skillset from his father, Vincent Craig. Vincent was a prominent citizen of the Navajo Nation as a multitalented, multimedia artist, who, among many other things, created the *Navajo Times*-published political cartoon "Mutton Man." He has had a huge influence on Dustinn's life, both in terms of creativity and striving for social and political justice. The maternal side of Dustinn's family comes from a part of the White Mountain Ndee community known as Whiskey Flats, a housing development just a few miles northwest of the fabled Fort Apache. Dustinn grew up at both Whiskey Flats and Fort Defiance (Navajo Nation), and today he lives in the former, although he acknowledges both his Diné and Ndee cultures. Dustinn and his family have been skateboarding in Indian Country as long as anyone, a fact documented by a unique photo published in *National Geographic* magazine in 1980.

The February issue of that year (volume 157) included a three-article spread on the White Mountain Apache Reservation. Two of the articles are titled "Their Past and Future" and "Seeking the Best of Two Worlds."

Today these titles would seem rather cliché; however, for this time period, the representations of Indianness through text and images in this three-article spread was anything but clichéd, myopic essentializing. I read it as a progressive deviation from *National Geographic's* more common practice of exoticizing and patronizing people of color by portraying them outside of contemporary time, as if "foreign" cultures were nothing more than insightful glimpses into the primitive past of the magazine's predominately white subscribers—a way for white American readers to understand their "civilized" modernity in contrast to "undeveloped" primitiveness of the rest of the world (see Lutz and Collins 1993; Torgovnik 1990; Fabian 1983; Huhndorf 2001). This "White Mountain Apache" feature is one of the most progressive (non-Indigenous produced) mainstream media pieces that I have read from the late 1970s: two of the three authors are N'dee, the article deals with both cultural traditions and modern engagement in the contemporary world, and the photographs sophisticatedly present the complexity of White Mountain Apache life in the past, present, and future (Lupe 1980; Quintero 1980; Hess 1980). A main reason why this piece had such a clear understanding of the complexity of contemporaneous White Mountain life is that the author and photographer Bill Hess had been living there for a few years—not just a drop-in to take pictures and leave. As he notes in his article, "Seeking the Best of Two Worlds," in college he met a White Mountain Apache woman, married her, and subsequently moved with her to live in Carrizo, a village on the reservation near Whiskey Flats (Hess 1980). Once there he befriended Vincent Craig, in large part because they were both outsiders who had married into the White Mountain community, even though the origin of their "outsiderness" was quite different: Vincent, Navajo and Bill, white.

The coda of the three-article spread is an image of two teenage boys playing in the street in Whiskey Flats. One teen is wearing an animated Bruce Lee T-shirt and blue jeans while riding a horse with a rope wrapped around the saddle horn. At the other end of the rope is a teen in jeans and a cutoff generic football jersey holding on with one hand while using the other to help balance on the plastic skateboard he's riding.

Arguably this picture is more like "land waterskiing" than what we would today (or even in the early 1980s), describe as skateboarding; however, the presence of the board, the way the boys are dressed, and the paved road they are on all signify a kind of Native modernity. What's more, these boys also happen to be Dustinn's uncles—the very people that a few years later introduced Dustinn to skateboarding.

The photo's caption describes the boy being towed, Dwayne Johnson, as a "skateboard novice" (Hess 1980, 290). While it is true that being towed behind a horse is a relatively rudimentary form of skateboarding and the board itself is not quite up to the technological level that, say, the Z-Boys and their progeny were riding at this same time, "novice" is probably a mislabeling of Dwayne. When this picture was snapped, Dwayne had, in fact, been skateboarding for a while. Indeed, Dwayne and his friends skateboarded so much that Vincent Craig (Dwayne's older brother-in-law) and Bill decided to hold a skate contest for the local White Mountain kids in 1978, two years *before* the *National Geographic* article was published. The contest more closely resembled "Freestyle" skateboarding, a style of moves that characterize the cohort of skaters whom the Dogtown crew were reacting against and ultimately, for the most part, replaced. This freestyle was based more on spins, balance tricks, and jumping tricks than the power-sliding aggressive surf-style of the Z-Boys.[9] Dwayne took first place in two events, so he was clearly more than just a novice. This was almost certainly the first skate contest in Indian Country even though it was not quite the form that skating would become.[10] Dustinn was about three years old at this time, and it is when his uncles started to put him on a board. As he grew older, the revolution in skating began to take hold at White Mountain, and Dustinn and his friends were emulating the moves of the Bones Brigade and other skaters who emphasized verticality over the flat ground tricks of freestyle.

Since this precocious introduction to skating from his uncle Dwayne and his friends, Dustinn has spent the last forty-some years of his life skateboarding, whether at Whiskey Flats or Fort Defiance, or in the Phoenix metro area when he was going to college and raising his own family, or at any other prime skate spot throughout the Southwest. Skateboarding was a ubiquitous feature in Dustinn's life, and he frequently had a crew of "homies" with whom he skated in these various spots. Nevertheless, it was not till the mid-1990s, when he had his own budding family, that Dustinn began to assume a role of skateboarding mentor the way his uncle Dwayne had with him. During this time Dustinn and his wife decided to settle their young family in his home community of Whisky Flats.[11] Once moving there, Dustinn began to work on a project out of the White Mountain Apache Youth Center called Healthy Nations that promoted health and wellness among tribal youth. He had not lived at White Mountain for a while; consequently, much of this time was spent reconnecting with his culture and the community, which he was able to do through film, multimedia, and art workshops that he ran with tribal youth on the Healthy Nations project. Dustinn was still skateboarding frequently during this time period, but mostly by himself, as he had thought the White Mountain skate culture died in the early 1990s, and he had not been aware of anyone else skating in White Mountain. Then, seemingly out of nowhere, an opportunity came up: his colleagues at Healthy Nations were running weekly events called "play dates" meant to get kids outside, moving around, and athletically active. These colleagues knew how much Dustinn was involved in skateboarding, so they asked him to run a skate expo and contest for one of these play dates. It took a little convincing, but Dustinn agreed, and in so doing he essentially initiated a revival of skate culture at White Mountain.

Dustinn started by garnering some grant money, buying a bunch of wood, and setting to work building a skatepark inside of an empty warehouse that was part of the tribe's fairgrounds complex. Additionally, he used his connections in the Phoenix skate community and his intimate knowledge of the skateboard industry to contact skate shops and skate companies all throughout the United States to hustle free gear to be given away at the skate jam. This proved to be very fruitful, as he secured tons of free stickers, decks, and T-shirts as donations to pass out to participants and the audience. Ultimately, the event was a tremendous success. Dustinn was particularly touched by all his skate homies from Window Rock, Gallup, Chinle, Phoenix, and Tucson who show up to support him and this event for Native skateboarding. Even more of a revelation for Dustinn was the number of White Mountain *and* San Carlos Apache "skate rats" that "came out from under the rocks" to participate in the event (Dustinn Craig, interview, June 7, 2020). This was hugely significant because it illustrated to Dustinn that the potential for an Apache-based skate community was still there, and it set him off on a new life path. He now sought to be a mentor to this newer generation of local Ndee skaters in the same way his uncle Dwayne, his father, and Bill Hess all did for him.

After the skate jam, Dustinn was able to keep the ramps and ledges he built in the fairground warehouse so he and all these young White Mountain Apache skaters (and occasionally San Carlos Apache and Navajo skaters as well) could skate in their own community on a regular basis. Hence, the concept of the 4 Wheels War Pony team was born. Soon they were scouting new skate spots on the reservation and visiting ones where Dustinn skated when he was in his teens. The crew would also scavenge and salvage wood to build ramps elsewhere in the community. Perhaps the height of this White Mountain skate revival came in 2011 when one of the young riders that Dustinn had mentored reached out to the PBS television show *Design Squad Nation* to help them build another skatepark. *Design Squad Nation* was a show that started late in the first decade of the 2000s hosted by two young engineers who would solicit, from youth across the nation, civic engineering problems in their local communities that could be solved by the Design Squad Team's engineering know-how and labor and enthusiasm of local youth. The Design Squad Nation loved the proposal from the White Mountain kids and made their first episode about helping them build a skatepark behind the White Mountain Youth Center.[12] One highlight of the show is the host wearing a skate helmet with a 4 Wheels War Pony sticker prominently displayed across the front. Indeed, all the Ndee skateboarders featured in this show were part of the 4 Wheels War Pony team, including the young man featured as the community member who reached out to the Design Squad for assistance. This *De-*

sign Squad Nation episode was a highpoint of the 4 Wheels War Pony's influence and evidence of its successful model: a nationally broadcast show celebrating how Dustinn and his team riders took the concept of a "skate team" and indigenized it.

As discussed in chapter 6 with the Dogtown crew and the Zephyr Skate Team, in skateboarding (as in many other individualized sports) it is not uncommon for a team to form around a brand. "Riding" for a team means various different things, depending on a team's resources. It could be financial remuneration, sponsorships and contest entry fees, free branded gear, exposure and introductions to networks of greater resources, or merely the stamp of authenticity and approval—being part of a team means that someone believes that your skating has legitimacy. In some cases Dustinn was able to provide limited financial support (mostly in the form of contest entrance fees) and 4 Wheel War Pony gear, but the immaterial support of mentorship, friendship, and cultural education were perhaps Dustinn's and 4 Wheel War Pony's greatest asset. Just as his father and uncle did with him, Dustinn has shared his energy and love with his team riders—an intermittent group of five to ten Native skaters (mostly young men but including a few young women). One of the most significant ways he did this was by opening his house to young Indigenous skaters who were living in the Phoenix Valley or were part of a larger network of Indigenous skaters living on reservations or in border towns throughout the Southwest. This kind of loving mentoring is what Vincent Craig and the White Mountain Apache culture taught Dustinn, and he passed it on to those younger than him.

Surrogate family units are common in skateboarding. Sometimes they form around corporate skateboarding companies. Skaters who are sponsored by teams and brands with resources travel the world together doing expos and contests. These team structures and travel schedules often build fast and sometimes lasting friendships because of the intensity of the time spent together. Skaters who are talented and lucky enough to be on a corporate team are almost always in their formative years, and they are generally exposed to relatively grueling travel schedules often without the accompaniment of any (biological) family member. Hence a skate team can create the bonds akin to family to support each other. Additionally, there is a far more common and more organic version of surrogate skate family that happens on the grassroots level. Without discounting the incredible diversity of those who skate and of their backgrounds, it is safe to say that skateboarding tends to attract "misfits" — people who do not feel like they fit into their family, school, community, or society as a whole. Perhaps it is the counterculture nature of skating that draws them in or the creativity and relative freedom from rules and institutionalized structure (see Weyland 2002; Wheaton and Beal 2003; Kelly, Pomerantz, and Currie 2005; Atencio, Beal, and Winston 2009; Yochim 2009). Often these skaters, who come from dysfunctional families or feel alienated from normative society, are referred to as "skate rats." In many ways this is an endearing reference to these kids or young adults who tend to express their identity through skateboarding, adhere to a particularly "punk" or "goth" aesthetic, and espouse a DIY ("do it yourself") ethos.[13] Sometimes collections of skate rats form ad hoc "skate houses" by either squatting in an abandoned property or congregating and cohabitating for days at a time at the residence of a slightly older skate rat who lives on their own and has some means of paying rent.

For about a year in the mid-2010s, Dustinn sponsored his own version of a skate house. He had moved from White Mountain back down to Phoenix Valley in the early 2010s and was renting a house in Mesa, Arizona. Soon he began to open his home to folks in his skate crew in order for them to just hang out during the day or occasionally even crash overnight. His only request was that this emergent "skate house" not become a full-on party house. Dustinn had chosen to be sober during this period, and so while he never banned anyone from engaging in any activity, per se, he asked that they be discrete for his own sanity and as a way to make the house a place of support, not a place of lawless hedonism. Many of those who would come by were 4 Wheel War Pony riders, others were local friends of his oldest son, some were aspiring to be on the skate team, and almost all of them were in their late teens or early twenties.

In many ways this was an idyllic time for Dustinn. As he puts it, "Every skater's dream is to have a skate house and have a solid fucking crew, and you have editing and film equipment, and dope cameras" (Dustinn Craig, interview). In between his own work schedule, Dustinn would join them for several skate sessions a day to hone their skills, often he would feed them, and then at the end of the day he would give them a place to sleep for as long as they needed. By opening his house, Dustinn was building a skate family around youth who had unstable home lives and sometimes were on the verge of homelessness. He invited them in to be a part of his family; moreover, since many were Indigenous (mostly Apache or Navajo) he inflected this surrogate "family" with Ndee cultural values and Indigenous knowledge taught to him while he was growing up in Whiskey Flats and Fort Defiance. To reflect these values Dustinn started to call this crew "Young Raiders," as a way to connect these young adults with the way traditional Apache culture framed the stage in life in which many of them were.[14] Dustinn mentored these skaters in the importance of who they were as Indigenous people and how this identity and cultural base provided them with the life skills to be responsible to their community—whether that be a skate community, an Indigenous community, or any intentional social community.

While Dustinn definitely skated with these kids, he also spent a lot of time video-recording them skating. He was working on a short film that could act as a promotional video for the 4 Wheel War Pony team in a way that would gain exposure for several of the riders and increase the team's overall access to resources so that Dustinn and his riders could potentially make a career out of Indigenous skateboarding. Dustinn shared with me that the pinnacle of this time for their ad hoc skate house (and perhaps the 4 Wheel War Pony team) was the night when they had a backyard screening of the film he had been working on for a few years that he titled *Young Raiders* (Dustinn Craig, interview). It was a lively community event, with fifty-some people jammed into the side yard of the Mesa skate house to watch this thirty-five-minute movie and a few other shorts made by others in the crew. Additionally, they also raised over a thousand dollars through raffle tickets. This allowed

4 Wheel War Pony to buy the team riders new shoes, new boards, and other skate gear. This joyous evening celebrated the achievements and the bonds of friendship developed around skateboarding and the pan-Indigenous community in and around the Phoenix Valley.

While this "movie premier" was a first at their skate house, it was hardly Dustinn's first film. Indeed, Dustinn's own filmmaking is the central part of the 4 Wheels War Pony team and his role as a skate elder for these Indigenous skaters. At this point in his life Dustinn was a very accomplished filmmaker who had more than one nationally broadcast documentary. His most acclaimed piece is a documentary he wrote, directed, and produced for the renowned PBS series *American Experience*. In 2009 *American Experience* sponsored a five-part documentary on U.S. history from a Native American perspective called "We Shall Remain," and Dustinn directed *Part IV: Geronimo*. He was selected to direct this episode as part of a national search of Indigenous filmmakers in 2005. He was honored to have been selected because this was an important story for him personally, but it is far from an easy story to tell, given that the lore of Geronimo has been continuously manufactured for over a century. Portraying the life of Geronimo in the documentary required Dustinn to navigate a complex set of discourses that circulate around the "mythic" Apache warrior and the actual human being. Geronimo is coded by white America as both a ruthless savage outlaw and a noble savage warfare genius. Conventional American history tends to disconnect him from his community by absorbing him into the panoply of legendary rugged individuals of the "Old West." Within Indian Country as a whole, he is often coded as a relentless freedom fighter or revolutionary. And for the various Apache communities, he can be seen as both a cult hero or someone who terrorized different Apache bands as much as he did to the U.S. and Mexican federal governments. From a strict historical perspective, it is Ndee scouts from Dustinn's White Mountain Apache community that helped the U.S. Cavalry hunt Geronimo down, in part because Geronimo himself did not always treat the people from White Mountain fairly. However, like many contemporary Indigenous folks, Dustinn also admires the decolonial discourses that are embodied through Geronimo. All of this made the film a very personal project for Dustinn and provided the opportunity for a huge amount of self-reflection while making the film. Much of his self-reflection circulated around what it meant to be from White Mountain in relationship to other Ndee bands, what life was like for White Mountain Apaches in the nineteenth and early twentieth centuries, and what was the cultural role and significance of Ndee men and boys (Craig, interview, December 2, 2016). It was Dustinn's cultural exploration while making this film that planted the seed for how 4 Wheel War Pony could be an all-encompassing Indigenous skateboarding brand and team.

A key cinematic tool for all the episodes in the *We Shall Remain* docuseries was dramatic reenactment. This was particularly the case for the first four films, all of which cover events that happened before the widespread availability to video-record them. In *Geronimo* Dustinn chose to focus most of the reenactment scenes around "young raiders"—Ndee males, in their mid-teens to late twenties. Dustinn used these characters of young raiders both to portray the White Mountain Apache scouts who helped the Cavalry pursue Geronimo and in other scenes as Geronimo's band members who raided Mexican, American, and other Indigenous communities of the Southwest in order to obtain resources while on the run from the U.S. Cavalry. The actors that Dustinn enlisted to portray these roles were his own sons and a few of the "skate rats" from his White Mountain Apache crew. Despite the fact that most of these reenactment scenes were quite short (none more than about forty-five seconds long), Dustinn conducted a significant amount of research on traditions of Apache raiding because it was crucial for him to maintain cultural accuracy and legitimacy in these scenes. Many of the academic books and ethnographic reports that he read as part of his research—despite almost always being written by white men—reaffirmed much of what he learned from his extended family growing up at White Mountain about the importance of courage, responsibility to community, and how vital intergenerational mentoring was.

The process of shooting these reenactment scenes tremendously affected Dustinn and his family and friends who played the young raider roles (Craig, interviews, December 1, 2016, June 7, 2020). Most of these scenes were shot in the White Mountains—either on contemporary Apache reservation land or traditional land stolen at the inception of the reservation—and the regalia the actors wore was based on photographs from the late nineteenth century. Hence, Dustinn's family and friends, qua actors, were fully embodying the history of their people—at a critical juncture in the late nineteenth century when settler colonialism was rapidly devastating the cultural traditions of raiding, the close-knit social relations that came from living in small bands, and the model of informal leadership that had defined Ndee communities for thousands of years prior. This made the filming process inherently self-reflexive for Dustinn and his reenactors. For Dustinn, it was also when he began to fully embrace his role as an informal leader or mentor to younger Indigenous skateboarders. He began to recognize the Ndee responsibility and leadership necessary for headmen to maintain their relationship to the raiders that followed them in himself and his own relationships with the younger skateboarders he was mentoring. Intensely contemplating Geronimo and Dustinn's own ancestors who helped track Geronimo, while at the same time being dedicated to contemporary Ndee youth—particularly young men—and helping them mature in wellness and in healthy environments, Dustinn began to recognize the tremendous parallels between Indigenous "skate rats" of his present and Ndee raiders of his people's past.

Age was the most self-evident parallel between the raiders of the past and his skate crew in the present. A Ndee raider would being to train and hone their skills in their early teens, participate in raids in their late teens and early twenties, and then potentially begin to lead raiding parties in their late twenties (Craig, interview December 1, 2016; Opler and Hoijer 1940; Goodwin 1971; Watt 2002). This age span precisely corresponds to the ages of Dustinn, his sons, and the Indigenous skaters with whom Dustinn was rolling. This affinity in age and stage of life between the people Dustinn was directing for his movie (and skating with when not filming) and the young Apache warriors whom they were portraying had a huge impact on Dustinn. Soon he started calling the kids in his skate crew the "young raiders." He did this both colloquially when talking about them and formally in promotion videos for the 4 Wheel War Pony skate team.

One video in particular, titled *When History Becomes Real*, connects Ndee skaters of today with Apache Scouts of the past (Craig 2017). This short, less than two-minute promotion, starts with a black screen and then, in the yellow font Dustinn generally uses for 4 Wheel War Pony, appear the Ndee words *Dzilgaha Linbaha Dziltaadn*. The phrase generally translates to "the people of White Mountain," and as it emerges out of the black backdrop so too does the jangly, echoing electric guitar over a subtle but consistent bass line. The song adds an ethereal, dreamlike quality to the images that come through in faded grays, blues, browns, and reds of four young men walking through a high mountain meadow in Apache raider regalia all carrying rifles. These actors from Dustinn's film, who are all also his longtime skater friends, stride steadily and gracefully toward the camera to the beat of the baseline, as wind and their pace cause their long hair, loose shirts, and bandanas to flow across their bodies and faces. Approximately every five seconds a sharp guitar chord pierces the rhythm, and images slightly blur or shift as the chord reverberates. Frequently these shifts are to jump-cut edits to contemporary Ndee skateboarders wearing baggy jeans and T-shirts or hoodies that flow like the traditional regalia in the wind or holding their decks horizontally with the similar lines and angle as the rifles the scouts carry. There is no dialogue, but the visual and audio powerfully draw a connection between past and present. Toward the end of the promotion the camera pans and briefly captures faces of the actors as they pass by in their raiding regalia. On the last actor-skater's face, one can just catch a glimpse of a joyful grin—illustrating how much this young Ndee skater is enjoying playing the role of a traditional raider. Finally, the video fades to black, and then, just before the credits, the phrase "Decolonize History" materializes in the same yellow font as the beginning.

This short film is a powerful statement for the viewer to recognize how frequently Indigenous history has been represented by non-Indians and how a decolonized, self-representation of Indigenous history may more accurately depict how much Native people connect to their past and still live it into the present. The film speaks to a notion that American Indians (despite popular imagination) are still present and present in a way that acknowledges their deep history. For current Ndee tribal members, like the one smiling at the end of the video, this connection is empowering and an enjoyable reminder that no matter what happens or in what they like to participate, they will always be Ndee. Dustinn posted this promotional video to his Vimeo account (Craig 2017) and other social media platforms. Hence, the circulation of this short film enhanced the pride the actors-skaters have for their culture and for their current love for skateboarding.

The dual settler colonial practices of forced assimilation through the boarding school system and promotion of market capitalism have laid waste to the traditional practices of becoming an Apache "raider" (and the mentoring processes therein). Nonetheless, Apaches (like all human communities) still understand the significance and responsibility of mentoring youth through maturity. In most American Indian communities, missionaries explicitly aimed to convert Native processes of maturing to adulthood through new customs that center nuclear family development and the church. Youth were taught or forced to respect and learn from their parents (mainly fathers) and religious institutions above all else. Later market capitalist imperatives were similarly disruptive by regimenting secular education that forced learning into discrete time slots and subject matters and established value systems that mark gainful employment and individual economic independence as the sign of successful maturation to adulthood. In most cases these goals run completely counter to the values of Indigenous communities and arguably have been the main source of upheaval and devastation in American Indian communities over the last 150 years. Indigenous values such as that extended family is equally as important as nuclear family, that learning comes in a variety of forms and sources including intense self-contemplation, and that adulthood is marked not by accumulation and independence but by proving one's ability to be responsible to and support the community as a whole have been significantly disrupted by settler colonialism. Some Indigenous epistemologies around coming of age have survived, albeit with changes; this forced assimilation, particularly in the form of girls coming-of-age ceremonies. Native communities in the Southwest have perhaps the most consistent continuity with their girls' coming-of-age ceremonies, although they are certainly still vibrant in other parts of Indian Country (see Talamentz 2003; Risling Baldy 2018). Dustinn was exposed to the coming-of-age ceremonies for Navajo (*kinaaldá*) and Apache (*na'ii'ees*) young women as he was growing up and in his own fatherhood of a Ndee-Diné daughter.[15] He was also acutely aware of the relative paucity of parallel ceremonies for boys still in existence. This all came to a head for him while filming young Ndee skaters in traditional raider gear, gliding lithely across the high desert plains and holding rifles; this scene heightened Dustinn's contemplation of historic and contemporary young adulthood of Ndee men.

Dustinn notes that the optimal skateboarding body type is one that is lean, strong, lanky, flexible, and agile (Craig, interviews, February 16 and December 1, 2016). These physical features help street skaters get off the ground easier, contort their bodies to maintain balance or fall the proper way, and allow for the fast-twitch reflexes and synchronous movements necessary to manipulate the board and one's body around the board. At the same time, this is the body type that made Ndee raiders successful. They had to be strong without expending too much energy and be able to go for days on a small amount of food. They also needed agility to move stealthily around an encampment they were raiding and escape quickly. Additionally, skateboarding requires a disciplined and resilient mindset: you have to be willing to fail/fall (often with some painful consequences) over and over again in order to successfully pull off a trick. Ndee raiding as well requires the forbearance to be away from one's home comforts for several days and the fortitude to go with little food or water for several days at a time when swiftly returning home from a raid (Opler and Hoijer 1940; Goodwin 1971; Watt 2002). Seeing the physical and mental similarities, Dustinn had a brilliant breakthrough: skateboarding as a contemporary way to mentor young men through adulthood by cultivating their strength and discipline. He began to talk with the young adults with whom he skated more and more about historic Ndee culture. Sharing with them what he had learned about what it meant to be a "raider" and how similar that was to being a dedicated skateboarder.

Moreover, he began to think about his role as a mentor (as a skate elder, if you will), who, like headmen of old, would lead groups of young men merely by charisma and experience. Using this analogy, there was little doubt Dustinn had the skateboarding credibility to stake a claim of experience and legitimacy. He had been skating in Indian Country since he was a toddler, but he also had spent a lot of time skating in urban locales and had made himself very familiar with overall skate subculture and skate industry. His experience, his ability to think critically about his own experience, and then his ability to successfully communicate that to those around him are what make him a skate elder. With this skill set and the respect that came along with it, Dustinn helped guide and support young Indigenous skaters through the world of amateur contests, sponsorship offers, and sponsorship decisions—all the while teaching them a sense of self-determination to control their own media and brand representations. Additionally, he shared with them his own life experiences with family relations, settler colonialism, and cultural tradition in an effort to help develop life skills in general.

Just like with headmen of days past, these young skaters, whom Dustinn referred to as "young raiders," engaged with Dustinn because of the skills he could teach them and the wisdom and experience he offered. But also, just like in days past, this did not mean that they always followed him per se. Some would come in and out of his life (and his skate house in Phoenix), others would engage with other Indigenous skate crews at the same time or instead of 4 Wheels War Pony, and some would ultimately start their own skate teams and brands, potentially becoming mentors for a younger generation of skaters. As with historic Ndee headmen, leadership and mentoring were informal and often episodic. This nicely fits the skater's life as well, in that most people drawn to skateboarding appreciate it for its flexibility and creative improvisation—its freedom within structure. Furthermore, Dustinn does not necessarily view his mentoring role to these "young raiders" as merely metaphoric (Craig, interview, June 7, 2020). For sure he talks with them about leveraging existing resources of the skate industry for their own purposes—a sort of appropriating of someone else's resources for their own needs. However, he also shared with me how, on more than one occasion when skaters wanted to build their own DIY skatepark, he would round up a few skaters in his truck. They would then go out in the middle of night and visit three or four construction sites in reservation border towns and steal small amounts of wood and supplies from these construction sites in order to build themselves ramps or ledges. This is an actual enactment of Ndee raiding culture, trusting a headman to put together a plan to surreptitiously acquire resources. To Dustinn, 4 Wheels War Pony was more than just a way to indigenize skate culture; it was a way to enliven the long-held Ndee values of respect, mentorship, and courage. And this, as is true with the other lifelong Native skaters I discuss in this chapter, is what makes Dustinn Craig a skate elder.

CONCLUSION

One way to measure successful mentorship may not be so much in the length of the mentoring relationship, but rather whether mentees begin to see themselves as mentors to those coming up after them. The effect of replicating a mentoring relationship creates an open-ended transmission of tradition and culture from one generation to the next.[16] Many of the skate elders that I discuss in this chapter have been successful in this regard. Todd Harder and his Native Skates brand have positively impacted many skaters who have participated in the All Nations Skate Jam (ANSJ)—particularly those for whom Todd's event provided a venue to promote their own budding skate companies or brand. For example, Navajo skater Clint Dayzie used a booth at the ANSJ to promote his brand, Purity, and in turn he sought to model for his younger nephews the way American Indians could take control of their lives by starting their own businesses (Clint Dayzie, interview, July 1, 2015).

Jim Murphy and Walt Pourier, through their work with Stronghold Society and Wounded Knee Skateboards, have paved the way for other Native community–based skaters such as Leander Begay, a Navajo skater who founded Dead Pawn Skateboards. While not directly connected to Jim and Walt, he has followed their lead in getting involved in the skate community at Pine Ridge. Leander helps cohost the Toby Eagle Bull Classic, a skate contest held every summer at the Wounded Knee Four Directions Toby Eagle Bull Memorial Skate Park—the park that Walt and Jim got built through the Stronghold Society and WK4-Directions. The contest honors the life of a Lakota skater from Pine Ridge who tragically died in a car accident at age twenty. Leander is one of the main advocates of the Toby Eagle Bull Classic, an annual event that is composed almost completely of kids from age ten to twenty and promotes a joy for life through skateboarding. Leander is so dedicated to mentoring these young Lakota skateboarders that he makes the nearly 1,200-mile drive every year to be with them, and he has started to design an annual "Toby Classic" skateboard that his company, Dead Pawn Skateboards, sells with proceeds going to support the Toby Eagle Bull Classic. Walt and Jim did not directly mentor Leander, but their development of the skatepark at Pine Ridge and their influence on and support of skating on the reservation has made it possible for Leander to cohost the event with the Eagle Bull family, whereby he now directly mentors a new generation of Lakota skaters.

Furthermore, Doug and Dustinn have had a huge impact on Native skaters throughout Indian Country in and around the Southwest. In fact, in several cases they have inspired the same kids at different times in these young people's lives.[17] As a result of the momentous influence they have had on adolescent Indigenous skaters who ride either for the Apache Skateboards or 4 Wheel War Pony teams, a handful of these kids have gone on to start their own skate crews, companies, and brands with the explicit interest of mentoring younger skaters just like Dustinn and Doug did for them. This younger generation has established two of the most on-the-rise Native skate brands: Enchantment Skateboards and Maize Skateboards. Enchantment Skateboards, based in Gallup, New

Mexico, was founded by a young married Navajo skateboarding couple, Cecely and Jeremy Todacheenie. Maize Skateboards is the brainchild of Laguna Pueblo skater Victor Corpuz. Victor partnered with one of his skate buddies, Shawn Harrison, an artist from the Navajo Nation, to help him run and promote Maize skateboards and share in the creative labor and fun involved in running a skateboard brand. It is a collaborative effort between Diné and Pueblo skaters, and much of the activity comes out of either Farmington, New Mexico, where Shawn lives or central New Mexico where Victor splits his time between Albuquerque and Laguna Pueblo. These four skaters and business partners are part of a larger crew of Southwest Indigenous skaters, almost all of whom grew up skating together and in conjunction with Doug or Dustinn. Now, even though they have some of their own separate projects, they cross-promote each other's brands and spend a ton of their free time traveling between their various home communities throughout the Four Corners region. They all consider collaboration essential to what they want to do and the community of Indigenous skaters they want to build. To that end they try to connect in person as much as possible so they can skate together, bounce ideas and artistic visions off each other, and just generally enjoy the mutual bond to skate and Indigenous cultures that they share. These relationships through skating have developed into deep, loving friendships and support networks (Young Raiders, interview, December 2, 2016). I have been fortunate enough to spend time with them all on several occasions when they are hanging out and skating: it is pure fun and joy to get to be around them. Their positive relationships and the time they get to spend together most certainly challenges the narrative of deficit and despair that too often circulates around Indian Country.

Moreover, they all actively seek to bring this fun and joy to the generation coming up behind them, just as those coming up before them have done. For example, Cecely was one of two women who rode for 4 Wheels War Pony, and she received tremendous support from Dustinn. This support and Dustinn's constant progressive mind frame of working for the community helped guide Cecely and Jeremy to think about what they could do for the youth of Gallup (Cecley and Jeremy Todacheenie, interview, August 17, 2016). Cecely frequently participates in events specifically geared toward empowering girls to skate more (more on this in the next chapter). Additionally, she and her partner Jeremy sought to improve skateboarding for all the youth in Gallup, New Mexico. In 2015 they embarked on a project to get a new skatepark built in the historic downtown section of the city. They convinced the city council of their plan, were able to help design the skatepark, and secured external funding from charitable community-based organizations. In late June 2018 they finally realized their goal with the grand opening of the Gallup Skatepark. Moreover, they were also able to secure rental space in a storage facility adjacent to the skatepark, which they remodeled and reopened as the Enchantment Skate Shop—and recently they moved locations into an even larger shop. The Todacheenies are providing a valuable service here, given that it is the only skate shop for at least a hundred-mile radius. This helps all the youth in Gallup and the several reservations surrounding Gallup with an easy destination to buy skate gear they need. What's more, the skate shop and skatepark have become hubs of action where youthful skaters hang out for several hours a day, going back and forth between the shop and the park. Here they are creating a safe communal space for Native and non-Native youth. Indeed, it is one of the brighter spots in the Gallup community, and it exists because of Jeremy's and Cecely's commitment to build something for the benefit of the generation below them. Actions like this are indications that Cecely, Jeremy, Victor, and Shawn are working their way toward being skate elders in the not-too-distant future.

NATIVE WOMEN AND NONBINARY SKATERS

Perhaps the most important (if not most heralded) event of the last twenty years for Turtle Island Indigenous communities was the activism of the #NODAPL "Water Protectors" encamped on the Standing Rock Sioux Reservation who were fighting to prohibit the construction of the Dakota Access Pipeline under Lake Oahe, which borders the Standing Rock Reservation. This pipeline would have put the reservation's main source of clean water under grave threat by transporting more than a half-million barrels of shale crude oil a day. A leak in this pipeline (all too common) would devastate this community, and they were giving little say about the route of the pipeline. Thousands came to this site to help protect the tribe's water sources, and millions more used social media to support and promote the protest and protection of this sacred resource. One person who came to Standing Rock to get a firsthand glimpse of the situation was Dustinn Craig. Always the filmmaker, Dustinn decided to go and record footage of this historic moment.

In early fall 2016, a friend of Dustinn's called him up and suggested they make a plan to go to Standing Rock, despite the fact that neither really had enough financial resources to make the trip nor that Dustinn could afford some of the film equipment he would need. Nevertheless, they decided that they could figure that out on the way and that they would just start the twenty-two-hour drive from Phoenix to Standing Rock and see what would happen. One of the first stops they made was Gallup, New Mexico, where Dustinn met up with Jeremy and Cecely Todacheenie, a young, Navajo married couple described in chapter 7, both of whom Dustinn had been mentoring for a few years in connection to 4 Wheel War Pony. Dustinn had first met them a handful of years earlier when Cecely and Jeremy came to a skate jam he hosted at the Zuni Pueblo (forty miles south of Gallup). As their friendship developed, he helped them think about how to make careers in the skate industry. This mentoring relationship flourished when Dustinn invited Cecely to join his team of riders—establishing her as one of the first Native women to be a sponsored skater! As the relationship between the three of them blossomed, the Todacheenies began thinking about a large project to revitalize the skate scene in Gallup. They endeavored to reestablish a skatepark in downtown Gallup that had long been abandoned and torn down. Cecely and Jeremy successfully lobbied the city council to approve the construction and got to be intimately involved in the design and fabrication process. Dustinn had been advising them on different aspects of this project, including ways to raise some funds for part of the project (Jeremy and Cecely Todacheenie, interview, August 17, 2016). During the time period that they were having these ongoing conversations about how to get a skatepark built in Gallup, their tight community of Indigenous skaters was rocked by a local tragedy. Their dear friend Nick Humphrey passed away at the all-too-young age of twenty. As traumatic as this was, though, they were able to use their mutually collective love of skateboarding to find some healing from Nick's youthful passing.

Nick's passing happened about a year before Dustinn had passed through Gallup on his way to Standing Rock. By all accounts Nick was a lively spirit, and all who knew him loved to skate and hang out with him. In response to his passing, Dustinn worked with Cecely and Jeremy to create a 4 Wheel War Pony deck in honor of Nick. The deck was a mini collage of photos detailing Nick's love for life and skating. This "in memorial" deck helped bring some peace to those that Nick left behind and created a way for Nick's legacy to continue. Some of the proceeds from the deck went to the project to build the Gallup skatepark, thereby contributing to the well-being of Indigenous skaters who can now use it for generations to come. This sense of healing is heightened by the fact that emblazoned on the concrete at the center of the skatepark is a painted-on medicine wheel—a trans-tribal symbol of healing and harmony.[1] In essence, with this relatively small act of honoring their skate homie, Dustinn, Cecely, and Jeremy contributed to a perpetual cycle of intergenerational relations of wellness, even though kids who now skate at the Gallup Skatepark may have never met (or even necessarily heard of) Nick Humphrey. Similarly, the kids who will skate there in ten to twenty years may never meet Dustinn, Cecely, and Jeremy, but their efforts will live on.

The Nick Humphrey memorial board also had a more immediate impact on Dustinn's life. Dustinn stopped in Gallup to see Cecely and Jeremy while on his way to the Water Protector encampment at Standing Rock. On that day he met up with Cecely and Jeremy and explained to them his desire to go film the water protectors. Immediately Cecely and Jeremy offered Dustinn financial support for this endeavor, and they were able to do so because they had some extra money from the Nick Humphrey deck sales (Jeremy and Cecely Todacheenie, interview; Dustinn Craig, interview, June 7, 2020). The beautiful twist here is that the mentees could now help one of their mentors. Dustinn was able to get the film equipment he needed, he continued on to Standing Rock, and ultimately he recorded some unique footage that he is using to make a film about the events and people at Standing Rock. Sponsoring Cecely as a team rider for 4 Wheel War Pony, Dustinn was able to promote her career in skateboarding, and now Cecely returned the support by aiding Dustinn in his filmmaking career.

As valuable as this mentoring relationship has been, specifically between Dustinn and Cecely, it still has limitations, when we consider it from a perspective of gender analysis. There is no doubt that it was incredibly forward thinking of Dustinn to include a female skateboarder as part of his team, especially when we consider how male-dominated skateboarding has been for the last forty-some years. What's more, Cecely was not the only woman who joined the team. Around the same time Cecely was invited, Dustinn also asked Jazmine Barney, another Navajo female skater, and then later Navajo skater Di'orr Greenwood to ride for 4 Wheel War Pony (Cecely Todacheenie, personal communication, October 1, 2020, Di'orr Greenwood, interview, March 4, 2020). As significant as it was for Dustinn to be so equity minded in his development of the 4 Wheel War Pony team, it is safe to say that Cecely, Jazmine, and

Di'orr would equally (and perhaps even more so) benefit from female skate mentors. This relative absence of female skateboard mentoring is far from unique to Indian Country—it is an issue for skateboarding in general. This challenge is even further compounded by the fact that skateboarding itself has been male-dominated, and in many cases misogynist, making the need for female mentorship even more critical. Fortunately, as Dustinn's mentorship (and that of other skate elders such as Doug Miles, who also had significant influence on these women) illustrates, this is beginning to change as more and more women and nonbinary skateboarders are asserting themselves into the culture and challenging its masculinist norms. In many ways Cecely, Jazmine, and Di'orr are part of a feminist wave of skateboarding, as they have been working for the last few years to mentor young Indigenous skater girls coming up after them.[2]

When mainstream and specialty (skateboard or action sports) media outlets choose to promote skateboarding, they almost always depict boys or men on boards. Despite the paucity of attention or media coverage of female skaters, they have been skateboarding since the beginning. In the pre-Dogtown days, girls were sidewalk surfing as much as boys. Take Patti McGee, the most prominent exception to the axiom I just asserted about media coverage. She appeared on the cover of *Life* magazine in 1965 to depict the entire youthful fad (not just a gendered version) of sidewalk surfing (Beal 2013). Peggy Oki is an almost forgotten original member of the Zephyr Team, but she was there busting down the doors of conventional skateboarding just like her male teammates. I describe Oki as "almost forgotten" because although she is a key visual part of Peralta's movie, she is thoroughly underreported on. Sadly, but not surprisingly, she is barely heard from or talked about in the film—a true narrative shame when we consider how fascinating and unique her role was as the only girl (and the only one in college) among all these derelict boys. Post-Dogtown, there have been several female professional skateboarders. Women such as Laura Thornhill Caswell, Cara-Beth Burnside, and Elissa Steamer have competed just as hard as the men (see Porter 2003; Beal 2013). Yet these female professional skaters, and the hundreds of thousands of amateurs like them, are rarely connected to the mainstream (if even specialist) discourses about skateboarding.

This omission or obscuration of female skaters is likely connected to the hypermasculinized image of the rebellious skater originally promoted by the Dogtown crew, despite the fact that there was a woman on their skate team and other skaters like her in this era (Porter 2003). To be clear, I critique obscuration of women skateboarders not necessarily as a unique condemnation of the hard-charging, rebellious, anti-establishment skateboarding that emerged out of the early 1970s per se. That is, it is not as if American sports culture writ large in the 1970s and 1980s was any less rife with male chauvinism and misogyny. Moreover, this sexist undercurrent surely can still be found in most sports today, despite the dramatic changes initiated by feminism and Title IX. But when it comes specifically to skating, Emily Chivers Yochim (2009) has found that the antiestablishment ethic in skateboarding, in particular, still often reinscribes mainstream gender inequality. Yochim (2009) notes that for many (mostly white) boys and men, who for whatever reason feel alienated from conventional "boy" sports, skateboarding becomes an avenue to reassert their masculinity lost by not participating in football or baseball (see also Porter 2003; Beal 1995, 1996, 1998). Many of the young male skaters she interviewed for her research in the upper Midwest responded to the emasculation that came along with not being good at (or interested in) traditional American sports by channeling a similar sexism and misogyny found in these mainstream sports into their performances of skateboarding. Yochim (2009) finds many of these male skaters engaging in similar kinds of hazing and ostracizing that kept them out of football, baseball, and other mainstream sports. Similarly, research by Matthew Atencio, Becky Beal, and Charlene Wilson (2009) also reveals the way many male skaters believe that female skaters are less worthy or authentic because they are perceived not to take the same level of risks as male skaters do. Perhaps even worse, Deirdre R. Kelly, Shauna Pomerantz, and Daen Currie (2005) find that many male skaters think of the girls and women who hang out at skate spots and shops as not even skaters, but rather groupies who are just there to watch the guys skate or to try to pick up on them, creating a fairly toxic combination of egotistical chauvinism and sexism in certain skate scenes.

Like almost all other female-identified skaters, Indigenous women skaters have at least once in their lives had similar toxic experiences with male skateboarders. Selina Mullen, a Diné (Navajo) skateboarder and artist who now resides and skates in Salt Lake City, Utah, shared with me that she/they frequently experience the sexism in skateboarding.[3] She/they assert, "Skateboarding is for everyone, but it seems like it's very common for males to be a bit more recognized and respected [than female skaters]" (Selina Mullen, personal communication, October 5, 2020). Selina has a very sophisticated understanding of the ambivalences of female skateboarding. As she/they puts it:

> Being a female in the skateboarding community can be empowering but at the same time experiencing hate. Either people look at me and feel inspired because I'm a female skateboarder or I think people could totally judge me because I'm a female and assume that I can't skate because "I'm a girl or I don't know anything." They either praise or hate you. Both sides of the spectrum. It's because of my gender, that will cause different opinions. (Mullen, personal communication)

Selina loves to skateboard and the connections that she/they have made through skating, but at the same time she/they acknowledges the way the sexism in skateboarding can be discouraging. In part, this is what makes connection and mentorship from other female (or nonbinary) skaters so important.

Despite the "freedom-from-rules" and "antiestablishment" attitudes that draw many to skateboarding, skateboarding, like any subculture, has informal codes of behavior and practices. Stylistic concerns and discrete rituals are frequently used to regiment skater identity and regulate interpersonal and spatial relations when skateboarders are skating at the same spot. Many habits and behaviors are based on the practicality of not getting in the way of someone trying a trick or avoiding high-speed collisions between people wearing very little in the way of protective gear (if any at all). Nonetheless, there are also unwritten rules of style and attitude that both mark the "cool" skaters and can be intimidating for outsiders.[4] Much of this intimidation is based on relative skill. That is, the skateboarders pulling off the most difficult tricks or the ones that risk the most bodily harm are often awarded the most respect; therefore, novices tend to be hesitant to compete for space and time at a skate spot when relative experts are present. However, the demarcation of "cool" or "punk" is rarely based on merit or skill alone.

Like many kinds of antiestablishment subcultures obsessed with "cool" or "punk," the semi-covert codes that determine cool or punk also often help reproduce a patriarchy where men define the terms of insider/outsider, cool/square, or punk/mainstream. Skateboarding is no different. In most instances who is and who is not considered an authentic skater is determined by men. Not surprisingly, women or gender nonconforming people are often left out. Atencio, Beal, and Wilson (2009) document the way male skaters often mark female skaters as "posers" based largely on gendered norms. They find that male skaters connect the notion of "risk"—how much a skater is willing to do a trick whose consequences of failing are pain and injury—with "authentic" skateboarding, and therefore, if women do not take risks, they are not real skaters. This notion of bodily risk is highly gendered such that the risks male skaters will take with their physical bodies (mostly risks to their limbs and sometimes head) are valued over the risks of humiliation and emotional stress that female skaters open themselves to by entering a male-dominated sport. Moreover, given the chauvinist past of skateboarding, girls and women are potentially at greater risk of bodily harm in terms of sexual assault when engaging in skater scenes (Porter 2003). As Carabeth Burnside succinctly puts it, "Who wants to go skateboarding at age 13 and get made fun of by guys?" (quoted in Porter 2003, 25). Truly, what could be more unpleasant or even riskier for a teenage girl than that?

Although there is no data to suggest that male skaters are necessarily any more likely to commit assault than any other group of men in

America, since the late 1970s American skate culture has valorized hard-partying, sexual promiscuity, and explicit, semi-pornographic imagery of women that is clearly objectifying. Much of this fits squarely into what has become described as "rape culture" (see Donat and D'Emilio 1992). Additionally, more than one highly prominent professional skateboarder has publicly advocated for women to stay away from skating, the most recent of which was Nyjah Huston (in 2013!) saying, "Skateboarding is not for girls at all. Not one bit" (quoted in Borden 2019, 37). What's even worse is the fact that some prominent professional skaters have been convicted of sex-based violence.[5] This is all to say that perhaps women skaters who spend time in certain skate subcultures are taking more risks of bodily harm than any male skater trying to pull off an extreme trick.

The promotion of a devil-may-care attitude as "real" skateboarding can be easily traced back to Dogtown skaters who were valorized for more and more extreme skating in pools. This romanticization of risk was further intensified by the popularity of ramp skating in the 1980s and the ever-increasing effort to get bigger and bigger air. In many ways it culminated in the skater-influenced antics of MTV's *Jackass*, a show based around a one-upmanship of who was willing to do the most extreme, dangerous, or grotesque stunt. *Jackass* was cocreated by Jefferey Tremaine, who, at the time, was editor of the skateboarding magazine *Big Brother* (notably a publication of the pornographer Larry Flint's company). The show featured many professional skaters such as Bam Margera, Rob Drydek, and Jason Acuña. Promotion of this kind of skateboarding is not only overwhelmingly male, but it is overwhelming hetero-masculinist with the result of obscuring women in the history of skateboarding and thereby making it even more intimidating for girls, women, and non-cisgender-identified people to fully participate and identify as skaters (Beal and Wilson 2004). Nevertheless, despite this frequently unwelcome attitude, women have still skated and will continue to skate—indeed in all likelihood the future growth of skateboarding will largely depend on women and non-cisgendered people. Fortunately, the hetero- and hypermasculinist vibe of skateboarding has been changing over the last quarter of a century, due in large part to more women and non-cisgendered skaters claiming a place for themselves within skateboarding and to certain progressive male allies. Women have done so by creating their own crews of skateboarders; zines, videos, and social media accounts for and featuring female skaters; skate school and camps for girls; and all-woman skate events or female-only sessions within larger skate contests and jams (see Beal 1996; Porter 2003; Beal and Wilson 2004; Kelly, Pomerantz, and Currie 2005; MacKay and Dallaire 2012; Atencio et al. 2018; Borden 2019). All of this has created more accessible avenues for girls, women, and nonbinary folks to start skating without having to deal with much of the chauvinism in skating.

In spite of the overwhelming sexism, women have been a part of skating since skateboarding's amateur and hobby beginnings and then through the late 1970s and into the 1980s as skateboarding entered its first financial boom when being a "professional" skateboarder could even be a thing. During this time period, a significant cadre of female skateboarders were sponsored and participated in professional competitions despite the sport being predominantly male (Beal 2013; Borden 2019). Toward the end of the 1980s, select female skaters were beginning to get promoted in skate videos (the medium of most import during this time), and a handful occasionally received high-level promotion throughout the 1990s. Most notable is Cara-Beth Burnside being the first woman on the cover of *Thrasher* (in 1989) and the first woman to have a Vans signature shoe (in 1999). Elisa Steamer was also heavily promoted by her sponsor, Toy Machine and subsequently *Thrasher* magazine throughout the 1990s and early 2000s. However, despite this uptick in recognition of female skateboarders, most mainstream skateboard media were still portraying women as bikini-clad (if that much clothing) fans of male skaters, not active participants who also kicked ass at skateboarding. It was in response to this continued chauvinism and misogyny of mainstream skating that many feminist-identified skaters created underground zines to connect women skaters and build a community. These zines led to female skate crews that would regularly skate together in order to claim the space of a skate spot in opposition to sexist (and sometime even physically violent) male skaters (see Porter 2003; Kelly, Pomerantz, and

Currie 2005; MacKay and Dallaire 2012; Atencio et al. 2018; Borden 2019). In many ways this expansion of women into skateboarding reached a relative zenith with the advent of the All Girl Skate Jam founded by Patty Segovia in 1997 (Borden 2019). This female-skater-only event has been tremendously empowering to women skaters worldwide and was so successful that Vans bought the rights to promote the event and included it as part of Vans's annual Warped Tour—a multimedia touring event of skateboarding, rock concerts, and art exhibitions (Atencio, Beal, and Wilson 2009; Borden 2019). In addition, Atencio et al. (2018) also acclaim the critical importance of feminist skate organizations such as Girls Riders Organization, Skate Like a Girl, and MAHFIA.TV as successors to the All Girl Skate Jam. These organizations helped expand the reach of the All Girl Skate Jam to create supportive communities of skaters who explicitly opposed the sexism and misogyny found in skateboarding. As Nyjah Houston's recent comment illustrates, skateboarding is far from rid of misogyny, but certainly it has come a long way.

The Native women skaters with whom I have spoken all acknowledge either the significant influence professional female skaters have had on their own participation in skateboarding, or how the mere existence of woman- or girl-only skate crews and events has benefited their own personal self-confidence in skating. Most of these Native women began skating during the mid-1990s to early 2000s when this growth of female empowerment in skating was taking place. The timing for a young woman skater could not have been much better. Indeed, for each of the women I spoke with, another woman played a certain role in their development of becoming a skater.

For example, Selina Mullen talks about how in high school she/they once went to a friend's house after school, and the friend pulled out a skateboard and started to skate around the street. Selina was mesmerized by this and could not wait to try it herself/themself. "I was hooked the minute I saw her skating around. She handed me the board and said, 'You try it out!'" Despite her/their nervousness and a wobbly start, Selina's friend taught her/them how to stand on the board, and Selina was off.

She/they raves about how fun it was for her/them and how she/they felt "connected" to the board:

> Once I was on the board I didn't want to get off. I was having fun being distracted with it. [My friend] saw my face light up with joy and laughter which was something I didn't feel much at that time struggling with my mental health & depression, my friend knew that about me so I guess she was surprised to see me in a different atmosphere being happy which I rarely expressed at the time. I spent the whole evening skating around as I just practiced pushing around until I felt I was ready for my other foot to be on the board, once I accomplished that I was filled with excitement, I knew I wanted to keep practicing. (Selina Mullen, personal communication, August 6, 2020)

Selina's friend could recognize what a transformative experience this was for Selina, and when Selina was leaving her/their friend's house, the friend gifted Selina that board. This hugely impacted Selina and bound the ideas of friendship, mentorship, and joy into the creative act of skateboarding.

> I was shocked, and I was like you really just want to give me your board??? . . . So I thanked her and went home with my very first skateboard which was a used one from a friend. It was a 7.5 Tony Hawk Birdhouse skateboard. That one skateboard is special to me, Skateboarding became the outlet to forget about the worries, sadness, and issues I had at home . . . Every time I stepped onto the board all those bad feelings and worries disappeared . . . It's still this happy memory in my head, just the pure happiness and joy. (Mullen, personal communication)

This moment of generosity from her/their friend and the joy of skating blended together to create a foundational sentiment of peace and happiness inside Selina that is still with her/them today. As a result, skateboarding, or rather being a skateboarder, has become a central part of her/their identity, combining with Selina's own sense of her/their indigeneity and Navajo-ness, of her/their nonbinary notions of gender, and of the importance of mental health to her/them.

It is also worth noting that this event and the feeling are the result of female bonding. That is, Selina's entrée into skateboarding did not necessarily come as a result of oppositional identity per se, nor as a sort of activist recognition that skateboarding was male-dominated, and she/they was going to break down that barrier. Rather, it came from a moment of compassionate, sympathetic connection with another female and Indigenous-identified skater.[6] Selina's "origin story" of her/their skating (a response to me asking, "Do you remember what your first skateboard was?") illustrates how skateboarding can be an important nexus and outlet for Indigenous women and nonbinary folks. The antiestablishment and DIY sensibility that the Dogtown crew and others following them implanted into the culture of skateboarding can be channeled away from heterosexist masculinity by others who have been marginalized as much as the Dogtown crew felt they were. I argue that, in large part, when Indigenous skaters (men, women, and nonbinary) engage with the art and culture of skateboarding, they are using its rebellious tropes and ethos to equally protest settler colonialism.

Indeed, in association with her/their skateboarding, Selina makes fantastic pop art that uses skateboarding and punk culture to comment on oppressive gender normativity, white supremacy, and settler colonialism (Bucklew and Kamper 2025). Through the online market Redbubble, she/they sells stickers and wearables under the shop name Skidskunx Art: Indigenous Resistance.[7] Her/their most creative work is stickers that represent Navajo skate punks. Hardcore, heavy metal, punk, and goth music have always been very popular at the Navajo Nation (see Soltani Stone and Zappia, 2020), and Selina acknowledges this history with animation-style drawings of Diné women, men, and nonbinary folks. These animated figures wear various elaborate combinations of traditional velvet skirts, German silver belts, squash blossoms, turquoise rings and bracelets, *kélchí* (traditional Diné footwear of soft-soled shoes with leg wraps that cover the calves), *tsiiyééł* (traditional Diné hair buns), punk and heavy metal band T-shirts and logos (The Addicts, Circle Jerks, Megadeath, Black Flag, etc.), mohawks, leather jackets, leather studded bracelets and chokers, tattoos, piercings, anarchy symbols, rainbow Pride insignias, and upside-down American flags. Many of these figures are also skateboarding and wearing skate-branded T-shirts (such as Vans, Thrasher, Spit Fire, Independent, or Skate and Destroy). The combination of these symbols and signs establishes a distinctly contemporary vision of indigeneity. With these images Selina is declaring that Navajo youth can be both skaters and "traditional." She/they is claiming the countercultural movements of punk, heavy metal, and goth music and of skateboarding are as much a part of Navajo culture as they are a part of middle-class suburban whiteness *and* that these "American" countercultural elements may be as much Navajo as *tsiiyééł* hair buns, velvet skirts, or turquoise and silver jewelry are. Indeed—like many aspects of Indigenous cultures—German silver jewelry, just like skateboarding and punk music, originated outside of the Navajo Nation but became indigenized (even "traditionalized") by the Diné people.

Selina's Skidskunx Art is decidedly anti–white supremacy. Many images feature figures standing up to police brutality and donning ACAB ("all cops are bastards") slogans—clear references to the activism of the Black Lives Matter movement. Selina's art should also be read in the context of contemporary Indigenous, decolonial discourses. Selina has a T-shirt design with a Navajo woman doing a kickflip encircled by the phrase "You're Skating on Native Land." Perhaps the most politically powerful aspects of Selina's art are the words emblazoned across the bottom of the animated figures' skateboards decks, on their leather jackets, or in their earrings: the decolonial battle cry, "Land Back." Like Doug Miles's "You're Skating On Native Land" Apache Skateboards deck (see chapter 6), Selina's skate art is provoking an awareness to the theft at the hand of American settler colonialism. The phrase "Land Back" has become a key part of recent American Indian activism and is a radical call to action. It not only is raising awareness of settler colonialism but also calls for a proactive solution based in restitution. "Land Back" is the

FIG. 6. Skidskunx Stickers designed by Skidskunx (Selina Mullen). Author's collection.

notion that being serious about undoing and ending settler colonialism means figuring out ways to return some (if not all) of Indigenous land back to its traditional, precolonial caretakers.[8] Selina's skateboard-based art contributes to the constant messaging needed to wake people to the urgency of radical land reform in America.

What's more, her/their art also promotes progressive and tolerant understandings of gender and sexuality. Selina does so through images questioning heteronormativity by displaying various gender and sexual identities, such as images of two of Navajo women in romantic embraces. One remarkable drawing, labeled "Decolonial Drag," proudly promotes Indigenous nonbinary identity by featuring a gender-fluid person queering "traditional" Navajo grandma attire. Perhaps the most radical (and amusing) image is a young Navajo woman, adorned with several traditional clothing items and designs, acting as a dominatrix, holding a leash around the neck of an s&m, black latex–clad figure, on all fours and wearing the archetypical red MAGA ("Make America Great Again") baseball cap. This image radically combines a tolerance for an expansive notion of "normal" sexuality with a rebuke of the most recent expressions of white supremacy and settler colonialism (Bucklew and Kamper 2025). The Navajo woman making the white supremacist Trumper heel to her is walking tall, and her Indigenous pride inverts the power dynamic of white supremacy, belittling the white supremacist and putting a chain on their violence. Moreover, the red cap is not just an easily recognized symbol of Trumper white supremacism, but it is also an important symbol of the settler colonial aspects of Trumper white supremacy—the notion that Trumper white supremacy is going to restore America to greatness erases the fact that "America" is on stolen, Indigenous land. Indeed, one of the more popular Indigenous responses to the Trumpers is a decolonial twist on the MAGA hat. At many powwow booths over the last several years, one could buy black ball caps with the slogan "Make America Native Again"—clearly a Land Back inversion of MAGA. The power in Selina's Skidskunx Art lies in the way it forcefully subverts how white supremacy and settler colonialism have sexualized Indigenous female bodies to serve the rapacious appetites of white men (see Murdock 2020).[9] The transgressive ethos Selina directs toward settler colonialism and white power clearly parallels skateboarding's anti-establishment attitude. However, combining skateboarding (and skate imagery) with her/their own radical ethos of indigeneity, feminism, and embodied notions of gender and sexuality, Selina is able to "rebel" against dominant culture with transcendent possibilities in ways not commonly seen from the prototypical, disaffected rebellious white boy skater.

Selina's artwork can be found for sale on the Redbubble website (redbubble.com), but she/they also frequently posts her/their artwork to her/their social media accounts. Social media, particularly Instagram, plays a critical role in fostering a community of Indigenous female skaters. Although many were raised in reservation communities, today most of these Indigenous women skaters, like many Indigenous people in the United States, inhabit the nexus between urban centers and reservations—a constant back and forth between the diasporic Native communities in cities and family life in tribal nations (see Ramirez 2007). Consequently, many Native women skaters do not always find other Native women skaters to skate with when they are living in urban centers. Instead, social media can provide crucial connections.

Di'orr Greenwood is another Native skater-artist with whom Selina is connected to through social media. Di'orr was also raised at the Navajo Nation, but like Selina, she now spends much of her time in the urban off-reservation hubs, such as Phoenix and Los Angeles (with frequent trips back to her home reservation community). Di'orr's art is also intimately connected to her skateboarding, as she does her art right on the surfaces of skateboard decks of various sizes. Calling on her mastery of woodburning, precious stone inlay, and painting, Di'orr creates gorgeous skateboards with powerful images and designs that reference her Diné upbringing and culture and her love of skateboarding. Her decks display geometric shapes that allude to rug design patterns. These patterns are painted and burned into the wood of the deck. Frequently the patterns act as borders around representational images of birds, flowers, or corn stalks. Additionally, almost all of her designs also include systematically placed inlays of small pieces of turquoise, coral, or hematite. Depending on the design, these boards are both for display and for riding.

Di'orr's project of indigenizing skateboarding is not merely based on adding Navajo symbology and art to the decks she makes. Rather, it is Diné artistic knowledge as well: a cultural process that connects her to her culture in general and to her family and clan specifically. Di'orr's great grandmother, grandmothers, and mother were all weavers, so she grew up around that uniquely Navajo creative tradition. In addition, her uncle Virgil is a flute maker and wood burner, and he is the one who taught her the craft of woodburning. She would often hang out at his workshop after school when she was in her early teens. After a while she got into the mischievous habit of burning small piles of wood scraps and kindling laying around his shop. One day, after her uncle discovered that Di'orr had wasted a significant amount of his gasoline stock—she had used an entire five-gallon canister in order accelerate a bunch of mini bonfires—he sat her down and asked her if she had been starting fires and squandering his gas. She denied it even though it was obviously her doing; however, his response was not one of harsh discipline but rather one befitting of a common Indigenous mode of educating youth that is based on redirection, not punishment. Her uncle had recently purchased a new woodburning iron, and instead of getting angry at Di'orr for misusing the gas and not being truthful about it, he gifted Di'orr the tool. His solution was to teach her how to make art by woodburning to direct her away from burning wood to start little fires and toward something more harmonious, such as producing art.

Today, at least ten years later, Di'orr still uses this woodburning tool in her artwork, and whenever she uses it to burn a design into her skateboard decks, she thinks of her uncle, the compassionate way he mentored her, and this very Navajo style of transmission of cultural knowledge and skills. Indeed, when talking about her artistry, Di'orr asserts to me that she considers skateboard art intimately linked to her family's and tribe's artistic tradition. She never had any formal training in art, but she insists on not labeling her skill "self-taught." Rather, she believes that her artistic skill derives from an ancestral bond. That is, when she produces art, it is her ancestors expressing themselves through her (Di'orr Greenwood, interview, March 4, 2020). She likens producing the art on her decks to an out-of-body experience where she is not really thinking about or planning the design in advance. Instead, she begins with a few simple ideas of colors and imagery that she wants, and she lets it all morph into a complete design, trusting herself that it will get there. Dio'rr describes it this way: "The moment I start . . . woodburning the board, it feels like I shut down, and, like, my ancestor comes into me, like starts designing for me and then leaves, and then I'm just, like, left with a board that I didn't even make. It's a really strange, strange thing, but it's been working" (Greenwood, interview). She notes that she's tried to use pencil and paper and design the board in advance that way, but she can never get that to work. She gets a kind of "writer's block" when she tries to design a mock-up and can never complete a prototype. There is something about the actual process that gives her the inspiration and ability to accomplish the design on the board. Di'orr tells me that what she's been told by her family is that this is exactly what would happen with the older Navajo weavers—that they didn't design a pattern for

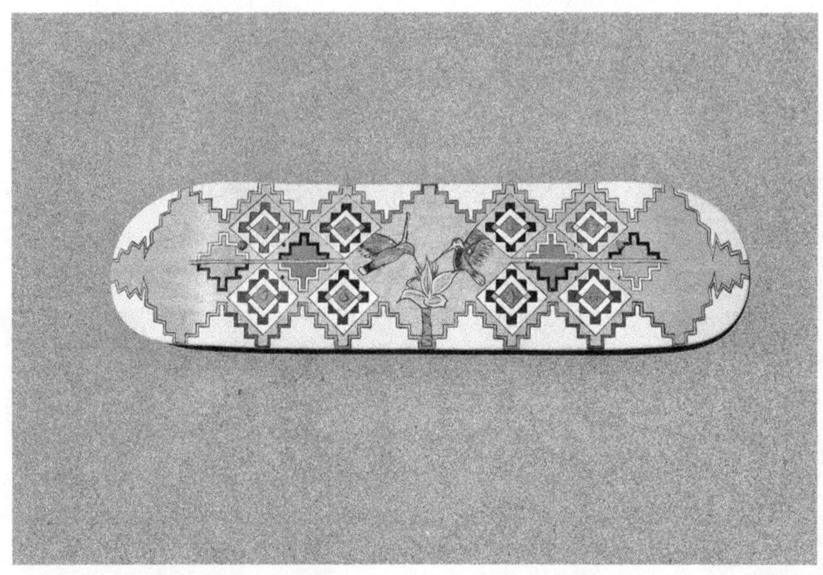

FIG. 7. Di'orr Greenwood custom deck designed by Di'orr Greenwood. Author's collection. Photo: Matthew Fowler.

their rugs in advance, but the pattern and design came to them once they sat in front of the loom and started to weave. In this way designing skateboards is clearly a very intimately Indigenous practice for Di'orr.

Interestingly, when I asked Di'orr if skateboarding invokes the same kind of "in-the-zone," "out-of-body" experience, she said "no"—admitting that skateboarding requires much more intentional practice and trial and error for her. For sure, it took Di'orr more time to build up her confidence with skateboarding than it did designing skateboards. She shared with me, for example, her first encounter skateboarding with Cecely Todacheenie. Di'orr had met her at a skate event hosted by Dustinn Craig at White Mountain. Di'orr did not skate much that day because she was self-conscious that her skill was not as high as some of the other women, such as Cecely, skating that day. A year or so later she had her sister drive her into the town of Gallup to go to the skate park there. When they approached the park, Cecely coincidently was there already skateboarding by herself, but Di'orr felt intimidated by the difference in skill level, so Di'orr never even went into the park and immediately asked her sister to take her somewhere else so that she would not have to be seen by Cecely. Upon reflection, Di'orr now finds this amusing, especially given that she now knows that Cecely is one of the sweetest people you could meet and far from what most would consider intimidating. Today, Cecely and Di'orr are very close friends, so much so that Di'orr considers her like a sister (Greenwood, interview), and now they just laugh about her jitters to meet and skate with someone she so admired.

At the same time, this instance also speaks to the challenge for Indigenous female skaters to find a cohort of fellow supportive skaters. The practice of skater women, in general, forming crews in order to skate together and minimize harassment at a given skate spot is a relatively recent phenomenon. Many female skaters report that this is a highly empowering act and, in many ways, has made it possible to have the confidence to even begin skating (see Atencio et al. 2018). However, these crews and collectives of women or queer or nonbinary skaters tend to be found mostly in larger population centers, and it can be hard for Native women and nonbinary skaters to find supportive crews in less geographically convenient places. Currently there isn't a critical mass of Indigenous female skaters in any one geographic area (except perhaps some urban centers in Canada). Hence, Di'orr had to ultimately look outside of an exclusively Indigenous context to find a crew of women with whom she could share a solidarity in skateboarding (for discussion of women's skate collectives see MacKay and Dallaire 2012). Fortunately, she was able to find an incredibly supportive collective of women skaters when she first moved to Phoenix. While hanging around at a skatepark there, Di'orr met by happenstance Natalie Krishna Das, a sponsored skater and cofounder of an "all-girl" skateboard crew called La Chicaz. This collective of (mostly) women and nonbinary skateboarders from several different U.S. states and Canada meet up and go on what they call "skate adventures" as frequently as possible to build solidarity and mutual support among those who are not always welcomed into skateboarding. Natalie is incredibly supportive of women skaters, and she welcomed Di'orr to the Phoenix's women skate community by picking Di'orr up basically everyday (Di'orr did not have a car when living in Phoenix) of her first few weeks in town and taking her to skate. She helped Di'orr find a community almost from day one. One woman she met as a part of Las Chicaz was Natalie's close friend Hailey McGee, who happened to be the daughter of legendary female skater Patti McGee. Di'orr was thrilled to get to meet both Hailey and subsequently Patti, and ultimately Hailey and Patti asked Di'orr to be a "flow" member of their skate team, "The Original Bettys."[10] They gave Di'orr two decks, one which was her favorite because it had the 1965 image of Patti from the cover of *Life* magazine in which Patti is doing a handstand on her original Hobie skateboard.

The Las Chicaz collective has been incredibly beneficial to Di'orr, helping her grow as a skateboarder, learn new tricks, and realize the impact that she could have herself, mentoring younger women and girl skateboarders. Today Di'orr informally mentors young girls whenever she sees them at skateparks and also does so formally by offering paid skateboard lessons. She uses these lessons and her artwork to support herself financially. Moreover, in addition to being able to supplement her income by selling her skateboard art, she also uses her craft to support her community as a whole, especially during the height of the COVID-19 pandemic. The Navajo Nation was hit particularly hard by the pandemic, and although Di'orr had been living mostly in Los Angeles or Phoenix during the pandemic, she did not forget the suffering of her people during this time. Di'orr felt compelled to support not only her immediate family on the reservation but also the entire community. So she decided to start raffling a select number of her skateboards to raise money to purchase food and supplies for the Navajo communities hit hardest by COVID. Additionally, she started to make cloth masks, both to distribute for free at the Navajo Nation and to sell on the internet, with the proceeds going to the supplies she helped purchase for the people of her homeland. During the summer and fall of 2020, Di'orr made three separate trips to the reservation to bring the relief supplies that she collected with the proceeds from selling her art. All of these activities represent an even further way in which Di'orr is indigenizing skateboarding: she is using it as an avenue to financially support her home Indigenous community. This ethos of using one's skill toward the greater good of the community is part of the Diné values with which Di'orr was raised. Clearly, the mode by which a Navajo community member manifests their responsibility to the community as a whole is always evolving to be relevant to the contemporary context, and like many of her Indigenous skater peers, Di'orr uses the creative energy that she channels through skateboarding as a way to sustain her Indigenous community.

The most recent and perhaps most significant example of this is Di'orr's central role in the creation of the Diné Skate Garden, which is a multiuse site at the Navajo village of Tóhaaliní in the Two Grey Hills Chapter of the Navajo Nation.[11] A key part of this site is a skatepark built by The Skatepark Project, and there are future plans to build a sustainable, Indigenous garden adjacent to the skatepark that will promote food sovereignty by feeding the local community. The Skatepark Project (TSP), formerly known as the Tony Hawk Foundation, is the world leader in helping skaters with the knowhow and support to get skateparks built in the community. A grant from this organization helped construct the skatepark that Cecely and Jeremy developed in Gallup, and the Diné Skate Garden is particularly significant in that it is one of only two parks that the TSP completely funded, illustrating how impressed the organization was with the community-based proposal Di'orr helped with and how it recognized the importance of a project like this.[12] In April 2023 Tony Hawk even showed up for the grand opening. Di'orr was there, of course, to be part of the ceremonies, to gift one of her custom boards to Tony, and, most importantly, to skate with the kids. Now Di'orr currently makes trips to Two Grey Hills to teach local kids how to skate and often has girls-only days in order to support female empowerment in the same way she was mentored by women and nonbinary skaters.

Unfortunately, I did not make it to this opening of the Diné Skate Garden, but I was lucky to see Di'orr in person a few months later when she was traveling through San Diego, and she raved to me what a beautiful and joyful event the opening was and what an amazing place it is today. On this occasion Di'orr happened to be in town because she was on an all-girls and all-women skate trip . . . and all-Indigenous one! She confided to me how thrilled she was that this was her first ever all–Native female skate trip; perhaps, she noted, it was the first one ever (Di'orr Greenwood, personal communication, July 14, 2023). There were women and girls from ages twelve to early thirties on this trip from Navajo Nation, Hopi (including a skater sponsored by Naqwatsveni Skateboarding; see chapter 6), and Zuni Pueblo. Cecely also joined in this trip, and in the true spirit of both Cecely's and Di'orr's incredibly kind hearts and amazing dedication to their community, the main intention of the trip was to mentor the younger women and take them to the world-famous Woodward Skate Camp in Tehachapi, California. It was only day one of their trip, and both Di'orr and Cecely shared that they were having a fantastic time already (Di'orr Greenwood and Cecely Todoachenee, personal communication, July 14, 2023).

RE-VISIONING INDIGENOUS MASCULINITY

It might seem odd or even problematic that I started this chapter about Native women and nonbinary skaters with a story that centers on a male skater—Dustinn Craig. Undoubtedly this speaks to my own gendered bias. Moreover, any gaps or aporias in this chapter's telling of the story of nonbinary and Native women skaters is a comment on the inherent limitation in trust that a settler cis male anthropologist like me can gain (or even deserves) from Indigenous women and nonbinary folks. Indeed a few of the female-identifying skaters to whom I reached out politely declined participation in my research project. I respect their refusals and acknowledge the built-in limitations to this chapter and this book as a whole. There are so many amazing stories to be told about and by Indigenous women and nonbinary skaters; far be it for me to have any illusions about telling the definitive story on the subject. Moreover, these stories are already being told in short verse through fantastic Instagram follows such as @skaterosie, @hammersmahsedface, and @nationskateyouth.

Another reason why the story of Indigenous women and nonbinary skaters is in more of an emergent phase than Indigenous male skaters is the sexist history of skateboarding in general, as summarized earlier in this chapter. Compared to basketball's growth in gender inclusivity, skateboarding has a lot of catching up and a lot of work ahead to undo the hypermasculine collateral damage of the Dogtown skate revolution

Indigenous women were participating in basketball from its inception (see chapter 4). And white suburban girls were also certainly part of the beginning of skateboarding. Yet, while basketball certainly still suffers from its own forms and levels of sexism and homophobia, it did not have quite the same epistemic break found in skateboarding, where a new form of the sport nearly completely wiped out any memory of female participation. The latter is a key reason why my chapter on male skater elders is more fleshed out (and longer) than this chapter on female and nonbinary Indigenous skaters—there are just fewer non-male Indigenous practitioners of skateboarding—though that too is changing rapidly. Moreover, I want to make clear that while this term I have coined, "skater elder," might seem covertly gendered and heterosexist, I believe it is only a matter of time before there are women and nonbinary skate elders. Indeed, in this chapter I try to illustrate the budding mentor relationships happening between many Native woman and nonbinary skaters, and the recent story of the Di'orr's and Cecely's California all–Native female skate trip is an incipient example of female skate elders.

In a similar vein it is also important to recognize that many of the skate elders and male Indigenous skaters that I mention in the previous chapters do not mentor only male skaters, but do so for female and nonbinary Indigenous skaters as well. A handful of key male Native skaters have worked hard to include and support female and nonbinary skaters. Again, by mentioning them in a chapter that focuses on non-male skaters I am not trying to center on these Indigenous male skaters per se, but guys such as Dustinn Craig, Doug Miles Sr., Walt Pourier, Doug Miles Jr., Delvan Polelonema, Shawn Harrison, Jeremy Todacheenie, and Victor Corpuz have all worked to further all Indigenous skaters, not just cis male ones. They have done so variously: from sponsoring women skaters or holding women-only events or sessions at the skate jams that they host to standing up for female skaters through social media or in person at skateparks, or even just inviting them to go skate on a daily basis. Perhaps most significant is the overall friendship and respect these men have shown toward women and nonbinary skaters—a fundamental step in making skateboarding more gender inclusive.

These efforts to combat the hypermasculinity and overt sexism that can still be found in skateboarding take on an additional significance when we consider the way settler colonialism has attempted to control Indigenous communities through normative gendering. Take, for example, Dustinn Craig and Doug Miles Sr., who, although they hail from different bands and reservations, are both Apache and thereby have had to live under the weight of white and settler expectations about Apache masculinity that are a fundamental part of the discourses circulating around Geronimo. White mainstream portrayals of Apache men have long reified the trope of masculine Indian warriors embodied by physical fortitude and emotional stoicism. And while it should be acknowledged that Geronimo imagery does have utility for Native folks seeking symbols of rebellion against and resilience in spite of settler colonialism, these images also promote a particular flattening of Indigenous masculinity that is romanticized and can thereby create unhealthy ideals for Apache boys and men to try to live up to. In their creative lives, Dustinn and Doug have had to navigate their complex relationships to Geronimo (the historical figure and the legendary resistor), particularly in regard to how he has come to represent Apache manhood.

Through his own cinematic techniques, Dustinn, for example, has critiqued and reworked the conventional images of Apache scouts, common to twentieth-century westerns, as silently pillaging and ruthlessly killing in small raiding parties. Dustinn merges the cinematic tropes of historical documentaries with contemporary skate videos or "edits."[13] He has done this in a dual fashion, first by using the skaters that he mentored as part of the 4 Wheel War Pony team to play extras in his definitive cinematic biography of Geronimo for PBS and then, second, by using the costumes produced for the documentary in a more playful

fashion for a skate video for 4 Wheel War Pony, in which the Apache
skaters, dressed as Apache raiders, walk through the high desert to som-
ber music carrying guns and rifles. Then toward the end of the film they
smile as the rifles turn into skateboards, and they skate away from the
sage brush onto asphalt roads. The blending of these two genres in each
of the two films enunciates multiple commentaries on the relationship
between the "historical" and "modern" and past and present forms of
Apache-ness. Film scholar Joanna Hearne also notes the commentary
on gender and masculinity. She asserts:

> Contemporary Native youth culture—both in the form of skate-
> board culture and filmmaking itself—supplants armed violence as
> a form of resistance when the gun becomes a skateboard. Craig's
> transformative vision answers the depiction of violent masculinity
> in Western genre images of Apaches and particularly the pop cul-
> tural focus on Geronimo as an icon to Indigenous threat to white
> settlement. (Hearne 2012, 299)

Craig's work seeks to unsettle expectations about gender roles of Indigenous people.

Similarly, Doug Miles's suicide prevention film (see chapter 7) emphasizes an overt expression of emotional vulnerability among Indigenous
men, as the two main characters talk about their feelings of depression
and seek mutual support. This solution of open communication and emotional expression refuses the fulfillment of a settler stereotype of stoic
Indian masculinity. What's more, Doug's art as a whole, through media
such as skate decks, murals, and short films, seeks to further question
white settler patriarchy by frequently featuring strong Apache women.
The female figures in his art implicitly talk back to settler representations
of Apache "toughness" and tropes of Geronimo by employing a bold female gaze, whether through painting, photography, or cinematography.
Doug and Dustinn seem to intimately understand how settler misogyny
is bad for women *and* men, and they are committed to collaborative work
across gender and committed to teaching Apache boys and young men to

not embody the classic (predominantly white) "asshole skater boy" from their own youth in the 1970s, 1980s, and 1990s. They actively channel the rebellion inherent in skateboarding toward a rejection of settler society, which also means rejecting sexism and settler notions of gender.

CONCLUSION

It is only fitting then that I conclude here with a story connecting Di'orr and Doug. By her own account, Di'orr has been greatly influenced and mentored by both of Dustinn and Doug (Greenwood, interview). One of the first things I ask, when I interview skaters, is for them to tell me about their first board. This almost always provokes smiles and brightening of the eyes as they nostalgically think back to that magical moment of beginning to skate. Generally, skaters from tribal-based communities have fewer resources and less access to skate gear than other communities (fixing this is the exact thing Cecely and Jeremy are trying to address with their Enchantment Skate Shop in Gallup, New Mexico). Consequently, their first boards tend to be prefab, mass-produced ones bought at Walmart or similar low-cost, all-purpose stores. However, the Native skaters who continued to advance in their skating then proceeded to tell me about their first "pro model" (a more legitimate board designed for more durability and ability to pull off tricks). In Di'orr's case she had a crappy hand-me-down board as her first, and by the time she took it to the skate jam that Dustinn was holding at White Mountain, the wood on the nose and tail was so chewed up from overuse that the board was nearly unrideable. Dustinn took one look at her board and decided that would not do, so right then and there he gifted Di'orr one of his 4 Wheel War Pony decks and immediately helped her switch out the wheels and trucks so she could start skating on the new deck right away. And then Dustinn said three simple words to her: "Just keep skating" (Greenwood, interview). These words and this act of kindness and mentoring from Dustinn still stick with her today. Di'orr is moved by the fact that Dustinn recognized her skating potential and valued that enough to make a small investment in her both in material terms with the deck and in emotional terms with the encouragement. This mentoring has kept Di'orr going and modeled for her how to interact with and mentor younger skaters coming up behind her.

Similarly, a key way that Di'orr's mentoring relationship with Doug Miles has also manifested is through a skateboard deck exchange. In 2017 Doug announced, through his Apache Skateboard Instagram, Di'orr as the newest team rider (@instapache1, Instagram, April 24, 2017). Among other things, this meant that Apache Skateboard would now provide her with free decks as part of their sponsorship. One such deck she received was Apache Skateboard's groundbreaking "You Are Skating on Native Land" design. However, the one that Doug developed for Di'orr was an alternative version to the original one discussed in chapter 6. The first (and more common) design is painted on an all-white deck with black print type, and in the center of the board is an anime or graffiti art style image of a skull (with a headband holding back shoulder-length hair) of an Apache warrior. Overlaid on top of the bottom half of this graphic is a black-and-white photographic image of three seated Apache warriors flanked by an Apache woman and an older man in a suit. Above these images are the words "YOU'RE SKATING" (one line for each word) and below the words "ON NATIVE LAND" (again, one line for each word). Di'orr's board has the same layout of text but with a different graphic in the center.[14] The graphic on Di'orr's board is of an Apache woman "warrior." As noted above, a huge percentage of Doug's art includes strong images of Apache femininity, and this deck is no exception. This image is from the shoulders up with the woman staring powerfully back at the viewer, with long flowing black hair and with one fist strongly gripping two arrows. Across her chest, in an italicized font, is the word "DESTINY." Undoubtedly this is a tribute to powerful women of the Apache community and Indigenous women in general, and it is further empowering to be put on a deck that is being ridden by an Indigenous woman like Di'orr Greenwood.

The relationship between skateboard as art and skateboard as function is often fraught. Most diehard skaters will declare that the art on the bottom side of a skate deck is to be appreciated and an important part of why someone would buy a given deck, but a skateboard is to be used. Of course, there are people (even hardcore skaters) who also like art in the shape of a skateboard to hang on their wall. This is evidenced by Di'orr's own creations of woodburned, elaborately painted, and precious stone-inlaid skateboards . However, even Di'orr is under no illusion that a board is not meant to be ridden. Hence, as much as she loved the painted-on empowering message of her Apache Skateboard deck, "YOU'RE SKATING ON NATIVE LAND," she too knew she had to ride it, eventually scuffing and obscuring the bottom-side graphic. However, Di'orr did something unique with this deck at the point when the design started to fade from her board's nose and tail, and it was clear that the wood was about to give out and break in certain spots—making it no longer ridable.[15] Usually when this happens, skaters often just retire the board by stashing it on some random shelf, or some ride it until it actually cracks in ways that make it completely unrideable and just throw it out. (Incidentally, my favorite thing to see is when a skater knows their board is about to fail, and they try to do a trick that will completely crack through the deck, or, even better, in some cases they perform their best Pete Townsend impersonation by grabbing the board by one of the trucks and slamming it into the ground until is smashes into two pieces. This feat has produced the now ubiquitous meme of a "broken" board positioned in the shape of a heart—the broken halves meet at a 45-degree angle so that the curved part makes a heart shape up top). Instead of taking either of these options, Di'orr decided to turn her board into art that would honor Doug. In her Instagram post she describes it this way: "[This is a] skateboard deck I skated, retired, redesigned and gave new life as an art piece" (@ woodburnskateboards, Instagram, August 27, 2020). To produce the end result, she stripped the board of its original painted design and sanded it smooth. Then she recreated all the lines of the graphic with a woodburning tool and added new paint and inlaid pieces of turquoise. The result was a beautifully revived piece of art that honored the original design and added her own flair. The bold political statement on this board and Doug's investment in and support of her through a sponsorship were all too significant to just toss the deck aside when she could not ride it anymore. Di'orr had to commemorate this board, and in a way the board became an emblem of her relationship to Doug and Apache Skateboards. As she put it, "Every skateboard that I have recreated will last longer then [*sic*] I will be alive ♥" (@woodburnskateboards, Instagram, August 27, 2020). Di'orr's skateboarding art celebrates intergenerational relationships that heal communities through mentorship.

Di'orr is part of new generation of emerging (female) skate elders who use skateboarding to connect youth to their culture. Nothing illustrates this more than her recent project heralded on her Instagram account @ woodburnskateboard. Di'orr has returned to her reservation, the Navajo Nation, to work with young Diné skater/artists to create art from the upcycling old skateboards that were commercially produced outside of Indian Country into Indigenous art from inside of Indian Country. These projects are fully collaborative, where she works with teenage Diné boys and girls, having them draw designs on the board and pick out the colors; next she teaches them how to use woodburning and other tools to complete the recycled or upcycled decks. Then she advertises the decks for sale on her website, and all the proceeds go to the young artists, who are often using the money to support their own families or to purchase tools for their own art careers. What is more, each board has a small metal plaque identifying the artist, and with the most recent collaboration the young designer wanted to add the phrase to his plaque, "it's up to you if you want to succeed." While mentoring this young man, Di'orr was able to bring in one of her mentors, Cecely Todacheenee, to help them translate the phrase into Diné so the deck would have both the English and Navajo language on it—hence completing another circle of mentorship/relationship.

Indigenous thinker, writer, and poet Leanne Betasamosake Simpson (2017) describes "present" moments, in her Indigenous worldview, as collisions between the past and future. Di'orr's mentoring of these young Native creators through skateboard art is a productive collusion of the mentoring she has received (from her uncle, Dustinn, Natalie Krishna Das, Hailey and Patti Magee, Cecely, Doug, and many others) with the mentoring she is doing with future Indigenous skaters/artists (those heralded in her Instagram account and those to whom she teaches skateboard lessons). It is relationships all the way back and all the way forward establishing intergenerational (and intergender) joy and healing.

Midway through the COVID-19 pandemic, social media platforms became even more dominant than they were pre–global pandemic. As people spent hours locked indoors with not much to do, these platforms became one of the best ways to connect people in the absence of being able to interact in person. The possibility of becoming "social media famous" seemed to grow logarithmically as memes and short videos were easily shared the world over and then referenced and re-referenced (almost) endlessly as followers created their own version of the meme or video, thereby creating their own followers. One such video clip that became ubiquitous was a man cruising down a hill on a skateboard in time to Fleetwood Mac song "Dreams" while gulping from his half-gallon jug of Ocean Spray Cran-Raspberry Juice in between lip-synching Stevie Nicks's too-high note, head voice chorus. Nathan Apodaca became a social media sensation by posting this video to his @420doggface208 TikTok account. His original video reached over eighty million views. Apodaca's urban, Chicanx style was easily identifiable by his buzz-cut haircut, baggie black Dickies pants, and gray hoodie. But closer inspection also revealed an eagle feather tattoo on the back of his skull. Apodaca identifies as Chicano on his father's side and Northern Arapaho on his mother's side. In interviews and postings after his fame, Apodaca discussed the importance of his indigeneity, having spent significant time visiting the community of his mother's upbringing, the Wind River Indian Reservation. In an interview with the national newspaper *Indian Country Today*, Apodaca encouraged Native people to "stay strong" and use social media to build solidarity among Indigenous folks: "Get out there and make videos, go do what you want . . . Follow your fellow Natives, follow each other. Be one with each other. One nation, we rise" (Chavez 2020). One Navajo female skater took this exhortation "to be heard" literally.

As is common on TikTok, Apodaca's post set off an open-ended viral chain of copycat posts — including Mic Fleetwood himself, attempting to skateboard. Perhaps one of the most significant was an homage made by a Native skater, Naiomi Glasses. Naiomi is a Diné woman who uses her social media account to promote contemporary Navajo living and womanhood by posting images of herself that combine historic and modern Diné style and culture. Her Instagram bio describes her as "Cleft proud. Weaver. Dog mom. Sometimes, I model. Sometimes, I skate ." Many of her posts can be read as advocacy for beauty and acceptance of cleft palates as she smiles and prominently features her own cleft palate. Other posts often feature her proudly wearing the historic regalia of Diné women (long velvet skirts, long-sleeved blouses, silver and turquoise necklaces, bracelets, and belts) or slightly more contemporary western wear (blue jeans; snap-front, button-down western shirts), all of which is often mixed in with Indigenous pride T-shirts. In these posts she is weaving, herding, horseback riding, or skateboarding! In her skateboard posts, Naiomi is almost always wearing historic Navajo clothing, thereby creating a beautifully harmonious combination historic and contemporary symbols, images, and activities.

Naiomi's most viewed post is her homage to Dogface420 (Nathan Apodaca). She dons a crushed velvet turquoise-colored skirt, *kélchí* (traditional Navajo moccasins), a black tank top, a *sis lichii'i* (a traditional Navajo woven sash belt), a squash blossom necklace, two other turquoise and silver necklaces, silver and turquoise wrist cuffs and rings, and a *tsiiyéél* (a traditional Navajo hair bun tied with yarn). The music in the clip is, of course, Fleetwood Mac's "Dreams," and she is holding an Ocean Spray juice box as she skateboards down a Navajo Sandstone hill.[1] Combined, these features make her post a particularly Diné version of the Apodaca meme, but perhaps most striking is the skating over the natural terrain of Diné Bikéyah (Navajo territory). Naiomi has posted multiple clips of her skating on this terrain. Navigating the naturally bumpy slope looks to be no easy feat, and the posts are an illustration of her riding ability. But what makes this video so significant is the way that it combines an Indigenous connection to land (place) with a skater's connection to space (terrain, obstacles). Making Navajo Sandstone hills ridable, Naiomi is claiming skateboarding for Navajo people and, really, for all Indigenous people. Through posts like this, Naiomi embodies what it means to be Indigenous while skateboarding.

Describing the skating of Naiomi Glasses this way, I am here again following Philip J. Deloria's (2019) notion of being "native to modernity," the expression he uses to describe his great aunt, the artist Mary Sullivan. Deloria's turn of phrase brilliantly responds to the complexity and tension in how settler notions of time have been leveraged against Indigenous people for colonial domination (see also Rifkin 2017). "Modernity" or "modern" has been historically contrasted with notions of "traditional" in ways that are rarely value-neutral and rarely have benefited Indigenous peoples. "Modern" is coded with notions of progress, advancement, and superiority, while "traditional" is coded with the ancient, unsophisticated, and inferior. Moreover, "modern" is seen as part of or leading to the future, while the term "traditional" delimits cultural practices and behaviors to the past. That is, the term "traditional" struggles to account for processes of change. Moreover, it invokes notions of authenticity that can be hard to ever definitively prove, given the nature of cultural change.[2] These strict notions of authenticity are often marshaled against Indigenous communities by settlers creating an infinite regression where the bar on what is "traditional" continually gets pushed further and further backward in time. This creates an unwinnable political game for Indigenous folks, forcing them to endlessly prove their authenticity in order to be afforded settler cultural or political legitimacy.

What is so exceptional about Deloria's formulation, "native to modernity," is that rather than the temporal modifying notions of indigeneity (such as traditional v. modern), Indigenous cultural style, and values can be seen as ways of living in the world that are transhistorical or beyond time limitations—as applicable now and in the future as they were a hundred years ago, a thousand years ago, or since time immemorial. This is important because it allows us to say something even more powerful than Native people are "indigenizing" a preexisting cultural phenomenon that may have originated outside of Indian Country. Ultimately in this book, I am arguing that Native people are not "indigenizing" basketball or skateboarding per se, but rather they are already Indigenous to these activities. This is a recognition that Indigenous ways of being are not limited by time or a historical moment.

Indigenous thinker and creative writer Leanne Betasamosake Simpson brilliantly parallels Deloria's thinking on time and embodying indigeneity when she writes about what she calls "radical resurgence." One key place Simpson does this is in her book *As We Have Always Done*. As the title suggest, Simpson (2017) argues for singularity of time, space, and embodiment where past, present, and future are connected by and collapsed into the present. This interconnection of time disavows settler notions of "traditional" and "modern" that construct value judgments based on arbitrary, settler notions of progress by arguing that indigeneity is always embodied in an active present. Simpson (2017) notes, "My own interpretation . . . is that the present . . . is a colliding of the past and the future" (193) and that "Indigenous thought doesn't dissect time into past, present, and future" (213). This Indigenous present of which Simpson speaks is not tantamount to Western (or Eastern-influenced) self-help, anti-stress mantras, instructing people to "live in the present" in order not to be weighed down by the trauma of the past or undone by anxiety about the future. Rather, it is an understanding of the interconnectedness and unseverability of the past, present, and future. These temporal realms are all linked by Indigenous action. As Simpson asserts, "The future is here in the form of the practices of the present, in which the past is also here influencing" (213). And Indigenous action is key to what Simpson calls a radical resurgence of indigeneity that provides the means for Indigenous peoples and communities to thrive. Simpson declares, "Placing Indigenous bodies on the land in *any* Indigenous context through engagement with Indigenous practices is direct action" (236). Her emphasis on "any" is significant because she does not want to create a false (settler) temporal distinction between traditional and modern.

Allow me, then, to conclude this book with one last anecdote from the world of Rezball that exemplifies how basketball and skateboarding are forms of Indigenous action that replenish and support Native communities and Native people. As with Naiomi Glasses, this example too comes from social media. In February 2020 I "liked" a post on the Instagram page of "itanativesports." This account is run by Inter-Tribal Athletics (ITA), an organization that promote Indigenous youth athletes in order to gain them the same national recruiting attention afforded to non-Indigenous athletes through websites such as Rivals, 24/7 Sports, and MaxPreps. The ITA account mainly (but not exclusively) focusses on Rezball and Rezballers, posting their successes, publicizing the signings of letters of intent to play in college, and hosting an annual showcase of Rezballers for college recruiters. The post that had such an impact on me and many others, receiving thousands of "likes," was a repost of a picture taken of the Ignacio High School Bobcats girls basketball team. The town of Ignacio is in the heart of the Southern Ute reservation in southwestern Colorado. To bring awareness to the ongoing tragedy of Missing and Murdered Indigenous Women (MMIW), the team did a photo shoot in November 2019.[3] The image was a standard team picture with players lined up in rows on bleachers wearing their uniforms and holding basketballs. However, in this image all the girls had either a red or black handprint painted over their mouths, and the coaches donned Southern Ute tribal ribbon dresses and skirts and wore large beaded earrings and braid ties. This painted handprint over the mouth and covering much of the cheeks has become synonymous with the MMIW movement. It is used to represent both the absence of voice of those who are missing and to revive their voice in protest over the lack of attention or protection for Indigenous women and girls who have been caught up in this epidemic of abduction and murder. The paint and the handprint both reference important colors to many Indigenous communities and common practice among many tribes to use handprints as various forms of warpaint on horses and their own bodies and faces.

This team photo was the promotional supplement to a larger project of activism around MMIW: a game between the Bobcats and another local high school, with all the proceeds from the game going to the grassroots organization Voices of Our Sisters. This organization and the game itself helped raise local and national awareness for MMIW, and girls on the team used this photo and other posters to provoke open dialogue about the crisis and steps to end the theft of these female Indigenous lives. (Incidentally, the charity game was played in the gym at the Sun Ute Community Center, and this Southern Ute Tribal recreation center also houses a very large skatepark.)

This lasting and striking image created by the Ignacio Bobcats to honor MMIW with a team photo represents the kind of collision of past, present, and future heralded by Simpson. The women and girls are wearing a mix of historic and contemporary clothing referencing past and present in order to make a statement about the healthier and safer future they are demanding. It is not an ancillary coincidence that this comes in the context of Rezball. As discussed in chapter 4, the prominence of Rezball among girls in Indian Country (especially comparted to non-Indigenous communities) has provided a venue to embody and honor the crucial importance of femininity in Indigenous communities. In a similar way, Rezball in general has become a practice and space for enacting Indigenous values of community, resilience, responsibility, and strength. And the same could be easily said for Native skateboarders. For the girls on the Ignacio basketball team, even in the context of raising awareness about tragic death, ball is life for them, and in the same way, skateboarding gives life blood to Indigenous youth across Indian Country, now and into the future.

INTRODUCTION

1. Wounded Knee Skateboards is a skate company founded by Lenape skater Jim Murphy. This company's participation is part of the reason why the skatepark is called "WK," for Wounded Knee Skateboards, and the other, of course, is the more significant fact that the skatepark is about fifteen miles from the historic protest and massacre site of Wounded Knee. Stronghold Society was founded by Murphy's good friend and business partner, Lakota skater Walt Pourier, who grew up in a house about five hundred yards from where the skatepark is today, hence the specific location of the skate facility. Jeff Ament, skater and bassist for the legendary rock band Pearl Jam, started Montana Pool Service as a nonprofit, to help build skateparks in low-income communities throughout Ament's home state of Montana. There are only a few Montana Pool Service skateparks outside of Montana and some are next to predominantly Indigenous communities on or off reservations.

2. Of course, in many ways the global dominance of professional sports increases, not detracts from, localized articulations of sport. The largest brands in professional sports (the elite English Premier League and Spanish La Liga soccer teams, several NBA teams, some NFL and MLB teams, and Indian Premier League cricket teams) have reached every nook and cranny in the world, influencing how people interact with and think about sport. Moreover, the massive economies created by these brands and their leagues have driven that professionalization of local versions of sport as athletes are now scouted, groomed, and trained from young ages for potential careers in sports.

3. That being said, in twenty-first century America, skateboarding and basketball are generally understood to be mainstream sports that have outlived the exclusive association with discrete racialized communities.

4. The few pseudonyms in this book are for the names of people who show up in the narrative of my consultants. Given that these people showed up as reported speech without me gaining permission to use their names, I have made up imagined names for them.

1. BALL IS LIFE

1. It is not uncommon at all for high school sports coaches to assign wind spirits, or what are known as "suicides," for the losing team in a drill or when the team collectively (or

even individuals) are not doing the drills correctly or putting forth enough effort at practice. This has a multipurpose agenda of creating team discipline and team solidarity and improving stamina through the discipline. While no player really "likes" to do suicides, all acknowledge their purpose and function in practice and training.

2. The La Jolla tribal campground does not produce the revenue of a gaming casino, but by any measure it is a successful operation, having been open for over eighty years and continually reinventing itself to meet the public's interest.

3. By no means am I suggesting that wealth is a tribal community panacea or can be measured solely in monetary terms. Indeed, successful gaming tribes have their own community issues to deal with and are not free of despair despite having a great deal of economic promise. But in San Diego Indian Country, Native people are often very cognizant of the differences between being from a gaming tribe and from a non-gaming tribe—even if most white folks in San Diego cannot tell the difference and these days think that all Indians are "rich" (see Spilde 1999).

4. The LA '84 Foundation, a charitable organization established from the success and profits of the 1984 Los Angeles Summer Olympics, works to improve community-based sports and athletic facilities.

5. It is worth noting the African American asylum orderlies have their most prominent and extensive speaking roles in these scenes on the basketball court, embodying the prototypical working-class Black male who has mastered the game invented and promulgated by a white man (Randle McMurphy hence becomes the metaphorical James Naismith here). Moreover, an additional irony is that Nicholson is known to be perhaps the most famous NBA fan, attending nearly every Los Angeles Lakers home game in his courtside seats–often building filming pauses into his contract so that he won't miss playoff games.

6. The tournament is currently structured with 32 teams, half are girls' teams and half are boys' teams. Two 16-team, gender-based brackets are created, and both brackets have the same 16 high schools. In 2015, there were 13 all Native or reservation-based high schools and 3 non-Native teams from off-reservation communities. In 2016, there were 15 Native high schools participating and only 1 non-Native–based school.

7. Full-court pressure is when the defense starts to guard the offense all the way up the floor beginning with the inbounds pass under the opponent's basketball. Half-court pressure is when the defense starts to guard the offense immediately when the ball crosses midcourt. Half court pressure is not as extreme as full-court, but it is still more significant than normal defense. Both methods of pressure generally employ traps, which occur when two defenders try to make the ball handler pick up their dribble (often pinning them against a sideline, creating a virtual third defender) in order to try to swipe the ball out of the offensive player's hands or force them into making an errant pass that will get stolen by a defensive teammate.

8. For much of the history of basketball, play has been based around "big men" (the centers and power forwards), getting the ball passed to them while they have their back to the basket and holding their defender off behind them. Once this "big man" receives the ball, the rest of the offense would watch him either beat their defender one-on-one or pass the ball to a guard who would become open for jump shots when their defender helps to double-team the forward or center in the post. Currently, however, the most sophisticated basketball teams model their rosters and game plans around the three-point shot and lay-ups, as advanced stats have revealed that shooting 40 percent from the three-point line is better than shooting an average shooting percentage that most players shoot from all other two-point shots (other than layups). Dead-eyed shooters and quick guards who can take their defenders off the dribble and make a lay-up in traffic or force a defense to collapse close to the basketball to help prevent this guard from making a lay-up, then create space and opportunities for this driving player to "kick" (pass) the ball out to open shooters on the three-point line. Hence smaller, quicker offensive players have become much more valuable in today's basketball than they were in the past. This has sped up the game so that it looks more like the way Rezball has always been played.

9. A shot clock (usually thirty-five seconds in high school games) was originally installed in basketball games to prevent teams from stalling on offense and thereby preventing their opponent from getting chances to score. Before the advent of the shot clock, teams with the lead would try to run out the clock by slowing down their play, spreading to the four corners of the front court, forty feet from the hoop, and merely passing the ball without making any attempt to get near the basket. This would often happen as early as the beginning of the second half of a game. It was not until 1985 that the collegiate men used shot clocks. In NABI games, teams could potentially almost ensure themselves a win using this stalling tactic after achieving a modest 5- to 8-point lead, especially toward the end of games. However, although this would be a more strategic decision, it would not illustrate the best sportsmanship or the high pace of Rezball and is rarely employed in NABI games. I have witnessed similar sportsmanship at the LNI games as well.

10. Nonetheless, the ability of sport to be politicized should not be underestimated. Much of the academic research on sport critically examines the way sports are utilized to support or reflect political machinations in terms of race, gender and sexuality, class, nationalism, etc. (e.g., Cayleff 1996; Boyd 1997; Boyd and Shropshire 2000; Zirin 2005, 2009; Colás 2016, just to mention a few examples of this vast body of research). Locally, there have been occasions when a tribe's or tribal member's lack of participation in ITS is political in nature, relating to disagreement over institutional control of resources and decision-making.

11. One year I helped coach the ITS all-star girls' team, and we practiced at the Soboba tribal gym. Many practices we shared the floor (separated only by a large curtain) with a powwow dance "class." Often we could hear the recorded music during practice, and sometimes during breaks in the basketball action, the girls would even practice their powwow dances in time to the music.

12. The Pit's reputation extends well beyond the Albuquerque community. College basketball fans know the Pit as one of the hardest places in the country for a road team to play. The bleachers sit right on top of the court, creating a very loud and raucous atmosphere. Consequently, *Sports Illustrated* listed the Pit among its top twenty sports venues of the twentieth century (Hoffer 1999). This venue has also achieved national fame as host to some of the most significant NCAA March Madness games in the history of the sport, including the classic 1983 Final that included Akeem Olajuwon and Clyde Drexler's 31–1 Houston Cougars being upset by the North Carolina State Wolfpack on a buzzer-beater, put-back lay-up by Lorenzo Charles and the now famous image of NC State's Jim Valvano deliriously running around the court trying to find someone to hug after the victory.

13. The popularity of women's basketball in the Connecticut area is largely due to the veritable basketball dynasty established by the University of Connecticut Huskies women's team that has won a record eleven national championships, including four in a row from 2013 to 2016.

14. In 2023 the Sycuan Band of the Kumeyaay Nation became a minority partner in the Major League Soccer team the San Diego FC; however, that team will not officially join league play until spring of 2025.

15. I have never had this response when speaking to a Native American. That is, I have never met an Indian who is not familiar with the term Rezball.

2. SOME DAYS

1. "Forty-nines" are social songs sung to powwow rhythms. They are generally sung for fun and revelry late at night after a day of powwow. They are generally comic, even bawdy, and often with improvised lyrics. Alexie and Eyre use forty-nines a few different times in *Smoke Signals*.

2. The conventional history has Naismith inventing basketball in 1891 and Geronimo did not die until 1909, so sure, Geronimo could have learned the game after Naismith invented it, but I believe Alexie is trying to say something much more here.

3. On the contrary, the most recent journalistic revelation of Rezball in the *New York Times* deals with these issues in a way that is more sophisticated than most previous articles. Michael Powell has written two excellent *New York Times* articles about Navajo Rezballers in which he considers the athletes' aspirations for their personal educational achievement and their hopes for their community as a whole without

falling back on the idea that basketball is their ticket out of the community (Powell 2015, 2017).

4. I rely on this distinction between "Indigenous literary" writers and "Indigenous academic" writers not so much because I believe there is a difference in knowledge, epistemologies, or agendas, but rather just to distinguish between processes and modes of writing and scholarship. Writers such as Alexie and Diaz also embody an explicitly "academic" voice in metadiscursive commentary on the role of Indigenous literature, language, and intellectualism. Moreover, this distinction is easily crossed and often falls away quickly when we look at Indigenous thinkers who often betray the ambiguity of the categories of literature, art, and scholarship (see also Indigenous thinkers and literary writers such as Ella Deloria, Leslie Marmon Silko, Simon Ortiz, Gerald Vizenor, Paula Gunn Allen, Thomas King, Craig Womack, Robert Allen Warrior, Ofelia Zepeda, Joy Harjo, Cutcha Risling Baldy, and many others).

3. REZBALL, THE ANTI-FUNERAL

1. Inter Tribal Sports, "Mission," accessed March 2016, http://www.intertribalsports.org /Default.aspx?tabid=872319.

2. Similar collective game day events happen with the other sports offered by ITS, such as softball, flag football, and soccer.

3. TANF stands for Temporary Assistance for Needy Families. It is a federal social services program to support low-income families. Given that many Native American families qualify for TANF funding, the federal government has set up localized programming in and near tribal communities.

4. There are generally six regional Navajo fairs held in the different geographic regions of the Navajo Nation (Western, Central, Northern, Dine Bi Eastern, Southwest, and Ramah), a Navajo Nation Fair held in the capital, Window Rock, and the Gallup Intertribal Indian Ceremony held in the largest border town just off the Navajo reservation in far west New Mexico.

5. Unlike American's most prominent racial dividing line—that between Black and white—wherein "one drop" of African American "blood" is used to define someone as Black, American Indian identity has historically been a battle over whether or not someone has "enough" Native "blood" to be Indian. In contemporary America, this plays out in terms of phenotype and a notion of "blood quantum." In terms of the former, many American Indians can pass (or refuse to do so) in American society as either white or, particularly in California, as Chicano/a/x. Blood quantum itself is a product of settler colonialism and enlightenment pseudoscience and does not reflect Indigenous practices of defining community membership—despite the fact that it is used ubiquitously by the federal government, the American general public, and many tribal governments themselves. This debate about whether someone is Indian enough

has been acutely intense among many Southern California gaming tribes as notions of citizenship have changed. Some tribes have generated very public disputes as they have audited and amended their membership rolls and rules in ways that sometimes disenfranchised people who were previously tribal members. For discussions on Native identity and blood quantum see Circe Sturm (2002), Eva Marie Garoutte (2003), Renee Ann Cramer (2005), and Kim TallBear (2013).

6. "To burn" is a euphemism for smoking marijuana. It comes from the phrase "to burn weed." People who smoke a lot of marijuana are often described as "burners."

7. An "All Native +2" tournament is one in which only two of the five to ten players on a team can be non-Indian. This is a common format for Rezball tournaments or adult leagues. Sometimes it is adjusted to only a "+1" or, on rare occasions, a "+3."

4. REZBALL AND GENDER

1. It was only recently that the men's Final Four became officially labeled the "Men's Final Four" to distinguish it from the "Women's Final Four," which was always labeled as such. However, in common parlance and media coverage, the term "Final Four" is still used ubiquitously to mean the men's tournament, not the women's.

2. Although the official name of the tribal nation is the Soboba Band of Luiseño Indians, the community comprises people of both Luiseno and Cahuilla heritage. This is reinforced by the promotion and use of both languages.

3. As discussed in chapter 2, the "basketball-as-ticket-out" narrative is rarely employed in Indian Country; nonetheless, this does not mean that no one from Indian Country has been able to parlay their athletic abilities into a college scholarship or even a professional career. I have already noted that Natalie Diaz and Shoni Schimmel both have had prominent college and professional basketball careers. Moreover, in 2017 Winnebago tribal member Bronson Koening concluded a prolific college career at the University of Wisconsin by leading his team on an NCAA tournament run. Koening was entered into the 2017 NBA Draft but was not chosen in the first two rounds; however, he had workouts with several NBA teams and ultimately signed a free agent contract for the 2017 NBA Summer League (summer tournaments made up of teams consisting of first- and second-year NBA players who were drafted but need to improve their game and of undrafted players looking to gain a full contract with an NBA team). Recently, Koening was playing in the NBA G League (its minor/farm system league) for the Grand Rapids Drive, an affiliate of the Detroit Pistons. Similar to these three, Joe Burton played basketball at a college with a national profile from one of the five major collegiate athletic conferences.

4. A few basic differences in regulations do exist: for example, the women's ball is about an inch smaller in circumference than the men's—making it easier to grip with a smaller hand and more likely for jump shots to be made because the rim diameter

is unchanged, hence there is a bit more room for the ball to go in. Additionally, the WNBA the three-point line follows the men's and women's international rules for distance, making it about eighteen inches closer than the NBA regulation. Despite these few changes, the games are almost identical in terms of rules and regulations.

5. On average, teams in this age group usually have anywhere from five to ten players, depending on the reservation, and generally no more than three are girls. One or two is more the norm, and in some cases, there are none. In 2023 ITS experimented with girls-only teams for the oldest ages. So far, they were able to field five all-girls teams of sixteen- to eighteen-year-olds.

6. While I have noted significant changes in the popularity in girls' and women's high school, college, and professional basketball, on the whole the sport is still significantly undervalued compared to the boys' and men's game. We are seeing increasing instances of high attendance and television ratings for female athletes; however, this is the exception rather than the norm. Hopefully these exceptional instances are at the front of a significant wave of change, but female athletes still get way less promotion, attendance, and financial renumeration compared to male athletes.

5. SKATE (REZ) LIFE

1. Ironically, the trick is not named after Mullen, but rather for Alan "Ollie" Gelfand. Gelfand's nickname is "Ollie," and in 1976 he first did the trick by accident when he and his board fully cleared the lip of the concrete bowl he was skating. His friends originally labeled it an "ollie pop," and then as more skaters replicated the trick in pools and on ramps, it became known as an "ollie air." Until Mullen, ollies were exclusively done in pools, concrete skateparks, or half pipes. After Mullen popularized it on flat ground, everyone simply just used the term "ollie" (Brooke 1999; Louison 2011; Snyder 2015).

2. Published in San Francisco, *Slap* was founded by professional skater Lance Dawes and existed from 1992 to 2008. *Slap* was characterized as a more independent version of the popular skateboard magazine *Thrasher*.

3. The adjacent cities of Encinitas and Carlsbad are home to many professional surfers and skaters including, Tony Hawk, Danny Way, and Rob Machado. The Encinitas-Carlsbad YMCA has a massive half pipe, akin to the kind used in professional competitions, that is used for skate camps and lessons and is open to the public for practice. The Skatepark Project (formerly the Tony Hawk Foundation) is headquartered in neighboring Vista, California. And in the foothills outside of Encinitas, Danny Way built the first "mega ramp," which was replicated for several ESPN X-Games competitions. Moreover, the Del Mar Skate Ranch hosted some of the most important contests of the 1980s and was the training ground for some of the most influential skaters ever.

4. DC Shoes has been one of the more popular skate shoe companies of the last twenty years, reaching revenues of $1 billion in that time period. Danny Way is a popular professional skateboarder known for his near mythological willingness to launch himself to extreme vertical heights on a skateboard; he is a "daredevil" in a sport already known for high risk-taking athletes.

5. On deck art see Cliver (2004), Waterhouse and Penhallow (2006), Carayol (2014), Borden (2019), and Gordon and Rogers (2022), and for specifically Native American deck art, see Badoni (2009).

6. For debates about authenticity in skate subculture see Beal (1995, 1998), Atencio, Beal, and Wilson (2009), and Yochim (2010), and for more general debate about authenticity in subcultures see Hebdige (1979) and Hall and Jefferson (1990).

6. SKATER LEGENDS OF THE REZ

1. It is important to note, however, that as skateboarding becomes increasing corporate, like all thing that were once the height of rebellion and cool, skateboarding is increasingly mainstream and less outsider. Nonetheless, in American popular imagination skateboarding is still seen as a rebellious sport even if the reality of its demographics has dramatically shifted from the 1970s and 1980s.

2. While Stecyk's gonzo journalism of the Z-Boys came first and provides much of the basis for Peralta's film, Stecyk's work does not have the same reach, longevity, and completeness as Peralta's film. The latter includes significant material beyond Stecyk's original writings and photographs, and as a film, made in 2001 and distributed by Sony Pictures, it has been circulated far more widely on far more platforms than Stecyk's original work. Stecyk's original stories only appeared in *Skateboarder Magazine*, which had a small distribution in the 1970s and was out of print by 1980. It was not until 2000 that Stecyk's articles have been republished, and even then, it is most likely that the success of Peralta's film created the market for this book.

3. Murph has Lenni Lenape heritage on his father's side that is very important to him, but he is not enrolled in either the Delaware tribes of Oklahoma or the Stockbridge-Munsee Community in Wisconsin—all of which have federal recognition—or in the currently unrecognized tribes in Delaware and New Jersey. He recognizes the complex history of Indian identity and settler colonialism that left some Indigenous folks without a community, some with communities the U.S. government does not recognize, and others that do have federal recognition (for more on this complexity see Garroutte 2003). Given this complexity, Jim honors his family's heritage but is very cautious to not overstate his Indian identity out of respect for the differing notions of Indianness (personal communication, February 20, 2024). It is for this reason that I have not identified him as Lenape in this book.

4. The Hopi reservation is in northern Arizona and is surrounded by the Navajo Nation. In reality "Hopi" is a cultural identification that has as more to do with settler colonial administration from the nineteenth century onward than with being a uniform cultural and political identity. Hopis are organized into several villages or pueblos that still maintain a great amount of political, legal, religious, and social distinctiveness and autonomy. Most, but not all, of the villages are on one of three mesas, and people often identify themselves as being from First, Second, or Third Mesa or by their village name (see Levy 1992; Richland 2008).

5. Some of these tags are still visible when visiting Alcatraz National Park. The best photographic collection is compiled in Troy Johnson's *You Are on Indian Land: Alcatraz Island, 1969-1971* (1994). The meaning of most of these tags is self-evident; however, "Taken by Oakes" refers to Richard Oakes, a key figure and organizer of the seizure of the island, and "Dept. of Indians, Bureau of White Affairs" is a playfully rebellious inversion of the U.S. federal government's Bureau of Indian Affairs, the bane of many Native people's experience and lives.

6. Several contemporary Native artists such as Steven Paul Judd, Bunky Echo-Hawk, and Rico Wurl have all used skateboards as creative palettes to express their distinctive visions of modern Indigenous art. They have all made beautiful work on the back of skateboards, but for them skateboards appear to be one of many places to produce their art rather than embracing the totality of skate culture and how it overlaps with Indigenous cultures.

7. SKATE ELDERS

1. I fully recognize there is some irony in arguing that a white man is "co-opting" the terms "tribe" or "elder," given that these terms actually originate from early Anglo American and European ethnological and social scientific nomenclature (from the likes of Lewis Morgan, Elman Service, and Morton Fried), but through the paradox of modernity Indigenous communities have reclaimed these terms (not without internal critique; see Kahnawake Mohawk scholar Alfred 1995, 1999), and they have specific legal and cultural meaning in context. A resurgence of white folks using the term "tribe" or "tribalism" in popular discourse to describe both a return to small-scale communal bonds (e.g., Junger 2016) or increased factionalism in sociopolitical life (e.g., Hanson 2021) is, in my mind, another form of "playing Indian" that further reifies settler fantasies of nobility and barbarism.

2. In addition to hosting one of the best skateparks in Southern California, the Pala Tribe also maintains the premier motocross facility in California, if not the whole country. All the top professionals train at this facility, and consequently motocross is hugely popular among the residents of the Pala Reservation.

3. Northwest Coast "style" art is one of the most appropriated Indigenous styles of design. It can be found all over products, signs, and logos in the U.S. and Canadian Pacific Northwest. One of Louie Gong's main goals of his company Eighth Generation is helping Indigenous artists regain control of their culture's imagery and aesthetics. One way he has done this is through his campaign "Inspired Natives, Not Native Inspired"—a campaign designed to educate the consumer public about cultural appropriation and the importance of Indigenous artists receiving the profit and compensation for their work, not non-Native mass production entities. What's more, as 8th Generation grew, instead of seeking mainstream corporate partners, Louie sold the company to Snoqualmie Indian Tribe as financial backer while maintaining his role as CEO (Tapahe 2022).

4. There are well over six hundred distinct tribes or Indigenous communities in the United States with often complex differences and relationships to each other, let alone the diversity even within these communities at the level of clan or initiate society. This diversity in Indian Country is frequently ignored and misunderstood by the rest of non-Indian America. Indeed, even the term "Indian" is a misnomer of false uniformity that is sustained mostly for the necessities of settler society and obscures distinctiveness and vast cultural, linguistic, political, and historical diversity.

5. I consider the term "skate elder" imperfect in that generally an elder is much older than the skaters I discuss in this chapter, *and* because this term comes from my estimation of what is going on in the community. I want to make very clear that this is not the term that these skaters use about themselves. When I floated the idea of this term to each of them, some liked it and thought it had connotative value, while others less so, but they certainly all demurred from calling themselves "elders," and no one said it was incorrect. More commonly, many of the skaters who had been mentored by these OG Native skaters showed much more enthusiasm for the term when I proposed this neologism to them. These younger skaters absolutely acknowledged the way the OGs acted as elders toward them: looking out for them and sharing knowledge. Ultimately, using this term is just me asserting my academic, analytic privilege for better or worse.

6. Probably the main reason for this dearth of equipment is that most reservations are rural and therefore are far from convenient trips to a skate shop. Add to this the fact that many Native families do not have surplus resources to spend on what might be considered a luxury item. Indeed, one of the standard questions with which I begin my interviews is: "Do you remember your first board?" Nearly everyone replied with some version of "a cheap board my parents bought at Walmart." This speaks to both the socioeconomics and geography of these Native skaters in that Walmart is frequently the most affordable and accessible place for their family to shop.

7. With some of these kids this may be one of the few times all year they leave the reservation.
8. Often there is an additional skate competition at Pine Ridge called the "Toby Classic."
   It is named after Toby Eagle Bull, one the best skaters from Pine Ridge who died in
   a tragic drunk driving accident in 2001 (Ecoffey 2015). In 2002 the Eagle Bull family
   decided to host a contest in his honor, and it is still going strong today. Walt Pourier
   and Jim Murphy have been instrumental in supporting this contest, and they worked
   with the Eagle Bull family in developing the skatepark at Pine Ridge, which is officially
   named the Toby Ray Eagle Bull Skatepark. For a longtime the Toby Classic was the
   only skate competition, and it ran in conjunction with the Wacipi & Fair. At some
   point, however, the ONE Gathering and the Toby Classic became separate events, often
   held just a week apart. In 2019 when I attended the ONE Gathering, the Toby Classic
   had been held just the weekend before. The Eagle Bull family showed up to the ONE
   Gathering event, and there did not seem to be tension between these two contests.
   Yet at the same time, it was clear Walt and Jim preferred not to discuss why there are
   now two separate events, and that is an ethnographic refusal I accepted without any
   further inquiry.
9. Spins were tricks where the skater attempted to spin 360 degrees (or more) while
   pivoting on the back trucks of the board. Balance tricks were based on a skateboarder's ability to stay on the board while putting all their weight on the nose or on just
   one leg or even doing a handstand on the board. Jumping tricks were usually two
   kinds: "hippie jumps" or "barrel jumps." In a hippie jump a skateboarder jumps off
   the board as it travels under a bar that the skater jumps over and then rejoins the
   board by landing on it cleanly after the board and the skater clear the bar. In a barrel
   jump a skater accelerates toward a row of barrels—usually plastic trash cans—
   lined up on their side, uses momentum to leap off the board at the first barrel and
   tries to clear the distance of the barrels in the air and successfully land on a second
   skateboarding waiting at a standstill at the edge of the last barrel in the row (for
   more detail on "freestyle" skateboarding see Weyland 2002; Borden 2019). In the
   conventional narrative, freestyle and the Z-Boys' new style came to a head at the
   1975 Del Mar Nationals when the Dogtown crew introduced themselves and their
   aggressive style of skating to the world. However, a more nuanced understanding
   of the relationship between these two styles is that the Z-Boys were doing some
   of the same things as the freestylers, such as spins and some balance tricks, and it
   was not until they started pool skating and emphasizing verticality that these two
   styles significantly diverged (Brooke 1999; Weyland 2002; Beal 2013; Borden 2001).
   Moreover, freestyle prodigy Ty Page, who was the Z-Boys' major competition at the
   Del Mar Nationals, was just as influenced by surfing as the Dogtown kids and was
   doing the surfing-influenced power slides as early as them, if not earlier (Bolster

1977). Unlike the narrative implied in Peralta's 2001 movie about Peralta's Dogtown crew, Page did not get left in a wreckage of the Z-Boys' wake. He kept modifying and innovating his on-ground skating while the Z-Boys and Bones Brigade were going vertical. It is no stretch of the imagination to call Ty a progenitor of street-style skating that gained popularity in the 1990s as vertical skating began to decline. Page was likely a big influence on street-legend Rodney Mullen (Louison 2011), and Page created many tricks, such as "shove it" and "manual," that are still practiced today by skaters all over the world—including Indian Country.

10. Although not completely verifiable, in all my conversations with Native skaters none have mentioned anything earlier than this 1978 skate contest at White Mountain. Ultimately "first" does not really matter in this situation, but suffice it to say that Dustinn is one of the "O-est" of OGs when it comes to skateboarding in Indian Country.

11. Like Dustinn, his wife at the time was Native. She, like Dustinn's paternal side, is Diné (Navajo Nation).

12. The construction of this skatepark can be viewed in the first episode of the first season of *Design Squad Nation* filmed in January 2011. The full episode can be viewed on the Daily Motion website, https://www.dailymotion.com/video/x5kk44l.

13. These characteristics of skate rats map pretty cleanly on to depictions of the most prominent Dogtown skateboarders. As I argue in chapter 6, Dogtown became an origin myth that defined the kind of skateboarder coming out of the mid-1970s. Ever since, skateboarding has exploded with far more diversity than illustrated among the Z-Boys; nonetheless, the concept of a bad boy, devil-may-care, gritty skateboarder (i.e., a "skate rat") clearly has its origins in Dogtown.

14. While there is little doubt that the term "raider" is an implicitly gendered code, Dustinn was attempting to interpret this role in a modern context that could also include women. There is more to come on this gendered aspect later in this chapter.

15. Indeed, the three-essay article in *National Geographic* (Hess 1980) that features his uncles skateboarding in Whiskey Flats also features an essay from a young woman going through the *na'ii'ees* (or Sunrise) ceremony on the White Mountain Apache Reservation (Quintero 1980).

16. I use the word "generation" here broadly, not necessarily a strict definition of every twenty years, but rather the relationship between people of significantly different enough ages and life stages.

17. As noted in chapter 6, Doug and Dustinn do not work collaboratively, and so even though they have influenced the same skaters, they have not done so in any coordinated effort. Most likely this overlap is a product of geography and demography. The two live about a hundred miles apart, are both Apache, and spend significant time with the Indigenous community in Phoenix; hence, it is natural that there would be a lot of overlap in the Native skate community of this region.

1. Many American Indian cultures thrive on notions of balance and harmony derived from four to six cardinal directions. These conceptualizations of harmony are often metaphorically represented through color schemes and directional markings. The Lakota medicine wheel, a circle divided into four quadrants painted red, black, yellow, and white, has become the most ubiquitous and is frequently adapted in a pan-Indian format, as many communities now use this visual representation for conceptions of healing. While a trans- or pan-tribal use of the Lakota medicine wheel does risk some amount of cultural appropriation or dilution of significance through decontextualized, ahistorical usage, it's trans-tribal usage in the context of the Gallup skatepark seems appropriate, given the fact that Gallup is in many ways seen as a crossroads for several tribes of the Southwest. What's more, the Navajo have a similar construction of four sacred directions that are metonymically connected to a color scheme.

2. In using the term "feminist," I am using it in the broadest, pro-woman, anti-misogyny way possible here. But I also acknowledge the dynamic variation and diversity within feminism. With my broad usage here, I mean to evoke a general sense of female empowerment, but I am not trying to oversimplify the complex relationships that exist between mainstream (white) feminism and feminists of color or queer and nonbinary empowerment—particularly in regard to notions of Indigenous feminisms (for more on the Indigenous feminisms see Allen 1992 Mihesuah 2003; Goeman and Nez Denetdale 2009; Ross 2009; Goeman 2013; Barker 2017; Risling Baldy 2018).

3. This is Selina's preferred pronoun: "she/they."

4. Perhaps the most obvious and surface-level example of this distinction of cool is the term "mongo" or "to push mongo." Mongo designates a person who keeps their rear foot on the back of the board and pushes against the ground with their front foot. Arguably this version is (or at least is almost) as functional as "regular," but mongo is considered not as cool and demarcates a less than authentic skater. Or as the Urban Dictionary defines "pushing mongo": "a stupid way to skateboard" (Urban Dictionary, s.v. "pushing mongo," accessed February 15, 2021, https://www.urbandictionary.com /define.php?term=Pushing+Mongo).

5. The most extreme example is Mark "Gator" Rogowski, who pleaded guilty to assaulting, raping, and murdering a woman in 1991. Jay Adams went to prison in 1982 for a gay-bashing incident, and Sal Rocco committed what I would consider to be a grave act of symbolic violence against women by creating Bitch Skateboards, whose (sadly popular) logo was a man holding a gun to a woman's head.

6. I want to be clear that I am not suggesting that there is something innate in women that allows them to bond this way or that men somehow cannot. Rather, societal conditions have aligned in such a way to more easily produce transformative power

in female and nonbinary relationships than in many male-to-male or even male-to-female relationships.

7. Redbubble (redbubble.com) is an online marketplace for independent artists to promote their work. It is generally consistent with the DIY ethos of skateboarding and is used by many skateboard artists, especially Indigenous ones.

8. An important thing to note about the Land Back movement is that, like the Prison Abolitionist movement, it is grounded in pragmatism, not merely ideology. It is not calling for an immediate reversal of more than 150 years of practice and policy that would produce an inordinate amount of chaos. Instead, it promotes several critical small steps that would have a huge impact on current Indigenous relationship to land—such as working out leasing agreements, joint jurisdiction, or comanagement. The idea is not that all non-Indigenous people and entities should forfeit any land that they occupy (just as Prison Abolition does not mean immediate release of all prisons or no consequences for crime), but rather that America is way out of balance in terms of Indigenous control of land and that Indigenous people should have far greater access to land lost to settler colonialism.

9. One last beautiful irony here is that, as mentioned, Selina sells her/their art on the Redbubble website, which is very convenient in that it takes images created by artists and offers consumers the options of putting this art on stickers, bookbags, T-shirts, sweatshirts, and mugs. The website provides stock models displaying the various items available. There are a handful of multicultural, multiethnic models, but there are also some distinctly white models. Seeing these white folks model the transgressive imagery of Selina's adds a whole new (unintended, but nevertheless powerful) rebuke of whiteness.

10. A "flow" team member is a term used to signify when a skate team or company sponsors someone by giving them free gear—as in the slang "to flow," to give or to share something with someone. This is like an entry-level sponsorship in that the team or company is not paying the skater (either because the team does not have enough money to so or because the skater is just beginning a professional career) but is just giving them free skate supplies. This is meant to be a mutually beneficial arrangement: the skater gets free gear while the team or company gets free marketing.

11. Navajo "chapters" are regional governmental administrative units, similar to counties both in size and function.

12. With every other skatepark it has been involved in, the Tony Hawk Foundation (now The Skatepark Project) has provided financial support to help communities find grants, donations, and local public money—its model is not to fully fund projects but to support communities in finding funding. The Diné Skate Garden and a park planned in Sacramento to honor the life of Tyree Nichols (a Black skater murdered by Memphis police) are the only two parks the TSP has ever fully funded.

13. Many young skaters call their homemade skate videos "edits"—a reference to the process and ability to shoot and edit a video on one's own. This is a result of the technological advances and easy access to digital filming devices (GoPro cameras, inexpensive high-definition small cameras, and high-quality video cameras on smartphones) and video production computer programs (apps for laptop computers and even smart phones that allow for video and sound editing, effects, and sound mixing). Making "edits" has become even more popular given the omnipresent audience created by social media platforms.

14. Note, that when I write "Di'orr's board" I mean it in the informal sense of the board being presented to her, not the more formalized notion of a "pro-model," the highest level of sponsorship in which a skate brand custom designs a board for its top riders; their names go on the board, and the board is specifically referred to as a "[skater's name] model."

15. "Board," "nose," and "tail" slides are maneuvers when the skater ollies their board to land on a feature, such as a ledge, rail, bar, or bowl copping, at an angel that puts their board perpendicular to the feature and thereby uses their momentum to slide the bottom of the board across the feature as far as they can. A board slide occurs when the primary part of the board sliding across the feature is the section between the two trucks; nose or tail slides occur when the board slides along the smaller sections of the board that are between the trucks and either edge of the board.

EPILOGUE

1. Navajo Sandstone is the geologic descriptor of the formations typical to the Southwest that are burnt orange in color, smooth, but textured with the petrified ripples deposited over 150 million years ago by ancient seas and lakes.

2. Of course, it is important to note that settlers and Indigenous folks, alike, will use the word "tradition" in a positive way. But when used by the non-Natives, it too often accompanies the patronizing trope of the Noble Savage that ultimately still codes the modern as advanced and the traditional as primitive. Within Native communities, often the notion of "tradition" is used to regulate Indigenous identity in local power struggles, especially when aspects of indigeneity that engage the contemporary world are labeled inauthentically Indigenous because they are not "traditional."

3. For more on MMIW see Amnesty International (2007); Deer (2015); Anderson, Campbell, and Belcourt (2018); Lucchesi and Echo-Hawk (2018).

WORKS CITED

Abdul-Jabbar, Kareem, and Stephen Singular. 2000. *A Season on the Reservation: My Sojourn with the White Mountain Apache.* New York: William Morrow.

Alexie, Sherman. 1993. *The Lone Ranger and Tonto Fistfight in Heaven.* New York: Atlantic Monthly Press.

———. 2000. *The Toughest Indian in the World.* New York: Atlantic Monthly Press.

———. 2003. *Ten Little Indians: Stories.* New York: Grove Press.

Alfred, Gerald Robert. 1995. *Heeding the Voices of Our Ancestors: Kahnawake Mohawk Politics and the Rise of Native Nationalism.* London: Oxford University Press.

Alfred, Taiaiake. 1999. *Peace, Power, and Righteousness: An Indigenous Manifesto.* London: Oxford University Press.

Allen, Paula Gunn. 1992. *The Sacred Hoop: Recovering the Feminine in American Indian Traditions.* With a new preface. Boston: Beacon Press.

Amnesty International. 2007. *Maze of Injustice: The Failure to Protect Indigenous Women from Sexual Violence in the USA.* New York: Amnesty International USA. https://www.amnestyusa.org/wp-content/uploads/2017/05/mazeofinjustice.pdf.

Anderson, Kim, Maria Campbell, and Christi Belcourt, eds. 2018. *Keetsahnak: Our Missing and Murdered Indigenous Sisters.* Edmonton: University of Alberta Press.

Atencio, Matthew, Becky Beal, and Charlene Wilson. 2009. "The Distinction of Risk: Urban Skateboarding, Street Habitus and the Construction of Hierarchical Gender Relations." *Qualitative Research in Sport and Exercise* 1 (1): 3–20.

Atencio, Matthew, Becky Beal, E. Missy Wright, and ZáNean McClain. 2018. *Moving Boarders: Skateboarding and the Changing Landscape of Urban Youth Sports.* Fayetteville: University of Arkansas Press.

Badoni, Georgina. 2009. "Native American Art and Visual Cultural Education through Skateboards." Master's thesis, University of Arizona.

Barker, Joanne, ed. 2017. *Critically Sovereign: Indigenous Gender, Sexuality, and Feminist Studies.* Durham NC: Duke University Press.

Beal, Becky. 1995. "Disqualifying the Official: An Exploration of Social Resistance through the Subculture of Skateboarding." *Sociology of Sport Journal* 12 (3): 252–67.

———. 1996. "Alternative Masculinity and Its Effect on Gender Relations in the Subculture of Skateboarding." *Journal of Sport Behavior* 19 (3): 204–20.

———. 1998. "Symbolic Inversion in the Subculture of Skateboarding." In *Play and Culture Studies*, vol. 1, edited by Margaret Carlisle Duncan, Gary Chick, and Alan Aycock, 209–22. Greenwich CT: Ablex.

———. 2013. *Skateboarding: The Ultimate Guide*. New York: Bloomsbury.

Beal, Becky, Matthew Atencio, E. Missy Wright, and ZáNean McClain. 2017. "Skateboarding, Community and Urban Politics: Shifting Practices and Challenges." *International Journal of Sport Policy and Politics* 9 (1): 11–23.

Beal, Becky, and Charlene Wilson. 2004. "'Chicks Dig Scars': Commercialisation and the Transformation of Skateboarders' Identities." In *Understanding Lifestyle Sport: Consumption, Identity, and Difference*, edited by Belinda Wheaton, 31–54. London: Routledge.

Bloom, John. 2000. *To Show What an Indian Can Do: Sports at Native American Boarding Schools*. Minneapolis: University of Minnesota Press.

Bolster, Warren. 1977. "SkateBoarder Interview: Ty Page, 'I Don't Do Anything That's Easy.'" *SkateBoarder*, September 1977.

Borden, Iain. 2001. *Skateboarding, Space and the City: Architecture and the Body*. Oxford: Berg.

———. 2019. *Skateboarding and the City: A Complete History*. London: Bloomsbury Academic.

Boyd, Todd. 1997. *Am I Black Enough for You?: Popular Culture from the 'Hood and Beyond*. Bloomington: Indiana University Press.

Boyd, Todd, and Kenneth L. Shropshire. 2000. *Basketball Jones: America above the Rim*. New York: New York University Press.

Boykoff, Jules. 2023. *The 1936 Berlin Olympics: Race, Power, and Sportswashing*. Champaign IL: Common Ground Research Networks.

Brooke, Michael. 1999. *The Concrete Wave: The History of Skateboarding*. Toronto: Warwick.

Bruyneel, Kevin. 2007. *The Third Space of Sovereignty: The Postcolonial Politics of U.S.-Indigenous Relations*. Minneapolis: University of Minnesota Press.

Bucklew, Chase, and David Kamper. 2025. "Origins of the 'Radical': The Dogtown Imaginary and the Inheritors of the Z-Boy Revolution." In *Waves of Belonging: Indigeneity, Race, and Gender in the Surfing Lineup*, edited by Lydia Heberling, David Kamper, and Jess Ponting, 182–203. Seattle: University of Washington Press.

Cahn, Susan K. 1994. *Coming on Strong: Gender and Sexuality in Twentieth-Century Women's Sport*. New York: Free Press.

Carayol, Seb. 2014. *Agents Provocateurs: 100 Subversive Skateboard Graphics*. Richmond CA: Gingko Press.

Carrington, Ben, and Ian McDonald, eds. 2009. *Marxism, Cultural Studies and Sport*. London: Routledge.

Cayleff, Susan E. 1996. *Babe: The Life and Legend of Babe Didrikson Zaharias*. Urbana: University of Illinois Press.

Chavez, Aliyah. 2020. "Nathan Apodaca: Everyone's New Cousin." *Indian Country Today*, October 13, 2020. https://ictnews.org/news/nathan-apodaca-everyones-new-cousin.

Chiu, Chihsin. 2009. "Contestation and Conformity: Street and Park Skateboarding in New York Public Space." *Space and Culture* 12 (1): 25–42.

Churchill, Ward, and Jim Vander Wall. 2002. *Agents of Repression: The FBI's Secret Wars against the Black Panther Party and the American Indian Movement.* Cambridge MA: South End Press.

Cliver, Sean. 2004. *Disposable: A History of Skateboard Art.* Corte Madera CA: Gingko Press.

Cobb, Daniel M., and Loretta Fowler, eds. 2007. *Beyond Red Power: American Indian Politics and Activism since 1900.* Albuquerque: University of New Mexico Press.

Colás, Yago. 2016. *Ball Don't Lie: Myth, Genealogy, and Invention in the Cultures of Basketball.* Philadelphia: Temple University Press.

Colton, Larry 2000. *Counting Coup: A True Story of Basketball and Honor on the Little Big Horn.* New York: Warner Books.

Comer, Krista. 2010. *Surfer Girls in the New World Order.* Durham NC: Duke University Press.

Connell, Raewynn. 1987. *Gender and Power: Society, the Person, and Sexual Politics.* Cambridge: Polity Press in association with B. Blackwell.

Corwin, Zöe. B., Tattiya Maruco, Neftalie Williams, Robert Reichard, Maria Romero-Morales, Christine Rocha, and Constanza Astiazaran. 2019. *Beyond the Board: Findings from the Field.* Los Angeles: Tony Hawk Foundation, USC Rossier Pullias Center for Higher Education, and USC Annenberg School for Communication and Journalism.

Craig, Dustinn. 2017. "When History Becomes Real." https://vimeo.com/166297590 (no longer a working link).

Cramer, Renée Ann. 2005. *Cash, Color, and Colonialism: The Politics of Tribal Acknowledgment.* Norman: University of Oklahoma Press.

Cummins, Ann, Cecilia Anderson, and Georgia Briggs. 2005. "Women's Basketball on the Navajo Nation: The Shiprock Cardinals, 1960–1980." In *Native Athletes in Sport & Society: A Reader,* edited by C. Richard King, 143–69. Lincoln: University of Nebraska Press.

Deer, Sarah. 2015. *The Beginning and End of Rape: Confronting Sexual Violence in Native America.* Minneapolis: University of Minnesota Press.

Deloria, Philip J. 2004. *Indians in Unexpected Places.* Lawrence: University Press of Kansas.

———. 2019. *Becoming Mary Sully: Toward an American Indian Abstract.* Seattle: University of Washington Press.

Derby, Rick, dir. 2001. *Rocks with Wings.* Shiprock NM: Shiprock Productions.

Diaz, Natalie. 2012. "Reservation Mary." In *When My Brother Was an Aztec.* Port Townsend WA: Copper Canyon Press.

———. 2013. "Run'N'Gun: Sports Blog Series." https://prairieschooner.unl.edu/digital-schooner/runngun/.

Donat, Patricia L. N., and John D'Emilio. 1992. "A Feminist Redefinition of Rape and Sexual Assault: Historical Foundations and Change." *Journal of Social Issues* 48 (1): 9–22.

Dowling, Colette. 2000. *The Frailty Myth: Women Approaching Physical Equality*. New York: Random House.

Ecoffey, Brandon. 2015. "Skate Competition Continues to Grow." *Lakota Times*, July 30. https://www.lakotatimes.com/articles/skate-competition-continues-to-grow/.

Ellis, Clyde. 2003. *A Dancing People: Powwow Culture on the Southern Plains*. Lawrence: University Press of Kansas.

Ellis, Clyde, Luke Eric Lassiter, and Gary H. Dunham, eds. 2005. *Powwow*. Lincoln: University of Nebraska Press.

Eyre, Chris, dir. 1998. *Smoke Signals*, written by Sherman Alexie. Los Angeles: Miramax Films.

Fabian, Johannes. 1983. *Time and the Other: How Anthropology Makes Its Object*. New York: Columbia University Press.

Fagan, Kate, Howard Bryant, and Tom Haberstroh. 2021. "The NBA's Vaccine Problem." *The Dan Le Batard Show with Stugotz*, September 30, 2021, produced by Mike Ryan Ruiz, Roy Bellamy, Billy Gil, Chris Cote, Jessica Smetana, Anthony Calatayud, Luis Montejo, and Jeremy Taché. Podcast, https://youtu.be/wATOsCglZbk?si=TL2RHUCQCLMhNCoo.

Frazier, Ian. 2000. *On the Rez*. New York: Farrar, Straus and Giroux.

Garroutte, Eva Marie. 2003. *Real Indians: Identity and the Survival of Native America*. Berkeley: University of California Press.

Glick, Peter, and Susan T. Fiske. 1999. "Gender, Power Dynamics, and Social Interaction." In *Revisioning Gender*, edited by Myra Marx Ferree, Judith Lorber, and Beth B. Hess, 365–98. Thousand Oaks CA: Sage.

Goeman, Mishuana. 2013. *Mark My Words: Native Women Mapping Our Nations*. Minneapolis: University of Minnesota Press.

Goeman, Mishuana, and Jennifer Nez Denetdale. 2009. "Native Feminisms: Legacies, Interventions, and Indigenous Sovereignties." *Wicazo Sa Review* 24 (2): 9–13.

Goldman, Tom. 2003. "Basketball: A Ticket off the Reservation?" *All Things Considered*, produced by Matt Ozug, Oliver Dearden, Gus Contreras, Jason Fuller, Kat Lonsdorf, Jonaki Mehta, Erika Ryan, and Mallory Yu. Podcast, M3 audio, https://www.npr.org /2003/08/12/1385520/basketball-a-ticket-off-the-reservation.

Goldstein, David. 2009. "Sacred Hoop Dreams: Basketball in the Work of Sherman Alexie." *Ethnic Studies Review* 32 (1): 77–111.

Goodwin, Grenville. 1971. *Western Apache Raiding and Warfare*. Edited by Keith H. Basso. Tucson: University of Arizona Press.

Gordon, Betsy, and Jane Rogers. 2022. *Four Wheels and a Board: The Smithsonian History of Skateboarding*. Washington DC: Smithsonian Books.

Grassian, Daniel. 2005. *Understanding Sherman Alexie*. Columbia: University of South Carolina Press.

Hall, Stuart, and Tony Jefferson, eds. 1990. *Resistance through Rituals: Youth Subcultures in Post-War Britain*. London: Hutchinson.

Hanson, Victor Davis. 2021. *The Dying Citizen: How Progressive Elites, Tribalism, and Globalization Are Destroying the Idea of America*. New York: Basic Books.

Hardwicke, Catherine, dir. 2005. *Lords of Dogtown*. Culver City CA: Columbia Pictures.

Hargreaves, Jennifer. 1994. *Sporting Females: Critical Issues in the History and Sociology of Women's Sports*. London: Routledge.

Harjo, Joy, Gloria Bird, Patricia Blanco, Beth Cuthand, and Valerie Martínez, eds. 1997. *Reinventing the Enemy's Language: Contemporary Native Women's Writing of North America*. New York: W.W. Norton.

Hearne, Joanna. 2012. *Native Recognition: Indigenous Cinema and the Western*. Albany: SUNY Press.

———. 2014. "'This Is Our Playground': Skateboarding, DIY Aesthetics, and Apache Sovereignty in Dustinn Craig's '4wheelwarpony.'" *Western American Literature* 49 (1): 47–69.

Hebdige, Dick. 1979. *Subcultures: The Meaning of Style*. London: Methuen.

Hess, Bill. 1980. "Seeking the Best of Two Worlds." *National Geographic* 157 (2) (February): 272–90.

Hobsbawm, Eric, and Terence Ranger, eds. 2012. *The Invention of Tradition*. Cambridge: Cambridge University Press.

Hock, Jonathan, dir. 2011. *Off the Rez*. Silver Spring MD: TLC.

Hoffer, Richard. 1999. "Our Favorite Venues Certain Ground Rules Prevail When It Comes to Picking the Best Places in the World to Watch Sports: No Domes, No Condemned Buildings, No Hooters." *Sports Illustrated*, June 7.

Howell, Ocean. 2005. "The 'Creative Class' and the Gentrifying City: Skateboarding in Philadelphia's Love Park." *Journal of Architectural Education* 59 (2): 32–42.

Huhndorf, Shari M. 2001. *Going Native: Indians in the American Cultural Imagination*. Ithaca NY: Cornell University Press.

Irvine, Simon, and Sophie Taysom. 1998. "Skateboarding: Disrupting the City." *Social Alternatives* 17 (4): 23–26.

Jacob, Michelle M. 2013. *Yakama Rising: Indigenous Cultural Revitalization, Activism, and Healing*. Tucson: University of Arizona Press.

Jaskulski, Józef. 2014. "More Than a Game: Basketball as a Medium of History in Three Early Works of Sherman Alexie." *Americana: E-Journal of American Studies in Hungary* 10 (2).

Jenkins, Sally. 2007. *The Real All Americans: The Team That Changed a Game, a People, a Nation*. New York: Doubleday.

Johnson, Troy R., ed. 1994. *You Are on Indian Land!: Alcatraz Island, 1969–1971*. Los Angeles: American Indian Studies Center, University of California, Los Angeles.

Junger, Sebastian. 2016. *Tribe: On Homecoming and Belonging*. New York: Twelve.

Kane, Mary J,. and Susan L. Greendorfer. 1994. "The Media's Role in Accommodating and Resisting Stereotyped Images of Women in Sport: Challenging Gender Values." In *Women, Media, and Sport*, edited by Pamela J. Creedon, 28–44. Thousand Oaks CA: Sage.

Kane, Mary. J., and Helen Jefferson Lenskyj. 1998. "Media Treatment of Female Athletes: Issue of Gender and Sexualities." In *MediaSport*, edited by Lawrence Wenner, 200–215. London: Routledge.

Kelly, Deirdre M., Shauna Pomerantz, and Dawn Currie. 2005. "Skater Girlhood and Emphasized Femininity: 'You Can't Land an Ollie Properly in Heels.'" *Gender and Education* 17 (3): 229–48.

King, Thomas. 2008. *The Truth about Stories: A Native Narrative*. Minneapolis: University of Minnesota Press.

Klein, Alan. 2020. *Lakota Hoops: Life and Basketball on the Pine Ridge Indian Reservation*. New Brunswick NJ: Rutgers University Press.

Lawler, Kristin. 2011. *The American Surfer: Radical Culture and Capitalism*. New York: Routledge.

Levy, Jerrold E. 1992. *Orayvi Revisited: Social Stratification in an "Egalitarian" Society*. Santa Fe NM: School of American Research Press.

Lisec, John, and Mary G. McDonald. 2012. "Gender Inequality in the New Millennium: An Analysis of WNBA Representations in Sport Blogs." *Journal of Sports Media* 7 (2): 153–78.

Lomawaima, K. Tsianina. 1994. *They Called it Prairie Light: The Story of Chilocco Indian School*. Lincoln: University of Nebraska Press.

Lombard, Kara-Jane. 2010. "Skate and Create/Skate and Destroy: The Commercial and Governmental Incorporation of Skateboarding." *Continuum: Journal of Media & Cultural Studies* 24 (4): 475–88.

Louison, Cole. 2011. *Impossible: Rodney Mullen, Ryan Sheckler, and the Fantastic History of Skateboarding*. Guilford CT: Lyons Press.

Lucchesi, Annita, and Abigail Echo-Hawk. 2018. *Missing and Murdered Indigenous Women & Girls: A Snapshot of Data from 71 Urban Cities in the United State*. Our Bodies, Our Stories. Seattle: Urban Indian Health Institute.

Lupe, Ronnie. 1980. "At Peace with the Past, In Step with the Future." *National Geographic* 157 (2) (February): 260–61.

Lutz, Catherine A., and Jane L. Collins. 1993. *Reading National Geographic*. Chicago: University of Chicago Press.

MacKay, Steph, and Christine Dallaire. 2012. "Skirtboarder Net-A-Narratives: Young Women Creating Their Own Skateboarding (Re)Presentations." *International Review for the Sociology of Sport* 48 (2): 171–95.

Mandt, Maura, and Josh Swade, dirs. 2012. *There's No Place Like Home*. 30 for 30, aired October 16, 2012, on ESPN.

Martinez, David. 2013. "From off the Rez to off the Hook! Douglas Miles and Apache Skateboards." *American Indian Quarterly* 37 (4): 370–94.

Messner, Michael A. 1992. *Power at Play: Sports and the Problem of Masculinity*. Boston: Beacon Press.

Messner, Michael A., Margaret Carlisle Duncan, and Faye Linda Wachs. 2001. "The Gender of Audience Building: Televised Coverage of Women's and Men's NCAA Basketball." In *Contemporary Issues in Sociology of Sport*, edited by Andrew Yiannakis and Merrill J. Melnick, 323–34. Champaign IL: Human Kinetics.

Mihesuah, Devon A. 2003. *Indigenous American Women: Decolonization, Empowerment, Activism*. Lincoln: University of Nebraska Press.

Million, Dian. 2013. *Therapeutic Nations: Healing in an Age of Indigenous Human Rights*. Tucson: University of Arizona Press.

Morgensen, Scott Lauria. 2011. "Unsettling Queer Politics: What Can Non-Natives Learn from Two-Spirit Organizing?" In *Queer Indigenous Studies: Critical Interventions in Theory, Politics, and Literature*, edited by Qwo-Li Driskill, Chris Finley, Brian Joseph Gilley, and Scott Lauria Morgensen, 132–53. Tucson: University of Arizona Press.

Muñoz, Oscar A. 2022. "Hani'-cha Fiesta-yk: 'Let's Go to the Fiesta'; A Historical Analysis of Southern California Native Fiestas." PhD diss., University of California, Riverside.

Murdock, Esme G. 2020. "This Land Was Made for . . . : (Re) Appearing Black/Brown Female Corporeality, Life, and Death." *Hypatia* 35 (1): 190–203.

Neal, Kelly. 1999. "Leaving the Reservation," *The Native American Sports Experience: Outside the Lines*. Aired November 10, 1999, on ESPN.

Nolan, Nicholas. 2003. "The Ins and Outs of Skateboarding and Transgression in Public Space in Newcastle, Australia." *Australian Geographer* 34 (3): 311–27.

O'Connor, Paul. 2018. "Beyond the Youth Culture: Understanding Middle-Aged Skateboarders through Temporal Capital." *International Review for the Sociology of Sport* 53 (8): 924–43.

Olive, Rebecca. 2016. "Women Who Surf: Female Difference, Intersecting Subjectivities and Cultural Pedagogies." In *The Pedagogies of Cultural Studies*, edited by Andrew Hickey, 179–95. New York: Routledge.

Olive, Rebecca, Georgina Roy, and Belinda Wheaton. 2018. "Stories of Surfing: Surfing, Space and Subjectivity/Intersectionality." In *Surfing, Sex, Genders and Sexualities*, edited by lisahunter, 148–67. Abingdon, Oxon, UK: Routledge.

O'Neil, Dana. 2010. "Haskell Offers Haven for Hidden Talent." EPSN, January 13. https://www.espn.com/mens-college-basketball/columns/story?columnist=oneil_dana&id=4821534.

Opler, Morris Edward, and Harry Hoijer. 1940. "The Raid and War-Path Language of the Chiricahua Apache." *American Anthropologist* 42 (4): 617–34.

Oxendine, Joseph B. 1988. *American Indian Sports Heritage*. Champaign IL: Human Kinetics.

Peavy, Linda, and Ursula Smith. 2005. "World Champions: The 1904 Girls' Basketball Team from Fort Shaw Indian Boarding School." In *Native Athletes in Sport & Society: A Reader*, edited by C. Richard King, 40–78. Lincoln: University of Nebraska Press.

———. 2008. *Full Court Quest: The Girls from Fort Shaw Indian School, Basketball Champions of the World*. Norman: University of Oklahoma Press.

Peralta, Stacy, dir. 2001. *Dogtown and the Z-Boys*, New York: Sony Pictures Classic.

Porter, Natalie L. 2003. "Female Skateboarders and Their Negotiation of Space and Identity." Master's thesis, Concordia University.

Povinelli, Elizabeth. 2002. *The Cunning of Recognition: Indigenous Alterities and the Making of Australian Multiculturalism*. Durham NC: Duke University Press.

Powell, Michael. 2015. "Games on a Reservation Go By in a Blur." *New York Times*, March 2. https://www.nytimes.com/2015/03/03/sports/amid-the-red-rock-a-fever-pitch-for-rez-ball.html?smid=nytcore-ios-share&referringSource=articleShare.

———. 2017. "For Navajo Team, a Season of Change and Challenge." *New York Times*, February 26. https://www.nytimes.com/2017/02/26/sports/basketball/navajo-basketbal-rez-ball.html.

———. 2019. *Canyon Dreams: A Basketball Season on the Navajo Nation*. New York: Blue Rider Press.

Quintero, Nita. 1980. "Coming of Age the Apache Way." *National Geographic* 157 (2) (February): 262–71.

Raibmon, Paige Sylvia. 2005. *Authentic Indians: Episodes of Encounter from the Late-Nineteenth-Century Northwest Coast*. Durham NC: Duke University Press.

Ramirez, Renya K. 2007. *Native Hubs: Culture, Community, and Belonging in Silicon Valley and Beyond*. Durham NC: Duke University Press.

Richland, Justin B. 2008. *Arguing with Tradition: The Language of Law in Hopi Tribal Court*. Chicago: University of Chicago Press.

Rickert, Levi. 2019. "Lakota Nation Invitational 'A High Holiday Sports Classic' Underway in Rapid City." *Eastern Woodlands Indigenous News & Events*, December 20. https://indigenous.boston/lakota-nation-invitational-a-high-school-holiday-sports-classic-underway-in-rapid-city.

Rifkin, Mark. 2008. "Native Nationality and the Contemporary Queer: Tradition, Sexuality, and History in 'Drowning in the Fire.'" *American Indian Quarterly* 32 (4): 443–70.

———. 2009. *Manifesting America: The Imperial Construction of U.S. National Space*. Oxford: Oxford University Press.

———. 2011. *When Did Indians Become Straight? Kinship, the History of Sexuality, and Native Sovereignty*. New York: Oxford University Press.

———. 2017. *Beyond Settler Time: Temporal Sovereignty and Indigenous Self-Determination.* Durham NC: Duke University Press.

Risling Baldy, Cutcha. 2018. *We Are Dancing for You: Native Feminisms and the Revitalization of Women's Coming-of-Age Ceremonies.* Seattle: University of Washington Press.

Ross, Luana. 2009. "From the 'F' Word to Indigenous/Feminisms." *Wicazo Sa Review* 24 (2): 39–52.

Sauer, Patrick. 2014. "The Legend of Elvis Old Bull." *Vice,* October 30. https://www.vice.com/en/article/jpz9m8/the-legend-of-elvis-old-bull.

Schimmel, Jude. 2015. *Dream Catcher.* N.p.: 22i.

Seymour, Rachel Anne. 2014. "S'Klallam Teens Roll Out for Skate Park Opening." *Kitsap Sun* (Bremerton WA), April 12. https://archive.kitsapsun.com/news/local/sklallam-teens -roll-out-for-skate-park-opening-ep-453346445-355621041.html.

Shakib, Sohalia. 2003. "Female Basketball Participation: Negotiating the Conflation of Peer Status and Gender Status from Childhood through Puberty." *American Behavioral Scientist* 46(10): 1405–22.

Shakib, Sohalia, and Michele D. Dunbar. 2002. "The Social Construction of Female and Male High School Basketball Participation: Reproducing the Gender Order through a Two-Tiered Sporting Institution." *Sociological Perspectives* 45 (4): 353–78.

Simpson, Audra. 2007. "On Ethnographic Refusal: Indigeneity, 'Voice,' and Colonial Citizenship." *Junctures* 9: 67–80.

———. 2014. *Mohawk Interruptus: Political Life across the Borders of Settler States.* Durham NC: Duke University Press.

Simpson, Leanne Betasamosake. 2013. *Islands of Decolonial Love: Stories & Songs.* Winnipeg: ARP Books.

———. 2017. *As We Have Always Done: Indigenous Freedom through Radical Resistance.* Minneapolis: University of Minnesota Press.

Smith, Andrea. 2015. *Conquest: Sexual Violence and American Indian Genocide.* Durham NC: Duke University Press.

Smith, Gary. 1991. "Shadow of a Nation: The Crows, Once Proud Warriors, Now Seek Glory—But Often Find Tragedy—in Basketball." *Sports Illustrated,* February 18, 60–74. https://vault.si.com/vault/1991/02/18/shadow-of-a-nation-the-crows-once-proud -warriors-now-seek-glory-but-often-find-tragedy-in-basketball.

Smith, Paul Chaat, and Robert Allen Warrior. 1997. *Like a Hurricane: The Indian Movement from Alcatraz to Wounded Knee.* New York: New Press.

Snyder, Craig B. 2015. *A Secret History of the Ollie.* Cambridge MA: Black Salt Press.

Soltani Stone, Ashkan, and Natale A. Zappia. 2020. *Rez Metal: Inside the Navajo Nation Heavy Metal Scene.* Lincoln: University of Nebraska Press.

Spilde, Katherine. 1999. "Acts of Sovereignty, Acts of Identity: Negotiating Independence through Tribal Government Gaming on the White Earth Reservation." PhD diss., University of California, Santa Cruz.

Stecyk, C. R., and Glen E. Friedman. 2019 [2000]. *Dogtown: The Legend of the Z-Boys*. Brooklyn NY: Akashic Books.

Streep, Abe. 2018. "What the Arlee Warriors Were Playing For." *New York Times*, April 4. https://www.nytimes.com/2018/04/04/magazine/arlee-warriors-montana-basketball -flathead-indian-reservation.html.

Stronghold Society. n.d. "About Us." http://strongholdsociety.org/?page_id=28.

Sturm, Circe. 2002. *Blood Politics: Race, Culture, and Identity in the Cherokee Nation of Oklahoma*. Berkeley: University of California Press.

Suetopka Thayer, Rosanda. 2008. "'Louise Yellowman Park' Opens to Public in Tuba City." *Navajo-Hopi Observer*, May 20. https://www.nhonews.com/news/2008/may/20/louise -yellowman-park-opens-to-public-in-tuba-cit/#:~:text=The%20park%20officially%20 opened%20to,Rosanda%20suetopka%20thayer%2fnho.

Talamantez, Ines. 2003. "In the Space between Earth and Sky: Contemporary Mescalero Apache." In *Native Religions and Cultures of North America: Anthropology of the Sacred*, edited by Lawrence E. Sullivan, 142–59. New York: Continuum.

TallBear, Kim. 2013. *Native American DNA: Tribal Belonging and the False Promise of Genetic Science*. Minneapolis: University of Minnesota Press.

Tapahe, Erin. 2022. "Eighth Generation's New CEO Prepares to Take Brand to Global Market." *Tribal Business News*, February 7. https://tribalbusinessnews.com/sections /entrepreneurism/13789-eighth-generation-s-new-ceo-prepares-to-take-brand-to -global-market.

Tatonetti, Lisa. 2003. "*Drowning in the Fire* by Craig S. Womack" (review). *Western American Literature* 38 (1): 95–96.

———. 2007. "The Emergence and Importance of Queer American Indian Literatures; or, 'Help and Stories' in Thirty Years of SAIL." *Studies in American Indian Literatures* 19 (4): 143–70.

Thorpe, Holly, and Robert Rinehart. 2012. "Action Sport NGOs in a Neo-Liberal Context: The Cases of Skateistan and Surf Aid International." *Journal of Sport and Social Issues* 37 (2): 115–41.

Torgovnick, Marianna. 1990. *Gone Primitive: Savage Intellects, Modern Lives*. Chicago: University of Chicago Press.

Tuck, Eve. 2009. "Suspending Damage: A Letter to Communities." *Harvard Educational Review* 79 (3): 409–27.

Tuck, Eve, and K. Wayne Yang. 2014. "R-Words: Refusing Research." In *Humanizing Research: Decolonizing Qualitative Inquiry with Youth and Communities*, edited by Django Paris and Maisha T. Winn, 223–47. Thousand Oaks CA: Sage.

Veri, Maria J. 1999. "Homophobic Discourse Surrounding the Female Athlete." *Quest* 51 (4): 355–68.

Vizenor, Gerald R. 1994. *Manifest Manners: Postindian Warriors of Survivance.* Hanover NH: Wesleyan University Press.

Wasson, Michael. 2016. "3:33 Sports Short #28 // Small Meditations by Michael Wasson." *Prairie Schooner,* June 20. https://prairieschooner.unl.edu/digital-schooner/333-sports -short-28-small-meditations-michael-wasson/.

Waterhouse, Jo, and David Penhallow. 2006. *Concrete to Canvas: Skateboarders' Art.* New York: Watson-Guptill.

Watt, Robert N. 2002. "Raiders of a Lost Art?: Apache War and Society." *Small Wars and Insurgencies* 13 (3): 1–28.

Weyland, Jocko. 2002. *The Answer Is Never: A Skateboarder's History of the World.* New York: Grove Press.

Wheaton, Belinda, and Becky Beal. 2003. "'Keeping It Real': Subcultural Media and the Discourse of Authenticity in Alternative Sport." *International Review for the Sociology of Sport* 38 (2): 155–76.

Wikipedia. n.d. "Joe Burton (Basketball)." Last modified September 2023. https://en.m .wikipedia.org/wiki/Joe_Burton_(basketball).

Womack, Craig S. 1999. *Red on Red: Native American Literary Separatism.* Minneapolis: University of Minnesota Press.

———. 2009. *Drowning in the Fire.* Tucson: University of Arizona Press.

Woodard, Catherine. 2012. "March Madness Continued: Poetry Hoops with Natalie Diaz." *Best American Poetry,* March 19. http://blog.bestamericanpoetry.com/the_best_american _poetry/2012/03/poetry-hoops-with-natalie-diaz-by-catherine-woodard.html.

Woolley, Helen, and Ralph Johns. 2001. "Skateboarding: The City as a Playground." *Journal of Urban Design* 6 (2): 211–30.

Yochim, Emily A. Chivers. 2009. *Skate Life: Re-Imagining White Masculinity.* Ann Arbor: University of Michigan Press.

Zirin, Dave. 2005. *What's My Name Fool? Sports and Resistance in the United States.* Chicago: Haymarket Books.

———. 2009. *People's History of Sports in the United States: 250 Years of Politics, Protest, People, and Play.* New York: New Press.

———. 2016. *Brazil's Dance with the Devil: The World Cup, the Olympics, and the Fight for Democracy.* Chicago: Haymarket Books.

www.ingramcontent.com/pod-product-compliance
Lightning Source LLC
Chambersburg PA
CBHW030830250925
33143CB00001B/3